JESUS' DEATH AND HEAVENLY OFFERING IN HEBREWS

This book addresses two crucial, related questions in current research on the Epistle to the Hebrews: When and where did Jesus offer himself? And what role does Jesus' death play both in Hebrews' soteriology as a whole and specifically in Jesus' high-priestly self-offering? The work argues that the cross is not when and where Jesus offers himself, but it is what he offers. After his resurrection, appointment to high priesthood, and ascent to heaven, Jesus offers himself to God in the inner sanctum of the heavenly tabernacle, and what he offers to God is the soteriological achievement enacted in his death. Hebrews figures blood, in both the Levitical cult and the Christ-event, as a medium of exchange, a life given for life owed. Represented as blood, Christ's death is both means of access and material offered: What he achieved in his death is what he offered to God in heaven.

R. B. JAMIESON is an associate pastor of Capitol Hill Baptist Church in Washington, DC.

SOCIETY FOR NEW TESTAMENT STUDIES
MONOGRAPH SERIES
General Editor: Edward Adams, *Kings College, London*

172

JESUS' DEATH AND HEAVENLY OFFERING IN HEBREWS

SOCIETY FOR NEW TESTAMENT STUDIES
MONOGRAPH SERIES

Recent titles in the series:
162. *Feasts in John's Gospel*
     GERRY WHEATON
163. *Paul's Political Strategy in 1 Corinthians 1–4*
     BRADLEY J. BITNER
164. *The Pauline Church and the Corinthian Ekklēsia*
     RICHARD LAST
165. *Jesus and the Temple*
     SIMON J. JOSEPH
166. *The Death of Jesus in Matthew*
     CATHERINE SIDER HAMILTON
167. *Ecclesiology and Theosis in the Gospel of John*
     ANDREW J. BYERS
168. *The Book of Revelation and Early Jewish Textual Culture*
     GARRICK ALLEN
169. *The Origin of Divine Christology*
     ANDREW TER ERN LOKE
170. *Romans 7 and Christian Identity*
     WILL N. TIMMINS
171. *Inventing Hebrews*
     MICHAEL WADE MARTIN, JASON A. WHITLARK

Jesus' Death and Heavenly Offering in Hebrews

R. B. JAMIESON
Capitol Hill Baptist Church

CAMBRIDGE
UNIVERSITY PRESS

Shaftesbury Road, Cambridge CB2 8EA, United Kingdom

One Liberty Plaza, 20th Floor, New York, NY 10006, USA

477 Williamstown Road, Port Melbourne, VIC 3207, Australia

314–321, 3rd Floor, Plot 3, Splendor Forum, Jasola District Centre, New Delhi – 110025, India

103 Penang Road, #05-06/07, Visioncrest Commercial, Singapore 238467

Cambridge University Press is part of Cambridge University Press & Assessment, a department of the University of Cambridge.

We share the University's mission to contribute to society through the pursuit of education, learning and research at the highest international levels of excellence.

www.cambridge.org
Information on this title: www.cambridge.org/9781108464499

DOI: 10.1017/9781108565448

© Cambridge University Press & Assessment 2019

This publication is in copyright. Subject to statutory exception and to the provisions of relevant collective licensing agreements, no reproduction of any part may take place without the written permission of Cambridge University Press & Assessment.

First published 2019
First paperback edition 2026

A catalogue record for this publication is available from the British Library

Library of Congress Cataloging-in-Publication data
Names: Jamieson, R. B., 1986- author.
Title: Jesus' death and heavenly offering in Hebrews / R.B. Jamieson, Capitol Hill Baptist Church.
Description: 1 [edition]. | New York : Cambridge University Press, 2019. | Series: Society for New Testament studies monograph series ; 172 | Includes bibliographical references and index.
Identifiers: LCCN 2018022938 | ISBN 9781108474436 (hardback : alk. paper)
Subjects: LCSH: Bible. Hebrews–Criticism, interpretation, etc. | Jesus Christ–Death–Biblical teaching. | Sacrifice–Christianity–Biblical teaching.
Classification: LCC BS2775.6.S24 J36 2018 | DDC 227/.8706–dc23
LC record available at https://lccn.loc.gov/2018022938

ISBN   978-1-108-47443-6   Hardback
ISBN   978-1-108-46449-9   Paperback

Cambridge University Press & Assessment has no responsibility for the persistence or accuracy of URLs for external or third-party internet websites referred to in this publication and does not guarantee that any content on such websites is, or will remain, accurate or appropriate.

CONTENTS

Acknowledgments	*page* ix
Note on Style and Sources	xi

1 Introduction 1
  1.1 The Self-Offering of Jesus in Hebrews: When
     and Where, and What 1
  1.2 When and Where Did Jesus Offer Himself?
     A Taxonomy of Five Views 4
  1.3 Two Material Questions That Follow 12
  1.4 Methodology 15
  1.5 Preview 19

PART I THE FORMAL QUESTION 21

2 Locating Christ's Self-Offering in Heaven 23
  2.1 Introduction 23
  2.2 Appointed High Priest at His Entrance
     to Heaven 23
  2.3 Where and When Did Jesus Offer Himself?
     In Heaven, after His Resurrection 35
  2.4 Conclusion 70

3 Confirming Christ's Self-Offering in Heaven 71
  3.1 Introduction 71
  3.2 The "When" and "Where" of Christ's
     Self-Offering in Hebrews 10:5–14 71
  3.3 Locating Hebrews' Other Cultic Configurations
     of the Christ-Event 83
  3.4 What about the Veil and Christ's Flesh
     in Hebrews 10:20? 86
  3.5 Concluding the Broad Conversation 92

vii

PART II THE MATERIAL QUESTION ... 95

4 What Christ's Death Achieved — 97
4.1 Questioning a Conclusion — 97
4.2 Hebrews 2:9: Jesus Tasted Death for All — 99
4.3 Hebrews 2:14–15: He Destroyed the Devil, Defeating Death — 110
4.4 Hebrews 9:15–17: Jesus' Death Bears the Old Covenant Curse and Inaugurates New Covenant Blessing — 116
4.5 Conclusion — 126

5 Death and Blood in Christ's Heavenly Offering — 127
5.1 Coming Full Circle — 127
5.2 Death and Blood — 128
5.3 Blood and Offering — 160
5.4 Death and Offering — 165
5.5 Conclusion — 178

6 Conclusion — 180
6.1 Summing Up — 180
6.2 Concluding Both Conversations — 182
6.3 The Question of Coherence — 189
6.4 Place and Roots — 190

Bibliography — 194
Subject Index — 212
Scripture Index — 214
Index of Other Ancient Sources — 221
Author Index — 224

ACKNOWLEDGMENTS

This work is a very light revision of my PhD thesis, which was submitted to the University of Cambridge in 2017. It is my joy to thank those who have enabled, encouraged, improved, and endured this thesis. At every stage my supervisor, Simon Gathercole, has given generous support, searching feedback, and warm encouragement. I am also thankful to Tyndale House, especially its principal, Peter Williams, and its librarians. Tyndale House is a remarkable place to write a PhD thesis, even more for the people than for the books. Among readers I have had the privilege to know, I am especially thankful for the friendship of Mateus de Campos, Peter Gurry, Greg Lanier, Jim Prothro, Greg Salazar, and Will Ross. Dozens more could be named who have sharpened and supported me and my work. Thank you all.

I am grateful to Michael Kibbe for conversations on Hebrews that well predate the writing of this work, and for his engagement with parts of it. I am also thankful to George Guthrie for reading Chapter 2 and for his deeply encouraging friendship. Georg Gäbel, David Moffitt, and Madison Pierce also read material from the thesis and offered substantive, constructive feedback. I am likewise indebted to Nicholas Moore for fruitful conversations and helpful correspondence. Matthew Crawford deserves a special word of thanks, not only for offering abundant assistance as I applied for PhD programs, but also for a key piece of advice that helped click the structure of this work into place. I also thank those who heard and commented on portions of the thesis in person. Parts of Chapters 1 and 3 were presented to the Cambridge Graduate New Testament Seminar; material that found a home in Chapter 4 was presented at the Muted Voices conference in Durham in April 2015; a sketch of Chapter 5 was presented at the Oxbridge Biblical Studies Day in Oxford in April 2016; finally, a digest of the whole was presented to the Cambridge New Testament Senior Seminar in May 2017.

I am and will remain stunned by the generosity of those who have supported these three years of full-time research. Chief among these are the elders and members of Capitol Hill Baptist Church in Washington, DC, without whose gifts this never would have happened. Many other friends, family members, and partners in ministry gave to enable time here. My family and I thank God for you all. I am also thankful to the Hedley Lucas Fund of Cambridge's Divinity Faculty for some tuition assistance in my third year. And I thank my parents for their constant support and generosity.

I am grateful to my children, Rose, Lucy, and William, for being such delightful company on our English sojourn. I finished the book – *tiddely pom*! Finally, on the human plane, there is no one to whom I am more thankful than my wife, Kristin. You have given every day, in countless ways, so that I could do this. I will not forget it.

Greatest thanks to God: May this work be a sacrifice of praise, the fruit of lips that acknowledge his name.

NOTE ON STYLE AND SOURCES

Style and abbreviations generally follow the guidelines of *The SBL Handbook of Style* 2nd edition. References are given according to a modified Chicago author-date style. The critical editions of biblical texts used are, for the Masoretic Text, the *Biblica Hebraica Stuttgartensia* 5th edition; for the Septuagint, Rahlfs-Hahnart 2006 edition (for which I use the abbreviation LXX); for the New Testament, the Nestle-Aland 28th edition. Unless otherwise noted, translations of biblical texts are from the ESV; where they differ they are my own. Citations of biblical texts follow English chapter and verse numbering. Texts and translations of classical works, including Philo and Josephus, are from the Loeb Classical Library unless otherwise noted.

1

INTRODUCTION

1.1 The Self-Offering of Jesus in Hebrews: When and Where, and What

This thesis argues that, according to Hebrews' specialized use of sacrificial terms and concepts, Jesus' death is not when and where he offers himself, but it is what he offers. The first half of this statement is denied by many modern scholars who argue that Jesus' self-offering begins and ends on the cross. By contrast, among the relatively small number who affirm that Jesus offers himself in the tabernacle in heaven, none has as yet argued that Jesus' death – that is, the saving work Jesus' death accomplished – constitutes the sacrificial material that Jesus presents to God in heaven.

This thesis will therefore conduct both a broad and a narrow conversation, answering first a formal question, then a material one. In the broad conversation that constitutes Part I I will argue that, as high priest according to the order of Melchizedek, Jesus offers himself to God in the Holy of Holies of the tabernacle in heaven, after his bodily resurrection and ascension. I will argue this point in dialogue with a wide range of scholarly answers to the "formal" question, "When and where does Jesus offer himself?" In the narrow conversation that follows in Part II, I will take for granted my answer to the formal question, and will answer a twofold material one: "What role does Jesus' death play in Hebrews' soteriology as a whole, and specifically within Jesus' high-priestly self-offering?" Hence by "formal" I mean the way Hebrews sequences events and aligns terms; by "material" I mean the role Jesus' death plays in Hebrews' soteriology as a whole and specifically in Jesus' self-offering. The formal question addresses when and where Jesus offers himself; the material question addresses what role his death plays in that offering.

In the narrow conversation about the material question, my primary dialogue partners will be those who affirm, as I do, that Jesus offers himself in heaven. Does this affirmation require the conclusion that, for Hebrews, Jesus' death is not "atoning"? Does it even necessarily require that, in Hebrews' use of Yom Kippur and Levitical sacrifice more broadly, Jesus' death on the cross is not a focal point of atonement? I will argue that neither inference is necessary, and in fact neither is drawn by Hebrews. Put positively, Hebrews indicates that what Jesus' death achieved is in fact what he gives to God in heaven. What Jesus offers God in heaven is the life he gave in death.

Those familiar with the peculiar world of Hebrews scholarship will recognize that a major impetus for this thesis is the influential, powerfully argued 2011 monograph of David Moffitt, *Atonement and the Logic of Resurrection in the Epistle to the Hebrews*.[1] However, this thesis is not simply a response to Moffitt. For one thing, Moffitt approaches Jesus' heavenly offering in Hebrews through the side door of Jesus' bodily resurrection. Thereby Moffitt makes a fresh, innovative contribution. Yet he simply does not attempt the task of engaging directly with the full range of scholarly views about when and where Jesus offers himself. By contrast, I aim to enter this debate through the front door. That is, I inductively inquire after the issues that inform judgments about when and where Jesus offers himself, and exegetically argue a stance on each. As the taxonomy in the next section illustrates, I ask how scholars correlate three variables in determining when and where Jesus offers himself: his death, entrance to heaven, and self-offering. As a result, I identify five views on the question, with four decisive issues that distinguish each view from the others. In other words, I suggest that the issues raised by Moffitt's argument for a heavenly offering call for more systematic treatment in active engagement with a wider breadth of scholarship.

Further, asserting that Jesus offers himself in heaven necessarily raises crucial questions about his death. As Benjamin Ribbens observes, "The great difficulty with a heavenly sanctuary and cult is to determine how they relate to Christ's earthly ministry and suffering."[2] Franz Laub puts the question of Jesus' death pointedly: "This raises one of the most controversial issues in this context: in view of this sort of 'spatial' understanding of the cultic terminology of Hebrews in general, what salvific significance still belongs to

---

[1] Moffitt 2011.   [2] Ribbens 2016:132.

Introduction

Jesus' crucifixion?"[3] Finally, Georg Gäbel raises the question from the opposite angle, beginning from the position, which he rejects, that Hebrews figures Jesus' death as an atoning sacrifice: "If his death on earth is understood as an atoning sacrifice, how then does his high priestly work in heaven relate to this? Determining the relationship between the life and death of Christ on earth and his heavenly work sets the decisive course for each interpretation of Hebrews."[4] Hence, in Part II I offer an account of the relationship between Jesus' death and heavenly offering that is more detailed than any yet offered by an advocate of a heavenly self-offering, bar one. That one is Gäbel, who has made the fullest case to date for locating Jesus' self-offering in heaven, and whose treatment of the relation of Christ's death to his heavenly self-offering I will both extend and critique.

What is at stake in this debate about where and when Jesus offers himself, and what role his death plays in that offering? First, as asserted by Gäbel in the previous quotation, this issue serves as a kind of hermeneutical watershed for one's entire reading of Hebrews. How one relates Jesus' death on earth to his priestly work in heaven will shape – and be shaped by – a whole range of critical issues in interpreting the letter, and will bear decisively on one's exegesis of the letter's central expository section (5:1–10:18). Second, at stake is how similar to and different from the rest of the New Testament – especially Paul – Hebrews is, and in what ways. It is widely recognized, of course, that Hebrews alone in the New Testament describes Jesus' saving act as that of a high priest offering himself as the sacrificial victim. But how exactly does this cultic construal of the Christ-event differ from the rest of the New Testament? Is this priestly sacrifice simply a conceptual gloss on the event of Jesus' death? Or does it instead offer a soteriological elaboration of Jesus' entrance into heaven that is unique in the New Testament? We will return to such questions in Chapter 6. In the rest of this introduction,

---

[3] Laub 1991:67, "Damit ist eine der umstrittensten Fragen in diesem Zusammenhang aufgeworfen: Welche Heilsbedeutung kommt bei einem so gearteten 'räumlichen' Verständnis der Kultterminologie des Hebr überhaupt noch dem Kreuzestod Jesu zu?"

[4] Gäbel 2006:3–4, "Wird sein Sterben auf Erden als sühnender Opfertod verstanden, wie verhält sich dann sein hohepriesterliches Wirken im Himmel dazu? Mit der Verhältnisbestimmung von Leben und Sterben Christi auf Erden und seinem himmlischen Wirken erfolgt die entscheidende Weichenstellung für jede Hebr-Interpretation."

I will offer a brief survey of literature, discuss two material questions that arise in the wake of the formal one, lay methodological groundwork, and preview the argument.

1.2 When and Where Did Jesus Offer Himself? A Taxonomy of Five Views

To pinpoint the time and place of Jesus' self-offering in Hebrews, one must correlate three variables: Jesus' death, entrance to heaven, and self-offering. Here I briefly sketch something of how Hebrews discusses each, before offering a taxonomy of five ways scholars have put them together.[5] First, regarding Jesus' death, it is too rarely observed that, while Hebrews often mentions or alludes to Jesus' death, it never explicitly identifies Jesus' death as his "sacrifice" or "offering."[6] Apart from 9:28, the only time Hebrews alludes to Jesus' death within its overarching Levitical framework is 13:12, which correlates the cross not with sacrificial slaughter but with the post-requisite disposal of corpses at the conclusion of the Yom Kippur rite.[7] Second, Hebrews repeatedly asserts that Jesus entered heaven, specifically the true sanctuary there (6:19–20; 9:11–12, 24; cf. 8:1–2). Yet the timing and mode of Christ's entrance to heaven are debated. Third, Hebrews frequently says Jesus offered himself, or his body, without explicitly stating when and where this happened (7:27; 9:14, 25; 10:10, 14; cf. 8:3–4). Closely related to these explicit "self-offering" passages are those that say Christ entered heaven by means of his own blood (9:11–12; cf. 9:25; 10:19), and that he offered a "sacrifice" (θυσία, 9:26; 10:12). Finally, other passages that construe Christ's saving work in cultic terms similarly leave time and place referents implicit (1:3; 2:17; 13:12). Hence these three variables include one event (Jesus' death); one item that, as we will see, some

---

[5] The following summarizes, and sometimes repeats selections of, Jamieson 2017.
[6] For someone who does observe this, see Davies 1968:387, "Where Christ's death is the subject of a passage (2,9–14; 5,7–10; 6,6; 9,15; 12,2; 13,11–13) προσφέρω and such words do not appear." Jesus' death is explicitly mentioned only in 2:9, 2:14, and 9:15. Mention of Jesus' "suffering" likely includes a reference to his death in 2:10, 5:8, 9:26, and 13:12; 12:2 says he "endured the cross." As I will argue in Sections 2.3 and 5.4, in the phrase "having been offered once to bear the sins of many" in 9:28, the second half alludes to the servant's death in Isa 53:12 LXX, which means the first half, "having been offered," alludes to Christ's death.
[7] For discussion of 9:28 in relation to where and when Christ offers himself, see Section 2.3 ("Self-Offering on Earth in Hebrews 9:26 and 9:28?") and Section 5.4 ("Jesus' Death as Sacrificial Victim and Sin-Bearing Servant (Heb 9:28)").

Introduction

Table 1.1 *Summary of Views 1–5*

View 1: Jesus' self-offering begins and ends on the cross. His earthly self-offering precedes his entrance into the heavenly sanctuary.
View 2: Jesus' self-offering is an earthly event with heavenly significance. His self-offering on the cross is metaphorically described as his entrance into the heavenly sanctuary.
View 3: Jesus' self-offering begins with his death and culminates in his immediately subsequent spiritual exaltation to the heavenly sanctuary.
View 4: Jesus' self-offering begins with his death and culminates in his post-resurrection entrance into the heavenly sanctuary.
View 5: Jesus offers himself at his post-resurrection entrance into the heavenly sanctuary.

Table 1.2 *Taxonomy of Views 1–5*

Distinguishing Interpretive Decision	View 1	View 2	View 3	View 4	View 5
Jesus' self-offering begins and ends on the cross	Yes	Yes	No	No	No
Jesus' "entry" into heaven metaphorically describes the cross	No	Yes	No	No	No
Jesus' exaltation is spiritual ascension, not bodily resurrection	Either	Either	Yes	No	No
Jesus offers himself in heaven, not on the cross	No	No	No	No	Yes

take as an event and some as a metaphor (entrance to heaven); and one cultic concept that may or may not designate a distinct event ("self-offering"). Table 1.1 summarizes five ways scholars align these three variables. Table 1.2 offers a taxonomy that registers how each view answers four questions that, taken together, distinguish each view from the others.[8] These five views are admittedly pure types; some scholars' positions elude the consistency at which my taxonomy aims.

---

[8] Many recent works address some of the relevant issues, but do not answer enough of the decisive questions for their views to be located in my taxonomy. These include Johnsson 1973; Hurst 1990; Lehne 1990; Dunnill 1992; Johnson 2001; Gelardini 2007; Rascher 2007; Allen 2008; McCruden 2008; Jipp 2010; Stewart 2010; Easter 2014; Peeler 2014; Filtvedt 2015b; and Dyer 2017.

View 1: Jesus' Self-Offering Precedes His Entrance to Heaven

Many scholars argue that Jesus' self-offering begins and ends on the cross.[9] Hence Jesus' singular, completed, earthly self-offering precedes his entrance into heaven. According to this view, all of Hebrews' statements about Jesus offering himself, his body, and his blood describe his death on the cross. Some scholars advocating this view identify Jesus' self-offering with his death on the basis of the assertion in 9:25–26 that Jesus' unrepeatable suffering was necessary for his singular offering, and the comparison in 9:27–28 between the universal human fate of dying once and Christ's fate of being offered once.[10] The interpretive decision that distinguishes this view from Views 3–5 (a version of which is implicit in View 2) is the conviction that, in using the Day of Atonement as a model for the work of Christ, the author deliberately alters the sequence of events. As Hebrews narrates the Levitical Day of Atonement, the high priest enters the Holy of Holies with blood *in order to make* his offering there (see προσφέρει, "offers," in 9:7). By contrast, on View 1 Jesus enters the Holy of Holies in heaven *having already made* his offering on the cross. So F. F. Bruce, in a frequently cited comment,

> There have been expositors who, pressing the analogy of the Day of Atonement beyond the limits observed by our author, have argued that the expiatory work of Christ was not completed on the cross ... But while it was necessary under the old covenant for the sacrificial blood first to be shed in the court and then to be brought into the holy of holies, no such division of our Lord's sacrifice into two phases is envisaged

---

[9] Owen 1991:277, 280–81, 301; Westcott 1903:199, 217, 263, 275–76; Moffatt 1924:123–24; Spicq 1953:257–58, 268–70; Stott 1962; Vanhoye 1965:24–26; Vanhoye 1996:333–34; Hay 1973:145, 149, 151; Hughes 1973:207–12; Loader 1981:185–92, 199, 201; Young 1981:206, 208–9; Braun 1984:28–29, 71, 270; Rissi 1987:72–73; Bénétreau 1989a; Bénétreau 1989b:53; Bénétreau 1990:89–90, 93; Bruce 1990:31–33, 213–14; Lane 1991:2.223, 2.234, 2.247, 2.249; Lindars 1991:81, 84–86, 93, 94; Weiss 1991:464–68, 488–89; Isaacs 1992:103–4, 108, 145, 202, 209; Ellingworth 1993:70, 102, 448, 474; Schunack 1994:224–31; Schunack 2002:18, 120–25; Kleinig 1999:132; Cockerill 2001:185–89, 197; Cockerill 2012:394–95, 416; Stökl ben Ezra 2003:181, 188–89; Fuhrmann 2007:200–3, 220–26; Telscher 2007:255–60; Joslin 2008:230–32; Allen 2010:486–89; Philip 2011:56; Richardson 2012:29–45, 47; Kuma 2012:273–74, 282; Small 2014:204, 224, 252–53; Compton 2015a:150 n. 231; Compton 2015b; Schreiner 2015:238 n. 375, 244, 268, 285; Moret 2016:299–300; Church 2017:283, 386, 416–21.

[10] E.g. Loader 1981:185–86; Richardson 2012:39–40.

under the new covenant. When on the cross he offered up his life to God as a sacrifice for his people's sin, he accomplished in reality what Aaron and his successors performed in type by the twofold act of slaying the victim and presenting its blood in the holy of holies.[11]

On this reading, Jesus' entrance into heaven is an act distinct from his death, but it is not a sacrificial act. For View 1, Jesus' self-offering begins and ends on the cross.

View 2: Jesus' Earthly Self-Offering Is Described as His Heavenly Entrance

Other scholars argue that Hebrews' references to Jesus entering heaven (6:19–20; 9:12, 24) metaphorically describe his self-offering, which occurs in his death on the cross.[12] View 2 shares with View 1 the conviction that Jesus' self-offering takes place on the cross. But View 2 observes how closely Hebrews connects Jesus' offering with his entrance to heaven. For instance, while the high priests yearly entered the inner sanctum, Jesus entered its heavenly counterpart only once, because he needed to offer himself only once (9:24–26; cf. 9:7, 11–14). Sometimes aided by a Middle Platonic construal of Hebrews' cosmology, proponents of View 2 conclude that these descriptions of Jesus' entrance to heaven do not describe an event distinct from Jesus' death. Instead, these statements use spatial, cosmological terms metaphorically to describe the heavenly value or quality of Jesus' death. Harold Attridge, for instance, argues that in Hebrews, "language of cosmic transcendence is ultimately a way of speaking about human interiority."[13] For Attridge, 9:14 indicates that Jesus' earthly self-offering simultaneously took place "in a spiritual realm."[14] Based on this entire schema, Attridge concludes, "Christ's sacrificial death is not an act distinct from his entry into God's presence."[15] Similarly, Franz Laub argues that the heavenly "tent" in Hebrews is not a spatial designation, but instead designates

---

[11] Bruce 1990:213–14; Loader 1981:189; Young 1981:208–9; Lane 1991:2.223, 2.249; Lindars 1991:94; Ellingworth 1993:474; Stökl ben Ezra 2003:189; Cockerill 2012:394.
[12] Calvin 1963:106; Luck 1963:211; Laub 1980:168–72, 185–220; Thompson 1982:107–8, 147–48; Thompson 2008:186 (though see further under View 3); Attridge 1989:27, 146–47, 251, 262–64; Asumang 2008:116–17; Hermann 2013:305, 316, 319, 326.
[13] Attridge 1989:262.   [14] Ibid., 251.   [15] Ibid., 264.

the Christ-event.¹⁶ The distinctive judgment of View 2 is not necessarily that "entrance" passages have no spatial referent at all, since these authors affirm that Christ relocates to heaven after his death. But what is crucial for View 2 is that all such statements in Hebrews are indeed metaphorical in the sense that they ascribe heavenly value to an earthly event. For View 2, Hebrews' apparent assertions that Jesus offered himself in heaven refer not to an event distinct from Jesus' death but to its heavenly significance.

View 3: Jesus' Self-Offering Consists in His Death and Subsequent Spiritual Entrance

Third, some argue that Jesus' self-offering consists in his death and his immediately subsequent spiritual – that is, disembodied – entrance to heaven.¹⁷ View 3 takes shape when four elements are combined. First, View 3 shares with Views 1–2 the conviction that "self-offering" passages designate Christ's death. Second, View 3 observes that the way Hebrews draws on Ps 110:1 seems to set Christ's sacrifice and subsequent session in an immediate temporal sequence. After offering a single sacrifice for sins, Christ sat down at God's right hand (10:12; cf. 1:3). Third, View 3 takes Hebrews' relative silence about Jesus' resurrection to indicate that the author construes Jesus' exaltation as spiritual translation rather than bodily resurrection and ascent. Fourth, unlike View 2, View 3 ascribes to Jesus' exaltation its own decisive soteriological significance as the culmination of his self-offering. For View 3, Christ's self-offering begins on the cross, but it does not end there. For instance, Erich Grässer calls Jesus' exaltation, which immediately follows his death, the "entscheidende Heilsereignis."¹⁸ For Grässer, "Good Friday and Ascension Day together form the great Day of Atonement of Christianity."¹⁹ For View 3 Christ's translation to the heavenly sanctuary is a constitutive element in his self-offering, whereas a consistent View 2, like View 1, restricts Christ's self-offering to the cross alone.

---

¹⁶ Laub 1980:189.
¹⁷ Jeremias 1949:198–99; Hofius 1970b:181 n. 359; Grässer 1990:64–65, 245; Grässer 1993:148; Barth 1992:153–54; Rose 1994:330; Knöppler 2001:195–200; Eisele 2003:388–89; Stegemann and Stegemann 2005:14, 19; Backhaus 2009a:70, 87–88, 317–18; Backhaus 2009b:205, 207 n. 28; Rowland and Morray-Jones 2009:171–72; Ounsworth 2012:164, 171.
¹⁸ Grässer 1990:65.   ¹⁹ Ibid., 245; cf. Backhaus 2009a:87–88.

A key division between Views 2 and 3 is what their proponents mean by Jesus' "death." View 2 holds that Jesus' (metaphorical) entrance to heaven took place *while he was dying* on the cross. By contrast View 3 argues that Jesus entered heaven, as a spirit, *when he died* on the cross – that is, at his moment of expiration. Yet Views 2 and 3 sometimes combine.[20] For instance, View 3 does not rule out Jesus' suffering on the cross having a heavenly significance, and proponents of View 2 often construe Christ's exaltation as spiritual translation rather than bodily resurrection and ascent.

View 4: Jesus' Self-Offering Consists in His Death and Subsequent Embodied Entrance

View 4 argues that Christ's self-offering consists in his death and his subsequent embodied entrance into the heavenly sanctuary.[21] Like View 3, View 4 sees Christ's self-offering as a process, a single sacrificial script, spanning earth and heaven: Christ's death enacts the slaughter of the victim, and his entry to the heavenly sanctuary corresponds to the Levitical priest's "offering" of blood in the Holy of Holies. Contra View 1, for View 4 Jesus' sacrifice does not begin and end on the cross; instead, it begins on the cross and culminates with his self-presentation to God in heaven. In contrast to View 3, View 4 holds that Christ was resurrected bodily. However, for many proponents of View 4, Hebrews' affirmation of Christ's bodily resurrection is more assumed than argued.

The use of the phrase "sacrificial script" to describe this view likely originates with Richard Nelson, who says that "the cross was the first component in a larger sacrificial script."[22] He explains,

---

[20] See esp. Thompson 1982:107–8, 147–48; Thompson 2008:186.
[21] Delitzsch 1887:14, 27–29, 81–82, 88–89; Cody 1960:168–202, esp. 174–75; Michel 1966:281, 292–93, 312; Scholer 1991:159–76; Chester 1991:61, 65–66; Pursiful 1993:66–72; Guthrie 1994:106, 122–23, 127; Guthrie 1998:29, 49, 191, 195, 309–16; Guthrie 2007:970, 973; deSilva 2000:305, 313; deSilva 2006:298, 305–12; Koester 2001:109, 117, 411, 414–15 (though see Moffitt 2011:12–14 for tensions regarding resurrection); Nelson 2003:254–56 (though he straddles the line with View 3); Johnson 2006:20, 52, 71–72, 139, 222, 233; Mackie 2007:95–98, 158–59, 169–70, 175–82 (though p. 181 is ambiguous on resurrection); Mackie 2011:78; Cortez 2008:324–413, e.g., 359–62 (though Cortez sees covenant inauguration, not Yom Kippur, as Hebrews' central framework); Cervera i Vallis 2009:479, 485, 492–93, 497; Moore 2015:177, 185–86, 198–99, 218–19.
[22] Nelson 2003:254.

His willing death was the first phase of a complex priestly action that continued in his ascension through the heavenly realms and entrance with blood into the heavenly sanctuary. It concluded with a decisive act of purification and being seated beside God's throne, where Christ can continually intercede for his followers. The cross was no mere prologue to, or presupposition for, Christ's priestly work in heaven, but an essential first element in his multi-stage act of sacrificial offering. Suffering, entrance, offering, and sacrifice are firmly bracketed together in 9:25–26.[23]

According to Nelson, "The point of Christ's passage through the heavens is not the journey itself but its goal, his entrance with blood as high priest into the heavenly sanctuary. This, too, is a liturgical act, a component of his sacrifice."[24]

While View 4's differences from Views 1–3 are straightforward, its differences from View 5 are more subtle. The chief difference is this: View 4 argues that, as both high priest and victim, Christ "offers himself" on the cross, whereas for View 5, strictly speaking, Christ "offers himself" only in the tabernacle in heaven. So Nelson on 10:10, "His death was an offering of his body."[25] Similarly, Nicholas Moore identifies the cross as the sacrificial "altar" of 13:10, and Aelred Cody calls the cross a "priestly sacrifice."[26] By contrast, View 5 holds that Christ was only appointed high priest at or after his resurrection, and therefore was only qualified to offer himself in the heavenly sanctuary, after dying and rising again. Proponents of View 4, however, tend to see Christ as already appointed high priest during his earthly career, or officially becoming high priest in his self-offering on the cross, or acting as high priest on earth before being confirmed in office at his exaltation.[27] Hence, while View 4 answers "no" to each of the taxonomy's four distinguishing decisions, it is not a negative position but a complex one. Against Views 1–3, View 4 affirms that Christ's self-offering unfolds over the sequence of his death, resurrection, and entrance to heaven. Against View 5, View 4 argues that Christ already officiated as high priest during his death, and hence his death itself can be described as a high-priestly self-offering.

---

[23] Ibid., 255.   [24] Ibid., 256.
[25] Ibid., 255; cf. Koester 2001:440; Mackie 2007:169.
[26] Moore 2015:218–19; Cody 1960:174.
[27] So, respectively, Cody 1960:107, 177; Mackie 2007:213–14; Cortez 2008:317–22.

View 5: Jesus Offers Himself in Heaven, after His Resurrection

Finally, for View 5, strictly speaking Jesus offers himself only in the heavenly sanctuary after his resurrection, not on the cross.[28] Recently this view has been influentially argued by David Moffitt, who will be a major dialogue partner throughout, and especially in Part II. Since this is the view I will argue in Part I, it will here receive only the briefest introduction. As noted previously, a key factor in this view is the conviction that Jesus was appointed to high priesthood only at or after his resurrection. And Jesus, like every high priest, is appointed to offer sacrifice (5:1; 8:3). So, Jesus' appointment precedes his offering. He does not perform his high-priestly work until he is appointed high priest. Hence he offers himself in the tabernacle in heaven. However, this does not require the conclusion that Jesus' death is not sacrificial. Nor does it require the conclusion that Jesus' death is not "atoning" or soteriologically efficacious in any objective sense. Instead, most supporters of View 5 argue that Jesus' death corresponds to the slaughter of the animal victim, and is the first step in the sacrificial sequence. And, in Part II, I will give a fuller account than this of the role Jesus' death plays both in Hebrews' soteriology as a whole and in Jesus' heavenly self-offering.

It is important to note that Georg Gäbel, who will also be a primary dialogue partner, maintains a degree of ambiguity about Christ's postmortem ontology. He recognizes that Hebrews refers to Christ's resurrection in 13:20, but argues, "In view of Hebrews' account of the way of Christ, the concept of resurrection in Heb 13:20 does not go beyond Hebrews' statements about exaltation."[29] For Gäbel, this one assertion of resurrection does not say anything more specific than what the previous exaltation statements have said already, which he does not regard as decisively establishing Jesus'

---

[28] Barrett 1956:365, 284, 286, 388–89, 393; Davies 1968:386–87; Brooks 1970; Walter 1997:158–59; Eskola 2001:204, 208, 254, 267; Eskola 2015:227, 390–92 (though see pp. 226 and 394 for statements that fit better in View 4); Haber 2005:112, 117; Willi-Plein 2005:27, 33–35 (though no discussion of resurrection); Gäbel 2006:159–61, 200–1, 236–54, 279–310, 472–83 (though see below on resurrection); Mason 2008:35, 38–39, 194–95; Mason 2012:912–16; Moffitt 2011:215–96; Moffitt 2012; Moffitt 2016b; Moffitt 2016c; Barnard 2012:6, 92, 116, 134; Calaway 2013:28, 76, 145, 156; Kibbe 2014:30–35, 45; Kibbe 2016:162–67; Ribbens 2016:2, 99, 107–8, 118, 132–35, 219–20.
[29] Gäbel 2006:310–11, "Die Auferstehungsvorstellung in Hebr 13,20 führt im Blick auf die Schilderung des Weges Christi nicht über die Erhöhungsaussagen des Hebr hinaus."

bodily resurrection. By this criterion alone, Gäbel could potentially be grouped with View 3. However, to my knowledge no one who unambiguously asserts that Christ was spiritually translated to heaven, rather than being raised bodily, has also argued, as Gäbel has, that Christ was appointed priest only at his exaltation, and consequently offered himself only in the heavenly tabernacle. Since Gäbel takes Hebrews to locate Jesus' priestly self-offering consistently in the heavenly sanctuary, his view shares the most fundamental thematic affinities with other proponents of View 5.

1.3 Two Material Questions That Follow

Two material questions arise in light of the formal one that governs the taxonomy in the previous section, and will govern Part I. First, is Hebrews' sacrificial theology coherent? More specifically, does Hebrews consistently narrate the time and place of Jesus' self-offering? Some scholars answer "no." For instance, Kenneth Schenck argues, "Ultimately, the difficulty of interpreting Hebrews at this point derives from the fact that the author has used the heavenly tabernacle in several different metaphorical ways that do not necessarily cohere with one another."[30] Further, "The ambiguity in the author's thought as to whether the offering is the same as his death (9:27–8) or occurs in heaven (9:25) is a by-product of what is ultimately metaphorical language."[31] For Schenck, Hebrews' conceptions of Jesus' death as an atoning sacrifice and of his priestly self-offering in heaven are discrete metaphors that run on parallel tracks:

> The reason these images break down is because they are primarily metaphorical in nature rather than literal ... The heavenly Holy of Holies is not a structure in heaven, but heaven itself metaphorically conceived (9:24). Christ's entrance into this Most Holy Place is thus the same event as his exaltation to God's right hand. When Hebrews uses traditional Christian imagery, Christ's sacrifice is offered on the cross. When the author is arguing from his high priestly metaphor, it is offered in heaven.[32]

Similarly, in a perceptive essay on Jesus' death in Hebrews, Hermut Löhr argues, "The Christ-story oriented to sacrificial service is not so

---

[30] Schenck 2007:8; cf. the recent restatement in Schenck 2016.
[31] Schenck 2007:188.   [32] Schenck 2003:81.

Introduction 13

realized as a story that its narrative difficulty, indeed impossibility, could come to light. Also, no heavenly cult is described in detail, such as in the form of a vision."[33] Therefore, "Where the self-sacrifice of Jesus can be located in the worldview of Hebrews remains unclear in chapters 7 to 10. The sprinkling of blood undoubtedly occurs in the heavenly sanctuary (cf. 9:23). In Hebrews 13:12, however, the sacrificial language is clearly tied back to the crucifixion of Jesus on Golgotha."[34]

Closely related to this perception of narrative inconsistency is the judgment that Hebrews' sacrificial theology manifests conceptual incongruities. For instance, according to Christian Eberhart, Hebrews' innovative portrayal of Jesus as both priest and victim "remains ... partly contradictory."[35] Further, "In Hebrews it is repeatedly manifest that the sacrificial cult and the emphasis on death are simply incompatible." Finally, like Schenck and Löhr, Eberhart also sees temporal and spatial inconsistency in how Hebrews narrates Christ's self-offering.[36] I will briefly return to the question of coherence, both narrative and conceptual, in Chapter 6.

As noted earlier in this section, another material question arises from how one answers the formal question. If one takes Hebrews to assert that Christ offers himself in heaven, what role does his death play in Hebrews' soteriology, and how does Jesus' death relate to his self-offering in heaven? Some proponents of View 5 argue that Hebrews' appropriation of Levitical sacrifice rules out an atoning function for Jesus' death. For instance, Walter Edwards Brooks concludes, "In the light of the book of Leviticus, it is inconceivable how the author could think that death atoned."[37] Similarly Timo Eskola: "It is naturally important to note that atonement was obtained only in the Holy of Holies, and not at the moment when the sacrifice was slaughtered."[38] Hence Eskola denies that "the

---

[33] Löhr 2005:471, "Die am Opfergottesdienst orientierte Christus-Fabel wird nicht als Erzählung soweit ausgeführt, daß ihre narrative Problematik, ja Unmöglichkeit zu Tage treten könnte. Es wird auch kein himmlischer Kult, etwa in Form einer Vision, ausführlich beschrieben."
[34] Ibid., 471–72, "Wo das Selbstopfer Jesu im Weltbild des Hebr lokalisiert werden kann, bleibt in den Kapiteln 7 bis 10 undeutlich. Die Blutsprengung findet ohne Zweifel im himmlischen Heiligtum statt (vgl. 9,23). In Hebr 13,12 ist die Opfersprache aber deutlich rückgebunden an den Kreuzestod Jesu auf Golgatha."
[35] Eberhart 2013:143, "... bleibt ... teilweise in sich widersprüchlich."
[36] Ibid., 152, "Im Hebräerbrief ist verschiedentlich manifest, dass der Opferkult und die Betonung des Todes geradezu inkompatibel sind."
[37] Brooks 1970:210.   [38] Eskola 2001:267.

atonement is attached to the moment of Christ's death."[39] Many have taken David Moffitt's monograph to draw this conclusion as well.[40] For instance, commenting on the phrase "since a death has occurred for (εἰς) redemption of transgressions" in 9:15, Moffitt argues that Jesus' death is not "identified here as the agent that effects the redemption." Instead, the preposition εἰς has a "resultative" sense, and the verse presupposes that Jesus effects atonement not on earth but in heaven. For Moffitt, even in a passage such as 9:15, Hebrews "is not conflating Jesus' death and the atonement."[41] Again, the author "does not conflate that event [Jesus' death] with the atoning moment. Rather, he locates Jesus' death at the front end of a process that culminates in the atoning moment."[42]

One might suppose Moffitt intends these statements to be understood with an implicit qualification, such as, "Jesus' death is not the atoning moment within the predominant framework of Levitical sacrifice" – though Moffitt never offers such a statement. Such an implicit qualification would leave open the conclusion that Hebrews uses other conceptual frameworks to ascribe objective soteriological significance to Jesus' death. And it seems that Moffitt's more recent writings might affirm this conclusion. For example: "Nevertheless, Hebrews 2.9 and 2.14–15 especially identify Jesus' death as a key element within the larger narrative of the Christ event for how he accomplished the redemption of God's people from slavery."[43] However, in his 2011 monograph, Moffitt does not draw this conclusion. Instead, he repeatedly, emphatically denies that Jesus' death is atoning. He reads passages that might be taken to supply a distinct conceptual framework for Jesus' death – such as covenant inauguration in 9:15–17 – as expressions of the predominant Levitical one, and hence as assigning atonement exclusively to Christ's act in heaven. In Moffitt's treatment of Jesus' death he omits entirely 2:14–15, and does not discuss potential soteriological implications of Christ's tasting death "for everyone" (ὑπὲρ παντός) in 2:9. What Moffitt does say about Jesus' death is that it "serves as *the* paradigm of righteous suffering" and "stands as the event *sine qua non* for initiating the new covenant and in Jesus' *preparation* for his high-

---

[39] Ibid., 267 n. 55.
[40] Moore 2013:675; Kibbe 2014:30–35, 45–46; Compton 2015b:134; Moret 2016:291.
[41] Moffitt 2011:290.   [42] Ibid., 293.
[43] Moffitt 2016a:109; though what it means for Christ's death to be "key" is undeveloped.

priestly ministry and atoning offering."[44] So Moffitt denies any "atoning" significance for Jesus' death within the predominant Levitical framework beyond its role as initiating the sacrificial sequence. And when he treats Jesus' death more broadly he neither uses language of "atonement" to describe its other functions nor assigns it objective soteriological significance. Hence the conclusion about Moffitt's monograph drawn by the reviewers cited in Note 40 seems reasonable, however Moffitt's recent and forthcoming work might potentially qualify it.

Nevertheless, the need to reassess Jesus' death in light of his heavenly offering does not depend on Moffitt's work alone. Other scholars have explicitly drawn the conclusion that, in Hebrews, Jesus' death is not atoning. And the judgment that Jesus offers himself in heaven is sufficient warrant for a detailed re-reading of Jesus' death. In the final section of this introduction I will show how the structure of this thesis arises from the formal question regarding when and where Christ offers himself, and the material question of the significance of his death.

1.4 Methodology

First, however, I offer five brief points of methodological orientation. First, the argument of this thesis does not depend on any particular hypothesis regarding the authorship, date, provenance, destination, or specific occasion of Hebrews. On such matters there exists nothing remotely approaching scholarly consensus,[45] and nothing in what follows relies on any contested claim regarding Hebrews' origins.

A second methodological concern is the hermeneutical relationship between Hebrews and Levitical sacrifice. Some studies of Hebrews' sacrificial theology – including, I will argue, that of Moffitt – effectively read Hebrews in light of (modern reconstructions of) the apparent significance of various elements of Levitical sacrifice. While an element of this is inevitable, one potential pitfall is neglecting the formative role of Christian convictions regarding the saving significance of the Christ-event for how Hebrews reads the Levitical texts. In other words, it is possible that we will read straight from

---

[44] Moffitt 2011:285, emphasis original.
[45] Even the relative consensus, if one can call it that, regarding a Roman destination has been radically challenged by Mosser 2004.

what we take Leviticus to mean to what it must have meant for Hebrews, and miss something of what Hebrews took Leviticus to mean in light of Christ. In contrast to this approach, a key feature of my argument, especially in Chapters 2 and 5, is what we might call a dialectical engagement with Hebrews' appropriation of the Levitical cult. I will argue that Hebrews both reads the Christ-event in light of the Levitical cult and reads the Levitical cult in light of the Christ-event. That is, the Levitical rites, especially Yom Kippur, furnish the author with patterns and paradigms that he sees as singularly fulfilled in Christ's saving act (e.g. 8:5; 9:6–10, 23; 10:1). Equally, however, the author's interest in and interpretation of the Levitical cult is evidently shaped by early Christian convictions about the significance of Christ's saving act. So, because of the importance of the Levitical cult to Hebrews' sacrificial theology, at key points I will closely read the scriptural texts concerned with the cult that are most directly relevant to Hebrews' exposition.[46] But because Hebrews' engagement with the cult is shaped by its convictions about Christ, I will approach the Levitical texts through Hebrews, first sketching the use the author makes of the cult, then asking what the author of Hebrews took a Levitical rite to mean both for and in light of the work of Christ.[47]

Third, a terminological note on resurrection, ascension, and "exaltation." With Moffitt, I will argue for the presence and significance of Jesus' bodily resurrection in Hebrews. This implies that Jesus' entrance to the heavenly sanctuary is a bodily event subsequent to his resurrection. When I speak of Jesus' "ascension," this entrance is its endpoint. When I say "exaltation" I mean either

---

[46] Such texts are found predominantly in Leviticus, though portions of Exodus, Numbers, and Deuteronomy are also relevant. When I use "Levitical texts" as shorthand I mean those passages that prescribe or narrate the operations of the Levitical cult, whether found inside or outside Leviticus. Similarly, when I use "Levitical" as shorthand I mean matters pertaining to the cult as reported in these texts.

[47] This approach dovetails with the broader comments of Koester 2005:370 on the way Hebrews relates Christ and scripture: "On the one hand, what God disclosed through the prophets is prior to Christ in time, so that the scriptural words create the context in which the meaning of Christ's work can be discerned. The author does not begin with a fully developed view of Christ that he then relates to the OT, but discerns the significance of Christ's work by considering it in light of the OT. On the other hand, what God disclosed through Christ is prior to the prophets in importance, so that Christ's life, death, and resurrection provide the touchstone for understanding what had previously been said in the Scriptures." As Moore 2015:107 puts it, "There is then a hermeneutical circle whereby the OT explains the Christ event, and the Christ event in turn leads to a new understanding of scripture." Cf. also Rascher 2007:1.

resurrection and ascension considered as a unit, or entrance to heaven with resurrection presupposed. Such usage does not require either that, in Hebrews' portrayal, Jesus' ascent to heaven took place immediately upon his resurrection, or that Jesus' entrance to heaven corresponds to the ascension after forty days in Acts 1.[48]

Fourth, I offer a few lexical comments on how Hebrews' particular cultic idiolect uses, and how I will use, the terms "offering" and "sacrifice." In common English usage, unless it is used metaphorically, "sacrifice" is typically synonymous with "kill" or "slaughter." Further, in ritual studies some treat "sacrifice" or "offering" as synonymous with the slaughter of the animal.[49] This equation frequently supports the conclusion that Christ's self-offering in Hebrews is synonymous with his death on the cross. By contrast, the noun προσφορά (Heb 10:10, 14) typically denotes something presented to God (e.g. Sir 14:11).[50] Its cognate verb προσφέρω, common in Hebrews,[51] is the regular LXX equivalent for Hiphil קרב, which can refer to the act of offering as a whole (e.g. Lev 1:2–3, 10; 2:1) or to "bringing near" or presenting sacrificial objects as a climactic stage in the sacrificial process (e.g. Lev 1:5; 7:33; 9:9). The verb προσφέρω is not a synonym for slaughter, nor does προσφορά denote that which is slaughtered. Certainly, slaughter is necessary in animal sacrifice, but slaughter is not an act to which προσφορά draws attention.[52] Similarly, given that Hebrews highlights the high priest's entry with and "offering" of blood (9:7, 11–14, 24–25), when we encounter the noun θυσία ("sacrifice"),[53] we should understand slaughter to be presupposed but not necessarily highlighted. That in Hebrews "sacrifice" is not synonymous with "slaughter" is especially clear in light of Hebrews' frequent use of the verb "offer" with "sacrifice" as object.[54] Sacrifices are what priests, including Jesus,

---

[48] Zwiep 1997:129, for instance, argues that in Hebrews Christ's exaltation to heaven and enthronement immediately follow his resurrection. So also Hengel 1995:153; Eskola 2001:343. This strikes me as possible, but I remain uncertain on this point and nothing in my argument depends on it.

[49] For examples in definitions of "offering" see Eberhart 2013:41 n. 61.

[50] BDAG 887; GELS 600.

[51] 5:1, 3, 7; 8:3, 4; 9:7, 9, 14, 25, 28; 10:1, 2, 8, 11, 12; 11:4, 17. The verb has the sense "deal with" in 12:7. Cf. also ἀναφέρω in 7:27; 13:15.

[52] Similarly Moffitt 2011:229–30 n. 30.

[53] 5:1; 7:27; 8:3; 9:9, 23, 26; 10:1, 5, 8, 11, 12, 26; 11:4; 13:15, 16. Though one of the sacrifices to which 11:4 refers is non-animal, and the sacrifices of 13:15 and 13:16 are metaphorical.

[54] 5:1; 8:3; 9:9; 10:1, 8, 11, 12; 11:4.

offer. And the act of offering a sacrifice involves far more than slaughter – for both Levitical priests and Jesus, I will argue. As we will discuss in Section 2.3 ("Yom Kippur in Hebrews"), 9:7 is the one place where Hebrews explicitly spells out where and when the "offering" takes place on the Levitical Day of Atonement. What it there calls "offering" is the priestly manipulation of blood in the Holy of Holies. This is echoed by 13:11, where it is the blood brought into the Holy of Holies that is called a "sin offering."[55] Hence in Hebrews "sacrifice" includes slaughter but is not reducible to it. Throughout the thesis, when I use "offer," "offering," and "sacrifice," I intend to preserve the semantic range and nuances present in these cultic uses in both Hebrews and Leviticus.

Fifth, a comment on how I will use the word "atonement." One pitfall in this discussion is the breadth and ambiguity of this English word. Christopher Tuckett remarks, "In discussions about the NT, 'the Atonement' is generally understood to refer to the work of Jesus in putting right the human situation in relation to God." Tuckett notes that the New Testament uses a wide variety of "models and images to describe how the life, death, and resurrection of Jesus have changed the human situation."[56] In this common usage, "atonement" is a broad, inclusive term: under this heading Tuckett discusses sacrifice, redemption, reconciliation, victory over evil powers, and so on. Yet sometimes "atonement" is used in a narrower sense, one controlled by cultic terms, like the German "Sühne."[57] If "atonement" is used in this narrower sense, as a kind of translation equivalent for cultic uses of כָּפַר, ἐξιλάσκομαι, and so on, two consequences follow. The first is that exegetical and theological discourse requires another umbrella term for the saving significance of the Christ-event. The second is that, without some such term, our analyses of texts treating the saving significance of Jesus' death and resurrection might be restricted, with or without proper warrant, to passages that use cultic categories. In such a case it would not necessarily be clear what a scholar means by "atonement."

Given this potential ambiguity, when I address the material question of the saving significance of Christ's death, I will generally avoid using "atonement" as a master category. Instead, I will use phrases such as "objective soteriological significance," "soteriological achievement," and so on to describe how Hebrews portrays Christ's

---

[55] Again, see Section 2.3, "Yom Kippur in Hebrews."
[56] Tuckett 1992:518.
[57] E.g. Knöppler 2001.

death as setting right what is wrong with the human condition. These phrases, like Tuckett's broad sense of "atonement," presuppose some plight, some gap between the way things are (or were) and the way they should be.[58] Hence in Chapter 4 I will examine the fit between what Hebrews sees as wrong with the human condition and the ways in which Christ's death rights those wrongs.

1.5 Preview

As mentioned previously, this thesis has two parts engaging two conversations centered on two questions – and each part has two chapters. Part I, consisting of Chapters 2 and 3, will conduct the "broad" conversation concerning the question, "When and where did Jesus offer himself?" And I will answer, with View 5, "In the heavenly sanctuary, after his resurrection and ascent to heaven." Chapter 2 will argue that Hebrews depicts Jesus as being appointed high priest at his entrance to heaven and subsequently offering himself in the heavenly Holy of Holies. The first of these points is established by the way Hebrews aligns Jesus' perfection, resurrection, and appointment to high priesthood; the second by how Hebrews deploys Yom Kippur in 9:23–28, 8:1–5, and 9:11–14. Chapter 3 will first ask where 10:5–14 locates Christ's self-offering, answering that the passage figures Christ's bodily offering in heaven as the goal of his incarnation. Following this, I will briefly survey all of Hebrews' other, briefer passages that construe the Christ-event in cultic terms, and will conclude that they are all consistent with Christ offering himself in heaven, including the notoriously difficult apparent reference to "the veil of Jesus' flesh" in 10:19–20.

In Part II, Chapters 4 and 5, I will conduct the "narrow" conversation focused on the twofold material question of what role Jesus' death plays in Hebrews' soteriology, as well as in his heavenly self-offering. In Chapter 4, I will engage 2:9, 2:14–15, and 9:15–17, asking what conceptual resources each passage draws on to ascribe objective soteriological significance to Jesus' death. I will conclude that elements in both 2:9 and 9:15–17 prepare for how Jesus' death materially features in his heavenly offering. In Chapter 5, I will ask what role Jesus' death plays in his self-offering itself, and will argue that while Jesus' death is not where and when he is offered, it is what

---

[58] Tuckett 1992:518.

he offers. The primary focus of this chapter is Jesus' "blood." Contra Moffitt, who associates Jesus' blood exclusively with his resurrection life, I will argue the three-part thesis that (1) in a variety of cultic contexts, Hebrews conceptually equates blood with death, including using "blood" as a metonym for Jesus' death; (2) "blood" is one term for what Jesus offers in heaven; and (3) Jesus' death, as a soteriological achievement, is what he offers to God in heaven. To make this case, Chapter 5 will delineate three sets of conceptual connections in Hebrews' cultic construal of the Christ-event: those between Jesus' death and blood, his blood and offering, and his death and offering. In light of these connections between Jesus' blood and his death, Chapter 5 will conclude that the "blood" Jesus offers in heaven is the life he gave in death. Finally, in Chapter 6, I will return to the question of the narrative and conceptual coherence of Hebrews' sacrificial theology, and I will reflect briefly on how the reading of Hebrews offered here relates to other New Testament conceptions of atonement, especially those of Paul, and on the resources Hebrews drew on in formulating its singular high-priestly Christology.

Part I

The Formal Question

2

LOCATING CHRIST'S SELF-OFFERING IN HEAVEN

2.1 Introduction

According to Hebrews, when and where did Jesus offer himself? As we have seen, this question has prompted at least five answers, ranging from "on the cross on Good Friday" to "in the heavenly sanctuary after Jesus' resurrection." The goal of this chapter is to argue the twofold thesis that Christ was appointed high priest at his post-resurrection entrance to heaven, and that he offered himself to God, once for all, at his embodied entrance to the heavenly sanctuary. I will argue in Section 2.2 that Jesus' perfection is prerequisite to his appointment as high priest, that he is perfected at his resurrection, and as a consequence of this he is appointed high priest at his entrance to heaven. Because Jesus, like every high priest, is appointed in order to offer sacrifice (5:1; 8:3), his appointment after resurrection already indicates that he offers himself subsequent to his resurrection, in the heavenly sanctuary. Hence I address Jesus' appointment before his offering because that is a conceptual sequence Hebrews itself constructs.

Second, in Section 2.3 I argue that, in its deployment of Yom Kippur as a model for the work of Christ, Hebrews indicates that Jesus enters the heavenly sanctuary in order to offer himself there. To support this point I first briefly gauge Hebrews' interests in Yom Kippur and examine the ritual logic of Yom Kippur itself. I then ask where Jesus offers himself, answering, contra View 1 in particular, "the heavenly sanctuary." Finally, in dialogue with Views 2–4, I ask when Jesus offers himself, defending the answer "after his resurrection."

2.2 Appointed High Priest at His Entrance to Heaven

The question of when Jesus was appointed high priest has a significant, even decisive, bearing on when and where Jesus offered himself. Hebrews twice asserts that every high priest is appointed to offer

23

sacrifice: "For every high priest chosen from among men is appointed to act on behalf of men in relation to God, to offer gifts and sacrifices for sins" (5:1). And again, "For every high priest is appointed to offer gifts and sacrifices; thus it is necessary for this priest also to have something to offer" (8:3). Since a high priest is appointed in order to offer sacrifice, appointment necessarily precedes offering. Hence the idea that Jesus offered himself on earth, as Views 1–4 all affirm, requires that prior to his death Jesus was already appointed to the office of high priest. Conversely, if Jesus only became high priest after his resurrection, he could only offer himself after his resurrection, in the tabernacle in heaven. In what follows I will argue that Jesus was appointed high priest at his entrance to heaven, on the basis of the indestructible life he obtained at his resurrection. After surveying scholarly views on the question, I will argue that Jesus' perfecting is his becoming qualified for priesthood, this perfecting takes place at his resurrection, and he is appointed high priest when, at his entrance to heaven, God declares him high priest in the order of Melchizedek.

To survey views: First, many argue that Jesus was already high priest during his earthly career. Whether Jesus is seen as priest from eternity, or as becoming priest at his incarnation or baptism or an unspecified time, this view entails that Jesus already fills the office of high priest on earth, and offers himself in his death.[1] Second, a few scholars argue that Christ became priest in the act of offering himself on the cross.[2] Third, some argue that Christ's appointment to high priest was progressive: He acted as priest on earth, offering himself in his death, but was only formally appointed or confirmed in office after his death.[3] Fourth, many argue that Christ was appointed high priest after his entire earthly career, including his suffering and death.[4] Many in this broad camp associate Jesus' appointment with his exaltation to heaven, sometimes describing this in terms of

---

[1] So, with varying details, Cody 1960:107, 177; Laub 1980:120–22; Loader 1981:245–47; Rissi 1987:61–70; Scholer 1991:82–89; Grässer 1993:143–44; Rascher 2007:73, 114; Cockerill 2012:241–42; Richardson 2012:47–49; Sargent 2014:29 n. 78; Bates 2015:55.

[2] Peterson 1982:195; Wallis 1995:146; Fuhrmann 2007:102–17; perhaps Mackie 2007:213–14.

[3] Lane 1991:1.119, 1.154; Cortez 2008:317–22.

[4] E.g. Davies 1968:386; Hay 1973:144–45; Thompson 1982:105; Meier 1985b:506; Walter 1997:158–59, 161; Anderson 2001:204, 206, 216, 231–32; Nelson 2003:258; Lee 2005:275; Gäbel 2006:172–81, 236–54; Barnard 2012:130–43; Peeler 2014:127–29; Small 2014:249; Whitlark 2014:123–24; Ribbens 2016:107.

ascension. Others in this group specify that Jesus was perfected, and consequently appointed priest, at his bodily resurrection or subsequent entrance to heaven.[5] Fifth, some argue that Hebrews offers no clear answer to the question, whether because the author does not intend to or because of irreconcilable tensions in the argument.[6]

Space precludes detailed engagement with each view; here I simply argue that Jesus was appointed high priest at his entrance to heaven, on the basis of his being made perfect by resurrection.[7] I intend to argue the latter more definitely than the former. That is, I take Hebrews to indicate explicitly that Jesus had to be perfected in order to be appointed high priest, and that he was perfected at and by his resurrection. Further, somewhat more cautiously, I argue that Heb 5:5–6 presents God's installation of Jesus as high priest as a direct, in-person address, which occurs at Jesus' entrance to heaven. However, relatively little hangs on this latter assertion. The most important point is that Jesus was only qualified to become high priest once resurrected.

Hebrews' answer to the question of when Jesus was appointed high priest follows from its argument about what qualifications Jesus needed in order to become high priest. As many modern scholars recognize, Hebrews uses the term "perfection" of Christ to designate his qualification for the office of high priesthood, whatever other nuances it may have.[8] The process of Jesus' perfection consists in the whole series of prerequisites for his appointment to Melchizedekian high priesthood; his entrance into perfection is his acquisition of all he needed in order to become high priest. Jesus had to be perfected to be appointed priest. And, I will argue, he was only perfected at his resurrection.

We can pick up this trail at the three places where Hebrews says Jesus was perfected:

---

[5] For appointment at resurrection or subsequent exaltation see Brooks 1970:206–8; Kurianal 2000:219–33; Eskola 2001:259; Johnson 2006:187; Moffitt 2011:194–208; Barnard 2012:130–43; Easter 2014:94–99, 123; Kibbe 2014:38–42; Moore 2015:163 n. 69. Moffitt and Moore argue that, since Jesus was appointed priest at his resurrection, this occurred between his death and entrance to heaven.

[6] Attridge 1989:146–47; Pursiful 1993:81–85; Koester 2001:109–110; Stökl ben Ezra 2003:184 n. 181; Löhr 2005:458; Eberhart 2013:138 n. 31; Compton 2015b:134.

[7] For detailed recent treatments with which I generally concur and on which the following draws, see Kurianal 2000:219–33; Gäbel 2006:172–81, 236–54; Moffitt 2011:194–208. Cf. also Peeler 2014:124–28.

[8] See, e.g., Peterson 1982; Kurianal 2000:227–32; Gäbel 2006:163–70; Schenck 2007:66; Moffitt 2011:194–98; Small 2014:177, 222–23.

For it was fitting that he, for whom and by whom all things exist, in bringing many sons to glory, should make the founder of their salvation perfect (τελειῶσαι) through suffering. (2:10)

Although he was a son, he learned obedience through what he suffered. And being made perfect (τελειωθείς), he became the source of eternal salvation to all who obey him, being designated by God a high priest after the order of Melchizedek. (5:8–10)

For the law appoints men in their weakness as high priests, but the word of the oath, which came later than the law, appoints a Son who has been made perfect (τετελειωμένον) forever. (7:28)

In 7:28, Jesus' perfection is a perfect-tense reality: He is appointed high priest as one who has been made perfect. Jesus' appointment to high priesthood depends on his achieved state of perfection. And the two prior passages describe how Jesus came to achieve this state. In 2:10, the parallels with the preceding verse are instructive. In 2:9, Jesus is "crowned with glory and honor because of the suffering of death"; in 2:10, the author asserts that, in leading many sons to glory, it was fitting for God to "make the founder of their salvation perfect through suffering." This parallel indicates that the process of Jesus' perfecting included his suffering, his perfection was necessary in order for him to pioneer his people's salvation, and his perfection is somehow coordinated with his being "crowned with glory and honor."[9]

Further, 2:10 begins a discussion of Christ's solidarity with his human siblings that continues through, and culminates in, the purpose statement of 2:17: "Therefore he had to be made like his brothers in every respect, so that he might become a merciful and faithful high priest in the service of God, to atone for the sins of the people." This purpose statement draws an inference (ὅθεν) from the entire discussion begun in 2:10, and specifically from the assertion of 2:16 that Christ savingly lays hold not of angels but of humanity. In

---

[9] Kurianal 2000:228–29. Others who note the parallel character of 2:9–10 include Scholer 1991:84; Weiss 1991:204–7; Lane 1991:1.52–53. In light of 2:11 and 2:17, Moffitt 2011:196 further suggests, "That the Son's being perfected through suffering is necessary for the salvation of the many suggests that the perfection of the Son stands between his own endurance of suffering and his becoming the high priest whose service sanctifies his siblings."

order to become his people's all-sufficient savior, Jesus had to be made like them in every way. Because of the humanity he came to share with his people, he is not ashamed to call them brothers (2:11–12); because he became human to save, he embraced as children those whom God gave him (2:13). Because the children share in flesh and blood, he took on the same (2:14). This ontological solidarity is recapitulated in the assertion of 2:17 that "he had to be made like his brothers in every respect" (2:17). However, Jesus' being made like his brothers in every respect involved not only his assumption of flesh and blood but also his endurance of temptation through suffering: "For because he himself has suffered when tempted, he is able to help those who are being tempted" (2:18). Jesus' ability to serve as a high priest is grounded (γάρ, 2:18), in part, on his experience of temptation in suffering. What qualified Jesus to become high priest was not only his ontological solidarity with humanity, but his faithful endurance of the entire desperate human condition.[10] Therefore the implication of "become" (γένηται) in 2:17 is probably not that in his earthly life Jesus already was high priest but had to become merciful and faithful. Instead, the man Jesus had to *become* high priest (cf. 5:10; 6:20; 7:16). Hence 2:17–18 confirms that Christ's completed earthly career is prerequisite to his becoming high priest.[11]

This picture develops in 5:5–10. In 5:5, the writer cites Ps 2:7 ("You are my Son, today I have begotten you"), which he cited already in 1:5. The citation in 1:5 explicates the assertion of 1:3–4 that Jesus inherited a name superior to the angels when he sat down at God's right hand. Hence in 1:5 God speaks Ps 2:7 to Christ at his enthronement, the citation constituting an effectual speech-act that installs Christ in office as Messiah regnant.[12] Given this, we should probably understand the similarly structured address of Ps 110:4, cited in Heb 5:6, to install Christ in the office of high priest: "You are a priest forever, after the order of Melchizedek." This construal of God's oath in Ps 110:4 as installing Christ in high-priestly office is confirmed by the fact that the citation in 5:6 explicates the claim of

---

[10] For this characterization of Jesus' endurance of temptation, see Walter 1997:156.
[11] So Michel 1966:164, "Sohn war er (1:3, 5:7f.) und Hohepriester wird er (2:17, 5:10)"; followed by Ellingworth 1993:294; Gäbel 2006:179.
[12] Among scholars who comment on the temporal referent of Heb 1:5, a majority argue that God speaks Ps 2:7 to the Son at his enthronement. See, e.g., Spicq 1953:16; Vanhoye 1969:140–42; Loader 1981:12; Meier 1985b:505–6; Bruce 1990:54; Lane 1991:1.24–25; Weiss 1991:160–61; Guthrie 2007:929; Peeler 2014:42–46.

5:5 that Christ "did not exalt himself to be made a high priest" (γενηθῆναι ἀρχιερέα); that was accomplished instead by the one who spoke to him the cited words of Ps 2:7 and Ps 110:4. God's address to Christ in Heb 5:6 does not report something already true but makes something true.

So then, when did God speak Ps 110:4 to Christ? Since the citation of Ps 2:7 in 1:5 elaborates the assertion of Christ's enthronement in 1:3–4, it is clear that Hebrews understands God to have spoken the words of this psalm to Christ face-to-face, in the heavenly throne room. That the author links Ps 2:7 with Ps 110:4 in 5:5–6 suggests that he understands the latter address also to have been spoken by God to Christ in person. Hence, even before we see how Christ's appointment to priesthood is elaborated in 5:7–10, the most likely temporal referent for this address is Christ's arrival in heaven.[13]

In other words, 5:5–6 locates the moment when God speaks Ps 110:4 to Jesus after his entire earthly career. Then, after reporting this address of priestly appointment, in 5:7–10 the author describes Christ's earthly journey toward his appointment.[14] In 5:7 the author says Jesus prayed to the one able to rescue him out of death, with the result that he was heard because of his reverence.[15] Since Christ did in fact die, his "being heard" by "the one able to rescue him out of death (ἐκ θανάτου)" makes best sense as reporting Jesus' resurrection.[16] Jesus was not saved from dying. Instead, after submitting to death, he was delivered out of it (cf. 13:20).

Commenting on this sequence of events, the author asserts, "Although he was a son, he learned obedience through what he suffered" (5:8). The result of this process is described with two aorist participles and a finite aorist verb: "And being made perfect (τελειωθείς), he became (ἐγένετο) the source of eternal salvation to all who obey him, being designated (προσαγορευθείς) by God a high priest after the order of Melchizedek" (5:9–10). The parallels between 5:9–10 and 2:9–10 are striking.[17] God is the subject of τελειῶσαι

---

[13] Scholars who make this connection between Heb 1:5 and 5:5–6 include Hay 1973:144–45; Meier 1985b:506; Anderson 2001:204, 206; Gäbel 2006:180.

[14] Guthrie 2007:962 writes that though Jesus was "marked out for appointment, the path to that appointment lay along the way of suffering."

[15] For detailed discussion of this verse, see especially Gray 2003:188–205. For ἀπό as causal here, see Ellingworth 1993:290–91.

[16] Kurianal 2000:70, 230; Gray 2003:192–93; Jipp 2010:572; Moffitt 2011:188–93; contra Backhaus 2009b:207.

[17] For a visual synopsis of some of these points see Silva 1976:66.

("to perfect") in 2:10 and the implied agent of τελειωθείς ("having been perfected") in 5:9. In 2:10, Jesus-made-perfect is the founder of salvation; in 5:9 Jesus-made-perfect becomes the source of salvation. And in 2:10 Jesus is perfected through suffering, while 5:9 presupposes that perfection is the outcome of his suffering.[18] But what is new in 5:9–10, though implied in 2:17–18 (cf. 2:10), is that Jesus' appointment to Melchizedekian priesthood is the consequence of his being perfected. Only after being made perfect is Jesus designated by God as high priest. Thus the action depicted in the first participle (τελειωθείς) precedes that of the main verb, while the action of the second participle (προσαγορευθείς) is best taken as either coincident or subsequent.[19] What we have seen in 7:28 confirms this sequence: It is as one who has been made perfect that Christ is appointed high priest. In this way, 5:9–10 extends the sequence begun in 2:9–10. Jesus' suffering is one of the means of his perfection. Hence his being-made-perfect follows upon the conclusion of his suffering. This becoming perfect, in turn, is prerequisite to his appointment as high priest.

Hence, in relation to 2:10, 5:9–10 adds that not only is Jesus perfected through suffering, but he only attains the status of perfection after his suffering has concluded, namely after his death. The implicit sequence of 5:7–10 is: (1) Jesus learned obedience through suffering, up to and including his death; (2) after this suffering and death he was delivered from death and made perfect; (3) at that time or shortly thereafter, he was appointed high priest and so became the source of his people's salvation. In the second step, Jesus is perfected at his resurrection.[20]

---

[18] Kurianal 2000:230.

[19] Regarding the former participle, it is best to see Jesus' perfecting as at least logically preceding his becoming the source of salvation, since he saves by executing the office of high priest, and his perfection is prerequisite to his appointment as high priest. Regarding the latter participle, nothing serious rides on whether the action is coincident or subsequent. If subsequent, the sense may well be more logical than temporal: once perfected, appointed. For the former participle as antecedent and the latter as coincident see Moffitt 2011:197.

[20] Many take the phrase "offered up prayers and supplications" in 5:7 to indicate that Christ already acts as high priest during his earthly suffering. (So, e.g., Zesati Estrada 1990:128–42; Lane 1991:1.119; Scholer 1991:194; Koester 2001:298–99; Cockerill 2012:241–42; Richardson 2012:74–89.) However, against this view, as we have seen, 5:7 locates Jesus' offering of prayers within his learning obedience through suffering (5:8), which precedes both his perfection and his appointment to priesthood (Kibbe 2014:39–40). Within the chiastic structure of 5:1–10, 5:7 does correspond to earthly priests sacrificing for their own sins in 5:3. But the commonality in view is

The basis of Christ's qualification for high priesthood is elaborated further in Heb 7. Here Jesus' immortality, contrasted with the Levitical priests' mortality, is an essential ingredient in his superior priesthood. In 7:8 the Levitical priests are characterized as mortal, whereas of Melchizedek, Christ's precursor, "it is testified that he lives." In 7:16, Jesus "has become a priest, not on the basis of a legal requirement concerning bodily descent, but on the basis of the power of an indestructible life." In 7:23–24 the Levitical priests "were prevented by death from remaining in office," but Jesus "holds his priesthood permanently" because, like Melchizedek, "he remains forever" (cf. 7:3). This is why Jesus "is able to save to the uttermost those who draw near to God through him, since he always lives to intercede for them" (7:25).[21] Finally, 7:28 asserts that, while the law "appoints men in their weakness as high priests," the oath of Ps 110:4 "appoints a Son who has been made perfect forever." As I will argue in this section, all of these passages contrast the Levitical priests' mortality with Jesus' immortality, the latter an essential qualification for his appointment as Melchizedekian high priest.

I argued earlier that in 5:7–10 Jesus' attainment of perfection coincided with his resurrection. These passages in Heb 7 explain why: Jesus' resurrection perfected him. We should note again that 7:28 indicates Jesus was appointed high priest once he had attained the state of perfection. This perfection contrasts with the "weakness" characterizing those who were appointed as Levitical priests, which includes both moral weakness and mortality. Hebrews 7:27 explicitly refers to moral weakness in mentioning the Levitical priests' need to sacrifice for their own sins. This recalls 5:1–3, where the "weakness" that besets the Levitical high priests both requires them to sacrifice for their own sins (5:3) and enables them to "deal gently with the

---

human weakness, not priestly activity, since in 5:7 Jesus does not offer priestly intercession but prays for his own deliverance (Gäbel 2006:175). Finally, at least one early Jewish source uses προσφέρω to describe non-priests offering prayers and hymns to God, and both Jewish and pagan sources use it to describe the offering of petitions or entreaties to other people; these offer ample non-priestly parallels to its use here. (Non-priests praying: Josephus, *J.W.* 3.353; cf. T. Levi 3:8; T. Gad 7:2. Petitions to people: Josephus, *Ant.* 2.42, 45, 148; 4.107 (with δεήσις); Philo, *Joseph* 1.40; Longus, *Daphn.* 2.33.1; Achilles Tatius, *Leuc. Clit.* 7.1.3. See Gäbel 2006:176–78; cf. Attridge 1989:149 n. 154.) In other words, προσενέγκας in 5:7 employs a standard Greek idiom for petition, and so neither draws on nor influences Hebrews' description of Jesus offering himself as a sacrifice.

[21] Thus, as Stökl ben Ezra 2003:184 n. 181 observes, "Christ's high priesthood is εἰς τὸν αἰῶνα (5:6), but not ἀπὸ τῶν αἰώνων" (emphasis original).

ignorant and wayward." However, "weakness" in 7:27 also includes mortality. Hebrews figures the priests' mortality as an element of this same fabric of fallenness: the priests' sin and mortality are of a piece. This is evident from the way 7:23 presents the Levitical priests' mortality as a crucial limitation of their priesthood.[22] By contrast with the ultimately ineffectual Levitical priesthood, Jesus the high priest is able to save people utterly because he holds his office permanently. This unending priesthood is enabled by his unending life (7:24–25). And the contrast in 7:28 is between "men having weakness" and "a Son who has been made perfect forever." We have already seen that Jesus attained perfection at and by his resurrection. Further, while in his earthly life Jesus underwent temptation, Hebrews insists that he did so sinlessly (4:15). So the contrast in 7:28 is not primarily moral but ontological; the weakness that besets the Levitical priests, while including a moral dimension, also involves liability to death. Hence in 7:28, as in 7:8, 7:16, and 7:23–24, the contrast between Jesus and the Levitical priests turns on their mortality and his immortality.[23]

When and how did Jesus obtain this immortality? I argue that 7:16 answers, "his resurrection": Jesus "has become a priest, not on the basis of a legal requirement concerning bodily descent, but on the basis of the power of an indestructible life." Most scholars see 7:16 as describing the life Jesus obtained at his resurrection, and I concur for the following three reasons.[24] First, a reference to the life Jesus obtained at his resurrection makes best sense of 7:16 because this verse furnishes the basis for how Jesus' priesthood solves the problem posed by the Levitical priests' mortality.[25] Levitical high priesthood required perpetual succession; Christ is high priest perpetually.

---

[22] Cf. Moore 2015:168, "As with the plurality of priests (7.23–25), so also the plurality of sacrifices (7.26–28) is indicative of a weakness whose source lies elsewhere, in sin and mortality."

[23] So, e.g., Kurianal 2000:231–33; Moffitt 2011:197–98.

[24] E.g. Hay 1973:146; Peterson 1982:110–11; Bruce 1990:169; Lane 1991:1.84; deSilva 2000:271; Kurianal 2000:121 n. 388; Rooke 2000:91; Anderson 2001:259; Johnson 2006:188; Karrer 2008:84; Hays 2009:158; Moffitt 2011:203; Vanhoye 2011:214; Moore 2015:165–66; Compton 2015a:89; Schreiner 2015:222–23.

[25] As Moore 2015:165–66 comments on the repeated insistence on the permanence of Jesus' life throughout Heb 7, "These phrases all clearly characterize the enduring nature of Jesus' exalted state, yet the contrast with the priests is insufficiently accounted for unless a reference to the resurrection is also understood: since he himself underwent death, Jesus' exaltation alone does not explain how he is sufficiently different from the Levitical priests. It is in part the problem of *mortality* which must be overcome, and this is achieved only through resurrection" (emphasis original).

To confirm this assertion of Jesus' indestructible life, Hebrews cites Ps 110:4, "For it is witnessed of him, 'You are a priest forever, after the order of Melchizedek'" (7:17). The resurrection gives Jesus what Ps 110:4 implies the Melchizedekian high priest must have: life imperishable. Yet Jesus did not possess such indissoluble life before his resurrection. By coming to share "flesh and blood" (2:14), Jesus participated in precisely the frail, mortal existence the Levitical priests had, including its bitter end. Hebrews in no way qualifies or mitigates Jesus' mortality. Hence it is out of keeping with Hebrews' characterization of Jesus' human existence to introduce his divine nature as the source of his indestructible life in 7:16.[26] As Albert Vanhoye comments, "It is not true that, as from this first moment, the divine eternal life completely penetrated the human nature of Jesus. On the contrary, that human nature was weak, subject to suffering, mortal ... It was at the moment of the resurrection that the 'power of life indestructible' completely penetrated the human nature of Jesus and made it become immortal."[27]

Second, the parallels between 7:16 and 7:28 weigh in favor of a reference to Christ's resurrection life in 7:16. In 7:16, Jesus became priest on the basis of (κατά) an indestructible life, which presupposes his acquisition of such life; in 7:28 Jesus is appointed priest as one who has been made perfect. In both verses, a state Jesus did not always have but instead came to have warrants his appointment to high priesthood. This parallel confirms what I argued from 5:7–10, that Jesus' perfecting coincides with his resurrection. In 7:16, as elaborated in 7:23–25, Jesus' indestructible life is what enables him, in contrast to the mortal Levitical priests, to remain in office forever. In 7:28, Jesus' perfection names his decisive difference from the Levitical priests' mortal weakness. Hence the event that gave Jesus indestructible life is what perfected him, and his perfection includes his acquiring indestructible life.

Third, reading 7:16 as a reference to resurrection-imparted life best coheres with all three passages on Christ's perfecting (2:10; 5:7–10; 7:28). From 2:10 we learn that Christ's suffering was a means of his perfecting, and that this process was necessary for him to

---

[26] For a defense of 7:16 as rooting Jesus' "indestructible life" in his divine nature, see, e.g., Small 2014:170–71.
[27] Vanhoye 2011:214.

become the founder of his people's salvation.[28] From 5:7–10 we learn that Christ learned obedience through what he suffered, including death; that he was delivered from death; that his perfecting followed his completed suffering; and that all this was prerequisite to his appointment to high priesthood. From 7:28 we learn that Christ was appointed high priest as one who has attained perfection. In context of 7:23–25, this perfection only obtains after Christ has died and because he can no longer die. As Moffitt puts it, "[S]ince Jesus did in fact die, everything the writer has just predicated about Jesus' perfection and subsequent ministry can only apply to him *after* his death."[29] Before Jesus' resurrection, he is just as mortal as the Levitical priests, and therefore not yet qualified for Melchizedekian office. Only at Jesus' resurrection does he obtain the essential qualification of indestructible life. Hence Jesus is appointed high priest on the basis of his resurrection.

Corroborating evidence that Jesus is appointed high priest at his entrance to heaven, and hence only serves as priest in the heavenly sanctuary, can be found in 8:4. We read, "Now if he were on earth, he would not be a priest at all, since there are priests who offer gifts *according to the law*." The writer has already asserted that Christ can only serve as priest after suffering, dying, and being perfected by resurrection. Here he offers a complementary reason why Jesus' high-priestly ministry is restricted to the heavenly sanctuary: the priesthood on earth, prescribed by the Mosaic law, is one to which Jesus does not and cannot belong. This rationale resumes the argument of 7:13–14: "For the one of whom these things are spoken belonged to another tribe, from which no one has ever served at the altar. For it is evident that our Lord was descended from Judah, and in connection with that tribe Moses said nothing about priests." Since Jesus descended from Judah, he is not qualified for priesthood on the basis of the law. Hence in 7:15 and following, the author introduces that which did qualify Jesus for high priesthood – his indestructible life. As elaborated throughout Heb 7, Jesus' priesthood is not warranted by the Mosaic law but by the divine oath of

---

[28] Since Jesus was only perfected at and by his resurrection, we should understand 2:10 to indicate that his suffering was a necessary, though not sufficient, means of his perfection. Since Jesus needed both empathy gained by experience (cf. 2:17–18, 4:15) and indestructible life in order to become high priest, both suffering and resurrection are necessary conditions of his perfection.

[29] Moffitt 2011:198, emphasis original.

Ps 110:4, "which came later than the law" (7:28). Hence in 8:4 the author's implicit premise seems to be that the law is valid on earth. Therefore, Jesus was not qualified to serve as a priest on earth, and did not serve as high priest during his earthly career.[30]

Hebrews 8:4 presupposes two separate, even mutually exclusive, priesthoods, one on earth and one in heaven, one predicated on Levitical descent and the other on the event of Jesus' resurrection. In light of the passages discussed in this section, 8:4 confirms that Jesus did not and could not serve as high priest during his earthly life. Hence we must look to another time and place to discern when and where he offered himself. We will return to 8:4 and its whole paragraph (8:1–5) in the next section.

We have seen in 2:10, 5:7–10, and Heb 7 that Jesus had to suffer and die in order to be made perfect, was perfected at his resurrection, and was appointed high priest on the basis of this resurrection-conferred perfection. Since Heb 5:5–6 conjoins Ps 2:7 and Ps 110:4, and in Heb 1:5 God speaks the former to Christ in the heavenly throne room, it makes best sense to see Heb 5:5–10 as indicating that God also appointed Christ high priest, with the words of Ps 110:4, upon Christ's entrance to heaven. Yet these official installations do not occur at precisely the same moment. At Jesus' entrance to heaven, God appoints Jesus high priest by declaring, "You are a priest forever" (Ps 110:4; Heb 5:6). Then, after entering the heavenly Holy of Holies and offering himself there, Jesus is invited by God to sit at his right hand (Ps 110:1; Heb 1:3, 13). He does, and God declares, "You are my Son, today I have begotten you" (Ps 2:7; Heb 1:5).

In this section I have argued that Jesus is appointed high priest at his entrance to heaven, on the basis of his resurrection. As we saw from 5:1 and 8:3, Jesus, like every high priest, is appointed to offer sacrifice for sin. Since offering sacrifice is a defining purpose for which priests are appointed, the writer clearly presupposes that appointment to priesthood precedes offering sacrifice. There is no evidence in Hebrews that Jesus' self-offering precedes or somehow effects his priestly appointment. The scriptural logic Hebrews explicitly, repeatedly appropriates is that a high priest is appointed in order to make an offering.

---

[30] Gäbel 2006:248–49; Moffitt 2011:198–99; deSilva 2013:636–37; Ribbens 2016:107–8.

Hence, on the basis of this discussion we must already conclude that Jesus offers himself in heaven, after his resurrection. In order to be appointed high priest, Jesus had to be perfected. In order to be perfected Jesus had not only to suffer and die, but to arise with indestructible life. Jesus is only qualified for priesthood by his resurrection, and only appointed high priest on the basis of it. This helps explain why Heb 8:4 explicitly restricts Christ's high-priestly service to heaven. Further, as we will see in Section 2.3, Hebrews' deployment of Yom Kippur confirms this location for Christ's self-offering. Inasmuch as Views 1–4 all require Jesus to act as high priest in his death on the cross, this section's argument undermines each.

As Melchizedekian high priest Jesus offered himself in heaven, after his resurrection – only there, only then. This is not to deny that Jesus' death is sacrificial in the sense that it sets the Yom Kippur script in motion.[31] Nor is it to deny that Jesus' death is soteriologically efficacious in its own right, and is even incorporated into his heavenly self-offering, as I will argue in Part II. Nevertheless, we have seen that Jesus did not and indeed could not serve as high priest on earth. And, since high priests are appointed to offer sacrifice, Jesus offered his sacrifice in the only place where he served as high priest: the heavenly tabernacle.

2.3 Where and When Did Jesus Offer Himself? In Heaven, after His Resurrection

This section continues the argument for locating Christ's self-offering in the heavenly sanctuary, after his resurrection. Here I support and defend this conclusion by examining Hebrews' most explicit discussions of the time and place of Jesus' self-offering. The central contention of this section is that the manner in which Hebrews both narrates the earthly Yom Kippur rite and deploys it as a model for the work of Christ testifies conclusively that Jesus offered himself in the heavenly Holy of Holies upon his bodily ascent there. The argument of this section has four parts. First, I examine how Hebrews interprets Yom Kippur. Second, I read Yom Kippur in Lev 16 in light of Hebrews' interpretation.[32] Together these

---

[31] Rightly, Nelson 2003:255; Moffitt 2011:292–93; Ribbens 2016:132–34.

[32] Because most contemporary scholarship on Levitical sacrifice focuses on the Hebrew text, and in order to understand the Greek translation as a translation, I will read Lev 16 in both Hebrew and Greek. As I will discuss, Hebrews likely accessed a Greek version of Lev 16 in substantial continuity with that represented in Rahlfs.

sections both prepare for detailed exegesis to follow and offer their own support for locating Jesus' self-offering in heaven. Third, I argue that *where* Jesus offers himself is the Holy of Holies of the tabernacle in heaven. Fourth, *when* Jesus offers himself is his bodily ascent to heaven following his resurrection.

Yom Kippur in Hebrews

In this section I will survey Hebrews' interpretation of the sacrificial rite of Yom Kippur. In this survey I engage both Hebrews' references to the Levitical Yom Kippur and its references to Jesus' high-priestly sacrifice insofar as they shed light on Hebrews' interpretation of the Levitical rite. As I will discuss further, the question all of Part I seeks to answer turns largely, though not exclusively, on how one construes Hebrews' use of Yom Kippur. As we saw in Section 1.2, proponents of View 1 argue that our writer deliberately refashions Yom Kippur's sacrificial sequence. Such authors recognize that, in Hebrews' narration, the high priest enters the Holy of Holies in order to make his offering there (9:7), but they argue that Hebrews has rewritten this script such that Christ first offers himself on the cross, and then enters the Holy of Holies in heaven. I will argue throughout Section 2.3 that this interpretation misconstrues Hebrews' Christological appropriation of Yom Kippur. Instead, in narrating the Levitical Yom Kippur, Hebrews stages the sequence "enter in order to offer" precisely in order to indicate that Christ's self-offering follows the same sequence. Christ entered the heavenly tabernacle in order to offer himself there.

Yom Kippur is not the only sacrificial rite the author relates to the high-priestly work of Christ. He also mentions or alludes to the daily sacrifices (Exod 29:38–42; Num 28:1–8; Heb 7:27), the red heifer ritual (Num 19:1–13; Heb 9:13–14), and the inauguration of the Sinai covenant (Exod 24:1–11; Heb 9:18–21), among others. Yet Yom Kippur plays a programmatic, architectonic role in Hebrews' exposition of Christ's self-offering. Hebrews' chief proof-text for Christ's priesthood, Ps 110:4, names Christ "priest," but not high priest. The "high" in "high priest" derives from Hebrews' intense focus on Yom Kippur, in which the high priest himself performs the entire rite. And, as we will see, Yom Kippur is the only rite on whose sequence the author plots point-for-point correspondences with the self-offering of Jesus.

I will argue three points regarding Hebrews' reading of Yom Kippur.³³ First, the author tightly focuses on the high priest's entry with blood into the Holy of Holies. Second, according to Hebrews the Holy of Holies is where the high priest makes his offering. Third, the Yom Kippur offering purifies both God's people and his tabernacle.

In support of the first point, we turn first to the author's most detailed description of the Levitical cult in 9:1–10. This paragraph depicts the entire cultic operation of the wilderness tabernacle as a parable (παραβολή, 9:9) attesting its own ineffectiveness and pointing forward to Christ's achievement (9:9–10; cf. 10:1).³⁴ The description of the tabernacle and its furnishings in 9:1–5 frames a contrast between the ministry carried out in the "first tent," that is, the Holy Place, and that of the "second tent," the Holy of Holies. The priests enter the Holy Place throughout the year, performing their regular cultic duties (9:6). However, "Into the second [tent] only the high priest enters, once a year, not without blood, which he offers for himself and for the sins-in-ignorance of the people" (9:7). This contrast between the regular service and the once-yearly Yom Kippur is the crux of the parable Hebrews perceives in the first covenant's tabernacle. The key point is that during the rest of the ritual year, no one is allowed access to the Holy of Holies. That access is offered only to the high priest, only on Yom Kippur. Because access to the Holy of Holies is the author's chief concern, the only high-priestly acts he explicitly narrates are the high priest's entrance and his offering there (9:7). The slaughter of the animal is presupposed in "not without blood," but it is implied, not reported.

A similarly tight focus on the entry to the Holy of Holies is evident in Hebrews' exposition of Christ's sacrifice. In 6:19–20 believers' hope "enters into the inner place behind the curtain, where Jesus has gone as a forerunner on our behalf, having become a high priest forever after the order of Melchizedek" (cf. 9:3).³⁵ In 9:12 Jesus

---

³³ For detailed analysis of early Jewish and rabbinic discussions of the ritual actions that took place on Yom Kippur, followed by comparison of these sources with Hebrews' treatment of the same, see Gäbel 2006:254–79.

³⁴ Thus in Heb 9:1–10, the old covenant's sanctuary, as interpreted by the Holy Spirit (9:8), provides an instance of what G. B. Caird calls "the self-confessed inadequacy of the old order" that features so prominently in Hebrews' reading of the Old Testament (Caird 1959:47–49). For detailed, broadly complementary analyses of this "parable" see Stanley 1995; Cortez 2006.

³⁵ As Richard Ounsworth notes, the only published studies to question that 6:19 refers to the veil separating the Holy Place from the Holy of Holies are entries in a

"entered once for all into the Holy of Holies, thereby obtaining everlasting redemption."[36] In 9:24, "Christ has entered, not into a Holy of Holies made with hands, a copy of the true things, but into heaven itself, now to appear in the presence of God on our behalf." That a report of Christ's entrance to the heavenly inner sanctum is both repeated (9:12, 24) and used as shorthand for his priestly work (6:20) confirms its centrality to his eschatological enactment of Yom Kippur.

The author has carefully crafted the narration of Yom Kippur in 9:6–10 so that each detail will find its contrastive fulfillment in the work of Christ expounded chiefly in 9:11–10:18.[37] The high priest entered the earthly Holy of Holies; Christ entered the heavenly one (6:20; 9:12, 24; cf. 10:12–13, 20). The high priest entered once a year; Jesus once for all (9:12, 25–26; cf. 10:12, 14). The high priest entered with the blood of animals; Christ by means of his own blood (διὰ δε τοῦ ἰδίου αἵματος, 9:12; cf. 9:14, 25). In reporting both the Levitical Yom Kippur and Christ's eschatological rendering of the rite, the author demonstrates the same intense focus on the high priest's entry with blood into the Holy of Holies. It is the act of entry that structures the comparison.

This focus is also evident in 13:11, which mentions the burning of animal corpses "whose blood is brought into the Holy of Holies as a sin offering." Then 13:12 depicts Jesus' suffering outside the gate of Jerusalem in terms of the postrequisite ritual disposal of animal corpses on Yom Kippur.[38] Jesus suffered in order that his blood, which he himself brought into the heavenly Holy of Holies (cf. 9:12, 25; 12:24), would sanctify the people, as did animal blood brought into the earthly Holy of Holies. While 13:11–12 is unusual for Hebrews in its mention of the burning of corpses at the end of the Yom Kippur rite, its summary reference to blood brought into the Holy of Holies is consistent with its focus elsewhere.

For Hebrews, what is most notable about Yom Kippur is the unique access it affords to the Holy of Holies in contrast with the

---

debate conducted in the journal *Andrews University Seminary Studies*. For an overview of the debate, see Ounsworth 2012:142–45.

[36] On τὰ ἅγια as the Holy of Holies, and σκηνή as the entire heavenly tabernacle, see Section 2.3, "Heavenly High Priest, Tabernacle, Offering (Heb 8:1–5)."

[37] As Cortez 2006:537 argues with reference to 9:11–10:18, "The parable contains *in nuce* the argument for the central section of Hebrews." Cf. Guthrie 2007:973.

[38] On the burning of the sin offering corpses on Yom Kippur, see, e.g., Wright 1987:134–35; Milgrom 1991:1052–53; Gane 2005:239–40.

rest of the Levitical year. Accordingly, Hebrews singles out the high priest's entry with blood into the Holy of Holies as the rite's definitive moment: that which uniquely makes Yom Kippur what it is.

Apart from the single mention of the burning of animal corpses, Hebrews' depiction of Yom Kippur focuses exclusively on the high priest's entrance with blood into the inner sanctum. Hebrews never explicitly mentions the slaughter of the animals (Lev 16:11, 15), the application of blood to the outer altar (Lev 16:18–19), the people's self-abasement (Lev 16:29, 31), or any element of the so-called scapegoat rite (Lev 16:20–22). The high priest's entry to the Holy of Holies, his passing behind the veil, occupies virtually Hebrews' entire vision of the rite (6:19–20; 9:3; cf. 10:20).

Following from this focus on the high priest's entry with blood is our second point, that Hebrews describes the high priest's innersanctum blood manipulation as an "offering."[39] Again, we read in 9:7, "Into the second [tent] only the high priest enters, once a year, not without blood, which he offers (ὃ προσφέρει) for himself and for the sins-in-ignorance of the people" (9:7). In 9:7 blood is the material offered, and it is offered in the Holy of Holies.[40] In LXX depictions of Yom Kippur, blood is brought into the Holy of Holies (εἰσφέρω, Lev 16:15) and sprinkled on the mercy seat (ῥαίνω, Lev 16:14), but it is never "offered." And no other ancient description of Yom Kippur labels the high priest's inner-sanctum blood manipulation an

---

[39] See Gäbel 2006:276–79.
[40] Eberhart 2013:144 n. 149 has argued that, rather than the common translation of προσφέρει in 9:7 as "offers," it should be rendered "brings in." He argues this based on the analogy he sees between Hiphil קרב / προσφέρω in Lev 1:5 on the one hand, and Hiphil בוא / εἰσφέρω in Lev 16:15 on the other. Yet, contra Eberhart, in Lev 1:5, Hiphil קרב likely has a more technical sense than the bare "bring in" (so Milgrom 1991:155); indeed, the LXX rendering προσοίσουσιν may attest such an understanding. And if the author of Hebrews had wished to say the high priest "brings in" blood, following Lev 16:15, he could easily have done so by using the same verb, as he does in 13:11, where εἰσφέρεται corresponds to the aorist passive form of the verb in Lev 16:27. Further, when we arrive at προσφέρει in 9:7, the high priest has already arrived, with blood, in the Holy of Holies; ὃ προσφέρει κτλ describes what he does with it when he gets there. Finally, throughout Hebrews, cultic uses of προσφέρω and προσφορά refer to the act of offering (5:1, 3; 8:3, 4; 9:9, 14, 25, 28; 10:1, 2, 5, 8, 11, 12) and that which is offered (10:5 [from Ps. 40], 8, 10, 14, 18). That "gifts and offerings" are the object of προσφέρονται 9:9 need not, as Eberhart suggests, complicate the translation of προσφέρει in 9:7, with "blood" as its object, as "offer." Instead, while treating the act of cultic offering in general as an undifferentiated unity in 9:9, the author may be specifying, in 9:7 as in 13:11, that on Yom Kippur, "offering" happens when blood is brought into the Holy of Holies.

"offering."[41] In other words, Hebrews' choice to describe this act as "offering" is both unusual and deliberate.

This point is corroborated by 13:11, where the author restates Lev 16:27 LXX almost verbatim: "For the bodies of the animals whose blood is brought into the Holy of Holies by the high priest as a sin offering are burned outside the camp" (ὧν γὰρ εἰσφέρεται ζῴων τὸ αἷμα περὶ ἁμαρτίας εἰς τὰ ἅγια διὰ τοῦ ἀρχιερέως, τούτων τὰ σώματα κατακαίεται ἔξω τῆς παρεμβολῆς).[42] Since τὸν περὶ τῆς ἁμαρτίας designates the "sin offering" in Lev 16:27, it seems that in Heb 13:11 as well the phrase περὶ ἁμαρτίας has its frequent Septuagintal, cultic sense of "sin offering."[43] The phrase is therefore an object complement to τὸ αἷμα ("the blood").[44] Here in 13:11 the animal blood itself is likely designated as the Yom Kippur sin offering, and the Holy of Holies is where it is offered. Even if the phrase means "concerning sin," the blood is that which is "brought in" in order to deal with sin, which amounts to nearly the same sense. By stating that the high priest "offers" blood in the Holy of Holies (9:7), and labeling the blood-brought-in as a "sin offering," the author underscores his controlling interest in the high priest's entrance to the inner sanctum. In Hebrews' treatment of Yom Kippur the "offering" happens when the high priest brings blood into the Holy of Holies, and not before.

Third, the high priest's offering of blood in the Holy of Holies has a double effect: it purges God's people and place.[45] To begin with the latter, in 9:23 we read, "Thus it was necessary for the copies of the heavenly things to be purified with these rites, but the heavenly things themselves with better sacrifices than these." Since this assertion is elaborated (γάρ, 9:24) by the discussion of Jesus' high-priestly self-offering that follows (9:24–26), with several explicit Yom Kippur correspondences, I have argued elsewhere that Yom Kippur is a

---

[41] Cf. Young 1981:208; Lane 1991:2.223; Gäbel 2006:277. As Gäbel points out, blood is the object of προσφέρω in the sense of "offer" in LXX Lev 1:5; 7:33; Ezek 44:7, 15. Yet none of these narrate Yom Kippur.

[42] This near-verbatim use of Lev 16:27 LXX supports the inference that Hebrews accessed a version of Greek Leviticus that stands in substantial continuity with that of Rahlfs.

[43] LXX Lev 4:3, 14; 5:6, 7, 8, 9; 6:18; 16:3, 5, 6, 9, 11, 15.

[44] For a discussion of ἁμαρτία as a cultic term in the LXX and NT, see Büchner 2009. Those who see περὶ ἁμαρτίας as "sin offering" in 13:11 include Attridge 1989:397; Gäbel 2006:459; Büchner 2009:12.

[45] See, e.g., Gäbel 2006:412 n. 349, commenting on Lev 16:33, "Die Kombination von Person- und Heiligtumssühne entspricht dem Verständnis des Hebr, wie schon die Komplementarität von Hebr 9,14.23 zeigt."

decisive conceptual framework for 9:23 itself.[46] Hence, in a move that I will argue is well warranted, Hebrews derives from Yom Kippur the notion that a sacrifice can cleanse God's tabernacle of defilement caused by sin.

But in our author's reading of Yom Kippur it is not only the tabernacle that is cleansed of sin's effects, but also people. In 1:3, for instance, we read that Jesus accomplished "purification for sins" (καθαρισμὸν τῶν ἁμαρτιῶν). This likely alludes to Septuagintal depictions of Yom Kippur. Exodus 30:10 furnishes the closest parallel: Once a year Aaron is to place blood on the horns of the altar, making atonement "by means of the blood of the purification of sins" (NETS; ἀπὸ τοῦ αἵματος τοῦ καθαρισμοῦ τῶν ἁμαρτιῶν). Similarly, Lev 16:30, summarizing the high priest's activity on Yom Kippur, announces, "For on this day he shall make atonement for you, to cleanse you from all your sins before the Lord" (NETS; ἐν γὰρ τῇ ἡμέρᾳ ταύτῃ ἐξιλάσεται περὶ ὑμῶν καθαρίσαι ὑμᾶς ἀπὸ πασῶν τῶν ἁμαρτιῶν ὑμῶν ἔναντι κυρίου).[47] Hence in 1:3, the phrase "purification for sins" likely echoes biblical accounts of Yom Kippur. And, if the phrase includes a reference to purifying God's place, it does not exclude purifying God's people. Particularly in light of Lev 16:30, the primary sense of "purification for sins" in 1:3 is likely that the contaminating effects of sin are removed from God's people. Further, in 2:17, Jesus became a merciful and faithful high priest "in order to make atonement for the sins of the people" (εἰς τὸ ἱλάσκεσθαι τὰς ἁμαρτίας τοῦ λαοῦ). This brief formulation previews the fuller account of Heb 9:11–10:18 and seems to allude to Lev 16:30 even more clearly than 1:3 does. Jesus, like the Levitical high priest, made atonement for the people's sins, cleansing the people by his Yom Kippur sacrifice.

We have seen that in Hebrews' interpretation of Yom Kippur, the high priest's entry with blood into the Holy of Holies is the decisive event that distinguishes this rite from all others. Once in the Holy of Holies, the priest "offers" blood there. And this inner-sanctum offering of blood purifies God's people and his tabernacle from the defilement caused by sin.

---

[46] Jamieson 2016, esp. 577–78.
[47] Scholars who perceive influence from one or both of these passages in 1:3 include Loader 1981:65 n. 18; Attridge 1989:46 n. 132; Weiss 1991:148–49; Lane 1991:1.15; Heininger 1997:61–62; Löhr 2005:462.

Yom Kippur in Leviticus 16 in Light of Hebrews

We now consider the primary scriptural source for Hebrews' understanding of Yom Kippur, Lev 16. In reading this passage my goal is to shed light on Hebrews' use of its source material, in order to ensure that the sacrificial concepts we bring to the text of Hebrews are those Hebrews itself brought out of its sources. That Hebrews is acquainted with a Greek text of Lev 16 in substantial continuity with Rahlfs' edition of the Septuagint is evident, first, in the near-verbatim use of Lev 16:27 LXX in Heb 13:11 noted earlier. Further, it is likely that Hebrews' frequent use of ἅγια to denote the Holy of Holies and σκηνή to denote the tabernacle as a whole is influenced by the similar usage in Lev 16:20 LXX: τὸ ἅγιον καὶ τὴν σκηνὴν τοῦ μαρτυρίου.[48] One other small but significant confluence bears mention: In Lev 16:34 LXX, atonement is said to be effected for the people "once a year" (ἅπαξ τοῦ ἐνιαυτοῦ). This phrase occurs only four times in the LXX and New Testament: twice with reference to Yom Kippur in Exod 30:10, and once each in Lev 16:34 and Heb 9:7. That Hebrews uses precisely this Septuagintal phrase to describe Yom Kippur adds one more strand of evidence for Hebrews' use of a Greek text of Leviticus that substantially mirrors that of Rahlfs. Therefore it is worth attending not only to the LXX narration of Yom Kippur, but also to the Hebrew text it translates, since accounting for the lexis and syntax of Lev 16 LXX requires us to consider them as translation decisions, not as freestanding instances of Hellenistic Greek.[49]

Two features of the Hebrew text of Lev 16 are particularly relevant to Hebrews' appropriation of Yom Kippur. The first provides the source of Hebrews' conviction that, when the high priest manipulated blood in the Holy of Holies on Yom Kippur, he cleansed the tabernacle (cf. Heb 9:7, 23). According to Lev 16, on Yom Kippur the high priest enters the Holy of Holies and sprinkles blood over and in front of the mercy seat (Lev 16:15) in order to purge the Holy of Holies, cleansing it of the impurities and sins of the

---

[48] So Hofius 1972:57. For discussion see Section 2.3, "Heavenly High Priest, Tabernacle, Offering (Heb 8:1–5)."

[49] As Büchner 2010a:111 writes, "It can be shown, at least for Leuitikon, that the provision of lexical items as corresponding matches for Hebrew items was often more crucial than the production of perfect sense. All too often, lexicography of the Septuagint is carried out from the Greek context without taking this matter into consideration."

people: "And he shall purge the Holy of Holies of the impurities of the children of Israel, and of their transgressions, all their sins" (וְכִפֶּר עַל־הַקֹּדֶשׁ מִטֻּמְאֹת בְּנֵי יִשְׂרָאֵל וּמִפִּשְׁעֵיהֶם לְכָל־חַטֹּאתָם, 16:16). That הַקֹּדֶשׁ denotes the Holy of Holies is evident in that the space is described in 16:2 as "behind the veil," where the mercy seat is, and that Aaron may not enter it as and when he pleases. Verse 3 specifies that all of the following instructions describe the manner in which Aaron may enter הַקֹּדֶשׁ. Finally, the actions described in 16:15–17 take place "inside the veil" (16:12, 15). After purging the Holy of Holies, the high priest must do likewise for the tent of meeting, "which dwells with them in the midst of their impurities" (הַשֹּׁכֵן אִתָּם בְּתוֹךְ טֻמְאֹתָם, 16:16; cf. Exod 25:8; 29:45–46). In the summary statement of 16:20, the priest is again said to "purge the Holy of Holies and the tent of meeting and the altar" (מִכַּפֵּר אֶת־הַקֹּדֶשׁ וְאֶת־אֹהֶל מוֹעֵד וְאֶת־הַמִּזְבֵּחַ). Verse 33 repeats this nearly verbatim, only changing the Piel infinitive construct of כפר to a perfect, and for "Holy of Holies" substituting "most holy part of the sanctuary" (אֶת־מִקְדַּשׁ הַקֹּדֶשׁ), an evident synonym.[50] It is significant that 16:20 and 16:33 both attach the direct object marker to הַקֹּדֶשׁ or מִקְדַּשׁ ("the Holy Place/Holy of Holies"), אֹהֶל מוֹעֵד ("the tent of meeting"), and הַמִּזְבֵּחַ ("the altar"; cf. Ezek 43:20), indicating that the inner sanctum, outer shrine, and outer altar are all cleansed of defilement. Since these statements restate the earlier assertions of 16:16 and 18, which attach the preposition עַל to הַקֹּדֶשׁ and to a pronominal suffix referring to הַמִּזְבֵּחַ, the עַל-constructions are most likely equivalent to direct objects, which underscores that the Holy of Holies is that which is purged in the inner-sanctum rite.[51]

That the Holy of Holies, tent of meeting, and burnt-offering altar are themselves purified on Yom Kippur is reinforced by the ritual macrostructure of the event. In a complex interlocking series, blood from the sin offerings (חטאת) for the high priest and for the people is applied to the sanctuary and its appurtenances, beginning in the innermost room of the divine abode and working outward to its exit. Following the pair of sin offerings, the so-called scapegoat ritual removes the people's transgressions to the wilderness.[52] Just as one

---

[50] Milgrom 1991:1058.
[51] For similar analysis see Levine 1989:105, 110; Gane 2005:133–35.
[52] On the unified ritual macrostructure of Yom Kippur, see Gane 2005:217–41. On the scapegoat as elimination vehicle, see Wright 1992:73; Hartenstein 2005:130; Willi-Plein 2005:32; Gane 2005:242–66.

mops a kitchen, the divine housecleaning on Yom Kippur starts at the farthest point from the exit and works outward.[53] Combining the inner-sanctum rite and the scapegoat's banishment to the wilderness, Yom Kippur constitutes a ritual merism, the only yearly occasion when rites address both the most holy seat of YHWH and its polar opposite, the wasteland inhabited by Azazel.[54] As 16:17 indicates, such a comprehensive cleaning is necessary because God's house dwells amid an unclean people and thereby incurs defilement (cf. Lev 15:31; Num 19:13, 20). But it is not only the people's impurities that infect the tabernacle; sins defile it as well. Verse 16 indicates that what is purged from the Holy of Holies are not only impurities but also transgressions and sins (וּמִפִּשְׁעֵיהֶם לְכָל־חַטֹּאתָם). As YHWH declares in Lev 20:3: "I myself will set my face against them, and will cut them off from the people, because they have given of their offspring to Molech, defiling my sanctuary and profaning my holy name" (NRSV; cf. Lev 18:24–25). Once a year, on Yom Kippur, YHWH's dwelling is purged of all that defiles it, restoring cultic equilibrium and ensuring that, for now, he will not leave his people (cf. Ezek 8–11).[55]

The second notable intersection of Hebrews' interests and the Hebrew text of Lev 16 is that on Yom Kippur not only is God's place cleansed but God's people are cleansed. Aaron's first sin offering effects atonement for himself and his house (וְכִפֶּר בַּעֲדוֹ וּבְעַד בֵּיתוֹ, 16:6, 11). Further, Aaron offers burnt offerings for himself and for the people, to make atonement for both (וְכִפֶּר בַּעֲדוֹ וּבְעַד הָעָם, 16:24). Finally, the summary of 16:30–34 contains several references to atonement for the people that results in their cleansing from sin. Verse 30 declares, "For on this day atonement shall be made for you to cleanse you (יְכַפֵּר עֲלֵיכֶם לְטַהֵר אֶתְכֶם). You shall be clean before the LORD from all your sins." In 16:33, in addition to purging the sanctuary and so on,

---

[53] Gane 2005:237; Hundley 2011:160–61.
[54] Gorman 1990:98–99; Jenson 1992:201–3; Jürgens 2001:81; Nihan 2007:374–75.
[55] There is a broad scholarly consensus that one of the key goals of Yom Kippur as described in Lev 16 is the cleansing of the tabernacle, including the Holy of Holies. See, e.g., Elliger 1966:214; Milgrom 1976; Milgrom 1991:1010, 1033; Wenham 1979:28, 232–33; Levine 1989:103–4; Gorman 1990:51–52, 55, 61–102; Kraus 1991:45–59; Geller 1992:109; Jenson 1992:203; Jürgens 2001:108–9; Walton 2001:301; Dennis 2002:115, 125–26; Gilders 2004:136; Gane 2005:133–36, 144–62, 217–41; Hartenstein 2005:128; Sklar 2005:88, 121–24; Nihan 2007:370–75; Nihan 2015:105–6; Hundley 2011:159–72, 181; Eberhart 2013:86. Those who see Yom Kippur as restoring cultic equilibrium include Jenson 1992:101–2; Jürgens 2001:122; Walton 2001; Hundley 2011:177–78.

the high priest "shall make atonement for the priests and for all the people of the assembly." Finally, in 16:34 these instructions will be an eternal statute, "that atonement may be made for the people of Israel once in the year because of all their sins." From these statements it is clear that the people themselves are also the recipients of atonement on Yom Kippur. By it the people obtain a new state and standing before YHWH. Just as YHWH's dwelling is purified on Yom Kippur, so also are his people.[56]

But are both aspects evident in LXX Lev 16? Regarding the cleansing of the Holy of Holies, the crucial phrase in 16:16 reads ἐξιλάσεται τὸ ἅγιον. Verse 20 adds καὶ συντελέσει ἐξιλασκόμενος τὸ ἅγιον καὶ τὴν σκηνὴν τοῦ μαρτυρίου καὶ τὸ θυσιαστήριον, while 16:33 reads καὶ ἐξιλάσεται τὸ ἅγιον κτλ. Whatever one might make of the choice of ἐξιλάσκομαι as a translation of כִּפֶּר, the accusative case of τὸ ἅγιον and the rest indicates that the translator understands both the כִּפֶּר עַל clause of 16:16 and the כִּפֶּר אֶת clauses of 16:20 and 33 to designate the Holy of Holies and other items as the direct objects of atonement. Given the highly literal translation technique of Greek Leviticus, if the translator understood the כִּפֶּר עַל clause to indicate merely the place where atonement is effected, one would have expected a preposition such as ἐπί. As it is, the LXX provides an early attestation of the interpretation argued earlier, that on Yom Kippur the entire tabernacle complex is cleansed of impurity.[57]

Regarding the people's purgation, 16:6 and 16:11 attest that one of the sin offerings effects atonement for Aaron and his house (ἐξιλάσεται περὶ αὐτοῦ καὶ τοῦ οἴκου αὐτοῦ), 16:24 that the burnt offering atones for priest and people (ἐξιλάσεται περί κτλ.), 16:30 that atonement is made for the people in order to cleanse them (ἐξιλάσεται περὶ ὑμῶν καθαρίσαι ὑμᾶς ἀπὸ πασῶν τῶν ἁμαρτιῶν ὑμῶν), and 16:33–34 that atonement is made for the whole congregation, for all their sins

---

[56] For a variety of accounts of how Yom Kippur purifies the people as well as the tabernacle see, e.g., Milgrom 1991:1056; Jürgens 2001:118–23; Dennis 2002:125–26, 129; Gane 2005:230–33; Sklar 2005:188–93; Gäbel 2006:411–12 n. 349; Nihan 2007:371–75.

[57] John William Wevers notes that in Lev 16:16, in contrast to its usual prepositional complement(s), ἐξιλάσεται has an accusative object. He continues, "The verb is further modified by an ἀπό phrase, i.e. 'the making atonement from …' means that atonement involves cleansing, purification, i.e. getting rid of the ἀκαθαρσιῶν of the Israelites, and of their unrighteous actions." Finally, regarding the identical syntax of 16:20, "Note that the participle ἐξιλασκόμενος is modified by accusative nominals, demonstrating that atonement is a matter of purgation, of ritual cleansing" (Wevers 1997:249, 251).

(περὶ πάσης συναγωγῆς ἐξιλάσεται ... ἐξιλάσκεσθαι ... ἀπὸ πασῶν τῶν ἁμαρτιῶν ὑμῶν).[58] Whether or not the author of Hebrews read exactly these phrases in a Greek Leviticus scroll, this LXX evidence suggests that at least some roughly contemporary Greek-speaking Jews perceived and preserved Lev 16's portrayal of Yom Kippur as cleansing both tabernacle and people. And it is more likely than not that these very phrases influenced Hebrews' understanding of Yom Kippur.

Just as in Hebrews, the Hebrew and Greek texts of Lev 16 depict the day's rites as purging both the people and the tabernacle. Just as in Hebrews, Lev 16 highlights the high priest's activity in the Holy of Holies, which is part of what marks this day off from all others. While neither the Hebrew nor Greek versions of Lev 16 label the high priest's inner-sanctum blood manipulation an "offering," it is easy to understand why, in close engagement with a Greek text of Lev 16, the author of Hebrews would use that term for this act. While in Lev 16 this blood manipulation is one element in an indissoluble ritual unity, it is an act unique to this rite, and is integral to its overall goal. Only by sprinkling blood in the Holy of Holies can the high priest purify both people and place.

Hence, to combine the contribution of these two sections, I suggest that the overall manner in which Hebrews reflects on Yom Kippur constitutes evidence for Christ offering himself in the heavenly tabernacle. While confirmation of this point awaits the next section, these sections have contributed a weighty *prima facie* case against

---

[58] Given that ἐξιλάσκομαι occurs both with sancta as direct object and with prepositions governing persons and sins, it seems best to view the translator as using the verb as a translation equivalent for Piel כפר, to convey both "purging" (the sancta) and "making atonement for" (persons and sins). This fits Büchner's observation, cited earlier, that the Leviticus LXX translator's lexical choices are more often governed by a desire to match Hebrew forms one-to-one than to produce perfectly sensible Greek. Büchner himself persuasively argues that, in Hellenistic Greek up to the time of the LXX, ἐξιλάσκομαι has no attested uses meaning "expiate" or "purge." Based on this and on exceptional instances where the LXX renders Piel כפר with other verbs such as καθαρίζω, Büchner argues that in Lev 16:16, rather than being a cipher for the Hebrew, ἐξιλάσεται has the more intelligible Greek sense of "reverence" (Büchner 2010b). Nevertheless, in both this instance and others, this seems an overly complicated explanation, and gives insufficient weight to the translator's decision to render the על clause in the accusative. Thus, similar to Büchner's conclusion that ἁμαρτία takes on a hitherto unattested cultic sense in the LXX (Büchner 2009), I would argue that, as a translation equivalent for Piel כפר, ἐξιλάσκομαι means both "render propitious" (Gen 32:21) and "purge." Cf. Harlé and Pralon 1988:32.

Hebrews fundamentally rewriting the Yom Kippur script such that Jesus first offers himself, and then enters the inner sanctum. Hebrews' construal of Yom Kippur is unique among ancient Jewish literature in its laser-like focus on the high priest's entry with blood, and in its labeling the subsequent blood manipulation an "offering."[59] Most details of Yom Kippur that Hebrews incorporates converge on this point, and the thematic coherence of Hebrews' appropriation of Yom Kippur suggests that Hebrews is not cherry-picking convenient details, but is employing the logic of the whole rite. The high priest cleanses the tabernacle and the people by offering blood in the Holy of Holies; as we will consider in detail below, Hebrews' Jesus does precisely the same. While Hebrews certainly refracts Yom Kippur through a Christological prism, each of its key points of comparison is, as it were, lifted cleanly off the text of Lev 16. While Hebrews does not appropriate the whole of Yom Kippur, what it does use it appropriates whole. As I will argue below, Hebrews preserves intact the ritual logic of Yom Kippur whereby blood manipulation in the Holy of Holies purges God's people and place.

Where Did Jesus Offer Himself? The Tabernacle in Heaven

I now directly address the question of where Jesus offered himself, arguing that he offered himself in the tabernacle in heaven. In the following section I address "when," confirming, in light of Section 2.2, that this offering in heaven took place at Jesus' bodily, post-resurrection ascent to heaven. This section will engage three key passages that indicate where Jesus offered himself, in the order of most to least explicit: Heb 9:24–25, 8:1–5, and 9:11–14. I will leave Heb 10:5–14 to the next chapter because it provides fewer clues to the time and place of Christ's self-offering, and is best read in light of these three passages. After making this case I will address the objection that Heb 9:26 and 9:28 seem to locate Christ's self-offering on earth, at his death. Finally, I will conclude by critiquing View 1, which locates Christ's self-offering at his death, and sees Hebrews as radically reconfiguring Yom Kippur's sacrificial sequence.

---

[59] Again, for a detailed comparison of Hebrews' treatment of Yom Kippur with that of other early Jewish sources, see Gäbel 2006:254–79.

He Entered Heaven in Order to Offer Himself There (Heb 9:24–25)

Hebrews' most explicit statement of where Jesus offered himself occurs in 9:24–25: "For Christ has entered, not into a Holy of Holies made with hands, which is a copy of the true things, but into heaven itself, now to appear in the presence of God on our behalf. Nor did he enter in order to offer himself repeatedly, as the high priest enters the Holy of Holies every year with blood not his own." These verses draw on the script already narrated in 9:7 – the Levitical high priest enters the Holy of Holies yearly, with the blood of an animal, in order to offer it there. And the author explicitly plots Christ's sacrifice along this sequence. He denies that Jesus entered the Holy of Holies repeatedly; he presupposes that Jesus entered the heavenly sanctuary, specifically its Holy of Holies, in order to offer himself there.

This passage's decisive evidence that Hebrews locates Jesus' self-offering in the Holy of Holies in heaven is the syntax of 9:24–25, which indicates that Jesus entered heaven in order to offer himself there. That is, the subordinate clause οὐδ' ἵνα πολλάκις προσφέρῃ ἑαυτόν in 9:25 ("not in order to offer himself repeatedly") depends on the aorist indicative εἰσῆλθεν ("he entered") in 9:24. The only other verbs to which ἵνα ... προσφέρῃ could conceivably attach are the infinitive ἐμφανισθῆναι in 9:24 and πεφανέρωται in 9:26. As to the former, while a purpose clause depending on an infinitive is possible, it is unlikely here, since the infinitive designates Christ's present action, whereas the subordinate clause and its elaboration designate his past, completed sacrifice. As to the latter, while ἵνα clauses very occasionally precede the finite verbs on which they depend (Matt 17:27; Jn 19:28; Rev 19:31),[60] this is impossible here. The emphatic νυνὶ δὲ ("but now") in 9:26b introduces the complement to the contrast begun in 9:25, and inserts a boundary in the discourse through which a subordinate clause cannot pass. Further, οὐδέ in 9:25 has the sense of "nor"[61] and presupposes οὐ in 9:24; both particles qualify εἰσῆλθεν. Jesus did not enter a handmade Holy of Holies; nor did he enter in order to offer himself repeatedly. Hence 9:25–26a both contrasts with 9:26b and correlates with 9:24. Finally, confirmation that προσφέρῃ depends on εἰσῆλθεν is found in the repetition of the latter verb in 9:25: "as the high priest enters

---

[60] Cf. BDF §478, p. 253. [61] BDAG 734 §1.

(εἰσέρχεται) the Holy of Holies every year with blood not his own." What is being compared is the purpose of the respective entries. The purpose of Christ's entry was not to offer himself repeatedly but, 9:25a implies, to offer himself only once. Hence the sense of 9:25a is, "Nor did Christ enter the Holy of Holies in order to offer himself repeatedly."[62]

The point of contrast is not that, whereas the earthly high priest entered in order to offer himself, Christ entered having already offered himself.[63] Instead, the contrast consists in repetition versus singularity: Christ did not enter-to-offer repeatedly, since then he would have had to suffer repeatedly (9:25–26a); instead, now, in his singular eschatological appearance, he has set aside sin by his sacrifice (9:26b). The argument presupposes that Christ entered the heavenly Holy of Holies in order to offer himself there. If a physician were to say, "I entered the patient's room to offer not spiritual counsel but a medical diagnosis," the contrast does nothing to alter the sequence "enter to offer." Similarly, the grammar of 9:24–25 indicates that the sequence "enter in order to offer" is common to both the earthly high priests and Christ. Both the οὐ ("not") of 9:24 and the οὐδέ ("nor") of 9:25 qualify Christ's entry into "heaven itself." Christ did not enter a handmade sanctuary but its archetype in heaven; nor did he enter in order to offer himself repeatedly but only once. Both contrasts describe Christ's singular entrance into heaven in order to establish the superiority of the sacrifice he offered when he entered.

Confirmation that Heb 9:24–25 locates Jesus' self-offering in the Holy of Holies in heaven is found in the relationship between 9:23 and the two contrasts of 9:24–26. That is, 9:23 articulates a thesis: "Thus it was necessary for the copies of the heavenly things to be purified with these rites, but the heavenly things themselves with better sacrifices than these." The following verses, 9:24–26, elaborate

---

[62] Those who recognize the dependence of the ἵνα clause on εἰσῆλθεν include Ps.-Oecumenius, PG 119:381; Theophylact, PG 125:313; Michel 1966:325; Braun 1984:283; Weiss 1991:488; Ellingworth 1993:478; Grässer 1993:193 n. 59; Gäbel 2006:298–99; Moore 2015:169 n. 87. Without making the grammatical point, Delitzsch 1887:128–30; deSilva 2000:314; and Moffitt 2011:280–81 also recognize that 9:24–25 presents Christ as entering the heavenly sanctuary in order to offer himself there. Among English translations that I have consulted, only the NIV and NLT accurately reflect the verbal syntax of 9:24–25.

[63] Contra Lane 1991:2.249 (cf. 2.223), "The contrast between the Levitical high priest and the heavenly high priest is displayed in the sequence of the projected action as well as in its frequency." See also Young 1981:208–9; Cockerill 2012:394 (on 9:12).

(I.A)²³ Ἀνάγκη οὖν τὰ μὲν ὑποδείγματα τῶν ἐν τοῖς οὐρανοῖς τούτοις καθαρίζεσθαι,

(I.B) αὐτὰ δὲ τὰ ἐπουράνια κρείττοσιν θυσίαις παρὰ ταύτας.

  (II.A)²⁴ <u>οὐ</u> γὰρ εἰς χειροποίητα εἰσῆλθεν ἅγια Χριστός, ἀντίτυπα τῶν ἀληθινῶν,

  (II.B) <u>ἀλλ'</u> εἰς αὐτὸν τὸν οὐρανόν,

    (II.B.1) νῦν ἐμφανισθῆναι τῷ προσώπῳ τοῦ θεοῦ ὑπὲρ ἡμῶν·

  (II.C) ²⁵ <u>οὐδ'</u> ἵνα πολλάκις προσφέρῃ ἑαυτόν,

    (II.C.1) ὥσπερ ὁ ἀρχιερεὺς εἰσέρχεται εἰς τὰ ἅγια κατ' ἐνιαυτὸν ἐν αἵματι ἀλλοτρίῳ,

    (II.C.2)²⁶ ἐπεὶ ἔδει αὐτὸν πολλάκις παθεῖν ἀπὸ καταβολῆς κόσμου·

  (II.D) <u>νυνὶ δὲ</u> ἅπαξ ἐπὶ συντελείᾳ τῶν αἰώνων εἰς ἀθέτησιν [τῆς] ἁμαρτίας διὰ τῆς θυσίας αὐτοῦ πεφανέρωται.

Figure 2.1 Structure of Hebrews 9:23–26

this thesis by naming two respects in which Christ's sacrifice is superior to its Levitical precursors. It was offered in the Holy of Holies in heaven rather than its earthly copy (9:24), and it was offered once for all rather than repeatedly (9:25–26). Visually laying out the structure of 9:23–26 may help us perceive the point.

As seen in Figure 2.1, 9:24 (II.A–B) and 9:25–26 (II.C–D) both contrast Christ's sacrifice with its Levitical precursors. Each says "not this, but this."⁶⁴ In 9:24 Christ enters not an earthly Holy of Holies but heaven itself; in 9:25–26 he offers his sacrifice not many times but once for all. Further, these contrasts are parallel. The first opens with οὐ, the second with οὐδέ (9:24, 25). As we have seen, οὐδέ in 9:25 has the sense "nor," and 9:25–9.26a both contrasts with 9:26b and correlates with 9:24. That is, 9:25a introduces a second reason why Christ's sacrifice surpasses its predecessors: He did not enter-to-offer repeatedly but only once.

---

⁶⁴ See the underlined terms in II.A–D. A fuller version of Figure 2.1 and fuller structural discussion of 9:23–28 appear in Jamieson 2016:572–74.

These latter verses describe the same "sacrifice" named in the former. The conceptual link between 9:23 and 9:24 (γάρ, 9:24) confirms that the "better sacrifice" attested in 9:23 was offered by Christ upon his entry to heaven. Hebrews 9:24–25 justifies the superiority of Christ's sacrifice by reporting his entrance to heaven. To hold that Christ entered heaven after having already offered himself in his death is to sever the link between these verses and to obscure the logic of 9:23–26 as a whole.

Further confirmation that 9:23–26 locates Christ's self-offering in heaven is found in the connection in Hebrews' narration of Yom Kippur between the effect of the sacrifice and the place where it is offered. That is, 9:7 asserts that the Levitical high priest entered the Holy of Holies in order to offer blood there, and 9:23 presupposes that this offering purified the tabernacle. As we saw earlier, this is a key feature of Hebrews' scriptural source for Yom Kippur (e.g. Lev 16:15–16). The Levitical high priest purged the Holy of Holies when he offered a sacrifice there. According to Heb 9:23, Jesus' sacrifice purified the heavenly tabernacle itself.[65] When did Jesus offer a sacrifice that cleansed the heavenly tabernacle? Hebrews 9:24–25 answers: when he entered it.

In my view, Heb 9:24–25 is the clearest statement of the place of Jesus' self-offering in all of Hebrews. As we saw earlier, the author's narration of the earthly Yom Kippur focuses sharply on the high priest's entry with blood into the Holy of Holies. In 9:24–25, the parallel with 9:7 becomes explicit: Just as the high priest entered the inner sanctum with blood, which he offered there, so Christ entered the heavenly inner sanctum in order to offer himself there. Just as the earthly sanctuary was cleansed when the high priest offered blood in the Holy of Holies, so the heavenly sanctuary was cleansed when Christ offered himself there.

Heavenly High Priest, Tabernacle, Offering (Heb 8:1–5)

A second passage that, I will argue, locates Christ's self-offering in the heavenly tabernacle is 8:1–5.[66] It does this by juxtaposing two priesthoods, operative in two tabernacles, wherein each offered

---

[65] For a detailed defense of taking Heb 9:23 to assert that Jesus' sacrifice cleansed the heavenly tabernacle from antecedent defilement caused by sin, see Jamieson 2016.

[66] While the paragraph continues to 8:6, that verse segues to the new covenant discussed in 8:7–13. Hence I limit my comments to 8:1–5.

sacrifice: one on earth, one in heaven. We saw in Section 2.2 that, according to 8:4, Christ only served as high priest in heaven. Here I argue three further points from this paragraph in support of locating Christ's self-offering in heaven: (1) Heb 8:1–2 positions the heavenly tabernacle as a spatial frame for the entire ensuing expository section (8:3–10:18); (2) this paragraph posits a two-room tabernacle in heaven, clarifying the parallel with the earthly high priest's offering (8:1–2, 5); (3) Jesus' offering of his sacrifice is explicitly included in the priestly activity Hebrews ascribes to Jesus in heaven (8:3–5).

First, Heb 8:1–2 sets the heavenly tabernacle as a spatial frame for the following expository section (8:3–10:18): "Now the point in what we are saying is this: we have such a high priest, one who is seated at the right hand of the throne of the Majesty in heaven, a minister in the Holy of Holies, in the true tent that the Lord set up, not man." These two verses constitute a transition between an expository section largely treating Christ's appointment to high priesthood (5:1–7:28, minus the digression of 5:11–6:20), and one treating his high-priestly self-offering (8:3–10:18).[67] The key assertion of these verses is that Jesus is a high priest who serves in the true tabernacle in heaven.[68] To make this point in 8:1, the author alludes to Ps 110:1, "Sit at my right hand, until I make your enemies your footstool." The allusion to this verse in 1:3 locates God's throne "on high" (ἐν ὑψηλοῖς), but in 8:1 the throne is "in heaven" (ἐν οὐρανοῖς). This redaction provides an explicit spatial reference point for the entire following discussion. The point of departure for the previous expository section (5:1–7:28) is that "every high priest" is "chosen from among men (ἐξ ἀνθρώπων)" (5:1). Hence this section reports how Jesus shared fully in the human condition and came to transcend it through resurrection, which perfected him and qualified him for priesthood (5:7–10; 7:11–28). In 8:1–2, the writer shifts the spatial frame from earth to heaven, where it remains throughout 8:3–10:18.

---

[67] For details see Guthrie 1994:82–85, 104–5. The section stretching from 5:11–6:20 is rightly termed a digression since it interrupts exposition of Christ's appointment. Nevertheless, 5:11–6:20 is central to the epistle's hortatory program (so ibid., 110). Guzmán and Martin 2015 rightly insist on the passage's importance in the epistle, and may be correct that the passage does not fit the classical category of *digressio*. But in denying that the passage is a digression in even an informal sense, they underplay the abrupt break at 5:11.

[68] The following argument is indebted to Guthrie 1994:122–24. See especially his chart of the spatial movement of Hebrews' expository sections (122).

Table 2.1 Parallels in heavenly tabernacle descriptions

	8:2	8:5	9:11–12	9:23–24
Holy of Holies	τῶν ἁγίων λειτουργός		εἰσῆλθεν ... εἰς τὰ ἅγια	οὐ γὰρ εἰς χειροποίητα εἰσῆλθεν ἅγια Χριστός ... ἀλλ' εἰς αὐτὸν τὸν οὐρανόν
True/Greater Tent	τῆς σκηνῆς τῆς ἀληθινῆς	(ὑποδείγματι καὶ σκιᾷ)	διὰ τῆς μείζονος καὶ τελειοτέρας σκηνῆς	(ἀντίτυπα τῶν ἀληθινῶν)
Made by the Lord, not Humans	ἣν ἔπηξεν ὁ κύριος, οὐκ ἄνθρωπος	(Μωϋσῆς ... ἐπιτελεῖν τὴν σκηνήν)	οὐ χειροποιήτου	οὐ γὰρ εἰς χειροποίητα ... ἅγια

This spatial frame is crucial for the ensuing exposition since "one of the author's main arguments concerning the superiority of Christ's offering ... has to do with it being made *in heaven*."[69]

Second, 8:1–2 and 8:5 posit a two-room tabernacle existing in heaven, the original on which the earthly tent was patterned. This clarifies and confirms the parallel between Christ's offering in the heavenly Holy of Holies and the Levitical high priest's in its earthly counterpart. After locating Christ at God's right hand in heaven in 8:1, the author continues the description in 8:2, "a minister in the Holy of Holies, in the true tent that the Lord set up, not man." As seen in Table 2.1, references to the Holy of Holies, the "true" or "greater" tent over against its earthly copy, and the heavenly tent's divine, not human, origin recur in 9:11–12 and 9:23–24, and two of these concepts' opposites are in 8:5. Hebrews 8:2 therefore introduces defining characteristics of the heavenly tabernacle wherein Christ accomplishes his high-priestly ministry, which is a central focus of 8:3 to 10:18.

Three characteristics of the heavenly tabernacle are particularly relevant for locating Christ's offering. First, Hebrews envisions the heavenly tabernacle as an actual structure in heaven. Though heaven is a transcendent realm, in Hebrews it is a realm housing a tabernacle in which a glorified human ministers. This tabernacle was "pitched" by God (ἔπηξεν, 8:2). It is not eternal or self-existent but was created by God. This tabernacle is where Jesus presently is, as Heb 8:1–2

---

[69] Ibid., 123, emphasis original. See also Guthrie 2007:968.

emphatically underscores (cf. 1:3, 13; 10:12–13; 12:2). Jesus entered this tabernacle "now to appear in the presence of God on our behalf" (9:24). And, as 9:28 indicates, Jesus will remain in the heavenly tabernacle until he appears on earth "a second time ... to save those who are eagerly waiting for him." In order to reach this tabernacle Jesus traversed heavenly realms: He "passed through the heavens" (4:14) and is now "exalted above the heavens" (7:26). Making all due allowance for transcendent aspects of Hebrews' depiction of heaven, its heavenly tabernacle must be "real" enough for the resurrected Jesus to be there now.

Second, this tabernacle in heaven has two rooms, one implicitly the Holy Place, the other explicitly the Holy of Holies. Hebrews regularly uses σκηνή to designate the whole tabernacle and ἅγια for the Holy of Holies.[70] In 8:5, 9:21, and 13:10, σκηνή clearly denotes the whole earthly tabernacle. In contrast, in 9:25 the high priest enters εἰς τὰ ἅγια to offer the Yom Kippur sacrifice, and in 13:11 blood is brought εἰς τὰ ἅγια; both unequivocally designate the earthly Holy of Holies. In 9:8, after describing the old covenant cult's restricted access to the Holy of Holies, the author indicates that the way into the Holy of Holies (τὴν τῶν ἁγίων ὁδόν) is not open while the first tent has legal standing; here again ἅγια denotes the inner sanctum. Further evidence for a two-room tabernacle in heaven is found in 6:19–20, where Jesus has gone into "the inner place behind the curtain." Like its earthly counterpart (9:3), the heavenly Holy of Holies is shielded by a veil. Hence, we should understand Heb 8:2 to name Christ "a minister in the Holy of Holies (τῶν ἁγίων), in the true tent (τῆς σκηνῆς)." The first term is narrower, the second broader. Hence also in 9:24 Christ does not enter the Holy of Holies made with hands (χειροποίητα ... ἅγια) but its counterpart in heaven itself (αὐτὸν τὸν οὐρανόν). Both Hebrews' general use of σκηνή and ἅγια and the Yom Kippur framework of 9:24 confirm that the space Christ enters in order to offer himself is the Holy of Holies of the heavenly tabernacle.[71]

---

[70] My argument here draws especially on Ribbens 2016:104–6. See also Hofius 1972:57–73; Attridge 1989:218; Scholer 1991:159–61; Grässer 1993:82–83; Mackie 2007:165; Barnard 2012:93–94, 110–12. As Barnard notes, the only exception is "the carefully qualified discussion of the earthly sanctuary in 9:1–8" (ibid., 93 n. 17), where Hebrews sometimes uses σκηνή to describe not the whole tabernacle but its successive rooms (9:2–3, 6), and uses the full phrase Ἅγια Ἁγίων for the Holy of Holies (9:3).

[71] For critiques of the view that 9:24 identifies the heavenly Holy of Holies with heaven as a whole, see Hofius 1972:70–71; Ribbens 2016:123–25. Cf. the identical use of σκηνή and ἅγια in 9:11–12.

Third, this tabernacle in heaven is the archetype of Israel's tabernacle, its earthly copy. In 8:5 we read that, in contrast to the heavenly tabernacle wherein Christ ministers, the Levitical priests "serve a copy and shadow of the heavenly things (ὑποδείγματι καὶ σκιᾷ λατρεύουσιν τῶν ἐπουρανίων). For when Moses was about to erect the tent, he was instructed by God, saying, 'See that you make everything according to the pattern that was shown you on the mountain'" (citing Exod 25:40). Several factors support the conclusion that this verse also attests a tabernacle existing in heaven, on which the earthly one was patterned. First, we have seen that the entire paragraph of 8:1–6 contrasts two priesthoods that operate in two sanctuaries, on earth and in heaven. Second, the phrase "copy and shadow of the heavenly things" is repeated nearly verbatim in 9:23, only in the latter the earthly tabernacle and its furnishings are copies "of the things in heaven (τῶν ἐν τοῖς οὐρνανοῖς)." In 9:23 the spatial preposition is significant: that on which the earthly tabernacle was patterned is located in heaven. This parallel sheds light on 8:5, confirming that the Levitical priests serve in a copy of the tabernacle in heaven. Third, contra Lincoln Hurst, while elsewhere ὑπόδειγμα may never have the precise sense of "copy," it can indeed denote a crafted mimetic representation, which is all my reading of 8:5 requires.[72] For instance, it has this sense in Aquila's translation of Deut 4:17 and Ezek 8:10. In the former, ὑπόδειγμα describes idols as the "likeness" of animals and birds; in the latter, Ezekiel sees "likenesses" of "creeping things and loathsome beasts" engraved on the sanctuary walls.[73] Similarly, Heb 8:5 takes Exod 25:40 to indicate that the earthly tent is a derivative likeness of the heavenly one. What Moses saw was the tabernacle in heaven; what he created was its copy.

---

[72] Hurst argues, "There is no instance in known Greek literature where ὑπόδειγμα can be demonstrated to mean 'copy.'" He glosses all its uses as "sample," "suggestion," "symbol," "outline," "token," and "example." Regarding "example," he argues that this is "usually 'something suggested as a basis for imitation or instruction' – a basis for something which comes later." See Hurst 1990:13. In addition to the lexical discussion that invalidates his primary claim, we should note that ὑπόδειγμα is often used without any hint of temporal prefiguration. For instance, it can describe an example of something under discussion, or a specimen of a class. E.g. Polybius 6.54.6; 9.16.8; Philo, *Posterity* 1.122; *Confusion* 1.64; *Heir* 1.256; *Dreams* 2.3; Josephus, *J.W.* 1.374, 507; Dionysius of Halicarnassus, *Comp.* 17 (line 74). Since this accounts for all of Philo's uses of ὑπόδειγμα, there is no sense in which the term is for him a technical, philosophical one. Rightly, Gäbel 2006:114, n. 25.

[73] Noted by Attridge 1989:219 n. 41; Gäbel 2006:241 n. 12.

Hence, contra those who argue that Moses was shown only a blueprint or architectural model,[74] in 8:5 the tabernacle Moses built copied one God had already built (cf. 8:2). Contra those who argue that Hebrews attests a cosmic temple, in which earth and heaven together constitute the ultimate sanctuary,[75] in 8:5 the whole tent in heaven is the archetype of the whole tent on earth.[76] Contra those who argue that Moses was shown a preview of the eschatological heavenly tabernacle that was only established when Christ entered it,[77] the relationship 8:5 takes Exod 25:40 to attest is spatial, not temporal. Further, this reading makes the earthly tabernacle a model for the heavenly, whereas 8:5 asserts the opposite.[78] Hebrews' heavenly tabernacle was pitched by God (8:2), shown to Moses on the mountain as the pattern for its earthly likeness (8:5), and in the fullness of time entered by Christ (6:19–20; 9:11–12, 24; cf. 8:1–2).[79]

Finally, a third point from 8:1–5 in support of locating Christ's self-offering in heaven: Jesus' offering of his sacrifice is explicitly included in the priestly activity Hebrews ascribes to Jesus in heaven (8:3–5). To be sure, 8:1–2 names Christ's present service in heaven: "we have such a high priest … a minister in the Holy of Holies." Since Hebrews emphatically insists that Christ's priestly sacrifice is

[74] E.g. Laub 1991:71.
[75] For a survey of the temple as the cosmos in early Judaism, see Klawans 2006:111–28. For primary sources see especially Philo, *Moses* 2.77–108; *QE* 2.68–97; *Spec. Laws* 1.66–67; Josephus, *Ant.* 3.122–24, 179–87; *J.W.* 5.207–18. Scholars who perceive some variety of cosmic sanctuary in Hebrews include Moffatt 1924:xxxiii–xxxiv; Käsemann 1961:135; Luck 1963:208; Sowers 1965:106–10; MacRae 1978:184–88; Thompson 1982:113–15; Koester 1989:174–82; Grässer 1993:87–92; Sterling 2001; Eisele 2003:375–77; Stegemann and Stegemann 2005:20; Schenck 2007:151–55; Backhaus 2009a:55; Svendsen 2009:158–68.
[76] That the "greater and more perfect tent" is "not of this creation" (9:11) also undercuts this view, as does Hebrews' consistent habit of distinguishing the Holy of Holies from the tent as a whole, all of which it locates in heaven. For a fuller critique see Ribbens 2016:90–94.
[77] E.g. Peterson 1982:131–32; Hurst 1990:13–17; Cockerill 2012:359–60; Church 2017; similarly Schenck 2007:166–67. 2 Bar. 4:2–7, 32:4; 4 Ezra 7:26; 8:52; 13:36; 1 En. 90:28–29; and Jub. 1:16–18, 27–29 are sometimes cited as precedents.
[78] Rightly, Gäbel 2006:242 n. 126; Ribbens 2016:111–12.
[79] As many have argued, certain early Jewish apocalyptic texts, including those sometimes called "mystical," provide the closest parallels to Hebrews' depiction of the heavenly tabernacle. E.g. 1 En. 9:1; 12:4; 14:8–25; 15:3; 71:5–9; Jub. 31:12–17; 4Q400, 403, 405; 11Q17 21–22 IX, 3–5. For a very capable comparison see Ribbens 2016:52–81, 89–99. Others who highlight the commonalities between Hebrews' heavenly tabernacle and that in early Jewish apocalyptic texts include Löhr 1991; Eskola 2001:202–11, 251–69; Stökl ben Ezra 2003:182–84; Alexander 2006:139–40; Rowland and Morray-Jones 2009:167–73; Elgvin 2011:25–30; Mackie 2011; Moffitt 2011:203–4 esp. n. 140; Barnard 2012; Barnard 2013; Mason 2012.

singular and finished (7:27; 9:12, 26, 28; 10:10), the ongoing activity in view in 8:1–2 is likely intercession (7:25; cf. 4:16). Nevertheless, after shifting the spatial focus to heaven, in 8:3 the author indicates that Christ's priestly ministry in heaven includes rather than excludes his offering: "For every high priest is appointed to offer gifts and sacrifices; thus it is necessary for this priest also to have something to offer." In 8:1–2 the author tells us where Jesus serves as priest; 8:3 says this service includes offering a sacrifice. Thus the denial in 8:4 that Jesus serves as priest on earth cannot square with an earthly location for Christ's self-offering. This is confirmed in 8:5 by the reference to the priests who serve on earth: "They serve a copy and shadow of the heavenly things." These offer sacrifices in the earthly tabernacle; Christ offers his in the heavenly tabernacle of which the earthly is a copy.[80] When the author locates Christ's high-priestly ministry exclusively in heaven in 8:1–5, he has past self-offering in view as much as present intercession. Hence 8:1–5 confirms that Christ offered himself in the only place where he was qualified to serve as high priest, the heavenly tabernacle. By setting heaven as the spatial frame for the following exposition, describing the heavenly tabernacle as a two-room entity corresponding to its earthly copy, and including Christ's sacrifice within his heavenly priestly activity, Heb 8:1–5 confirms that, just as the Levitical priests offered their sacrifices in the earthly tabernacle, so Christ offered his in the tent in heaven.

He Entered Once for All (Heb 9:11–14)

I now argue that, while less explicit than 9:24–25 and 8:1–5, 9:11–14 also locates Christ's offering in the heavenly tabernacle. Regarding 9:11–12, I will show that, though these verses do not use the word "offering," they too plot Christ's self-offering on the sequence "enter in order to offer." On the other hand, 9:13–14 names Christ's self-offering, but with less explicit temporal and spatial clues. I will argue that these verses' setting within Christ's entrance to the heavenly

---

[80] Ribbens aptly limns the logic of 8:1–5 as a whole: "Having stated that Jesus is a high priest and minister in a heavenly sanctuary and that every high priest – including Jesus – offers sacrifice, the implication is that the earthly high priests offer sacrifice in the earthly sanctuary and the heavenly high priest in the heavenly sanctuary. Verse 4 begins to draw out this implication … [Jesus] is not a priest κατὰ νόμον and, therefore, does not present offerings in the earthly sanctuary. His priestly activity happens in heaven, where he offers himself as a sacrifice" (Ribbens 2016:107).

(I) ¹¹ Χριστὸς δὲ

    (II) παραγενόμενος ἀρχιερεὺς τῶν γενομένων ἀγαθῶν

        (III) διὰ τῆς μείζονας καὶ τελειοτέρας σκηνῆς   (A)

           (III.1) οὐ χειροποιήτου,   (B)

           (III.2) τοῦτ' ἔστιν οὐ ταύτης τῆς κτίσεως,

        (IV) ¹² οὐδὲ δι' αἵματος τράγων καὶ μόσχων   (B¹)

        (V) διὰ δὲ τοῦ ἰδίου αἵματος   (A¹)

(I¹) εἰσῆλθεν ἐφάπαξ εἰς τὰ ἄγια

    (VI) αἰωνίαν λύτρωσιν εὑράμενος.

Figure 2.2 Structure of Heb 9:11–12

tabernacle confirm the heavenly location of Christ's offering. We begin with 9:11–12, a sentence many have called the *summa* or highpoint of Hebrews' priestly Christology, and therefore of the whole letter.[81] The structure of these verses can be displayed as shown in Figure 2.2.[82]

The main verb of this sentence is εἰσῆλθεν ("he entered," I¹), and participial phrases precede and follow it: "When Christ appeared (παραγενόμενος, II) as a high priest of the good things that have come ... he entered the Holy of Holies once for all ... thereby obtaining (εὑράμενος, VI) eternal redemption."

In this meticulous appropriation of Yom Kippur, the chief foci are Christ's entry to the Holy of Holies and its redemptive effect. Because words for "offering" do not appear in 9:11–12, we must ask: How does 9:11–12 relate to the Yom Kippur sequence that 9:6–7 has just narrated? We have noted that the description of the high priest's inner-sanctum blood manipulation as an "offering" in 9:7 is singular among ancient narrations of Yom Kippur. The word choice is not incidental but motivated; it signals Hebrews' controlling interest in this inner-sanctum rite. Hebrews 13:11 is also relevant, since it arguably describes the blood brought into the inner

---

[81] E.g. Lane 1991:2.235; Laub 1991:67; Weiss 1991:462; Grässer 1993:142; Koester 2001:411; Gäbel 2006:283; Backhaus 2009a:314.

[82] Following Gäbel 2006:284 with one modification. Similarly, Fuhrmann 2007:192.

sanctum on Yom Kippur as "a sin offering." However, some who have noted the lexical peculiarity of 9:7 still argue that the omission of "offering" from 9:11–12 indicates a radical rewriting of the Yom Kippur script. Such scholars, supporting View 1, argue that Jesus entered the heavenly Holy of Holies having already made his offering rather than in order to make his offering.[83]

Against this I note that 9:11–12 explicitly spells out the points of contrast between Christ's high-priestly offering and that of the Levitical high priest. Jesus appeared as high priest of the good things to come, not their parabolic anticipation (9:11; cf. 9:6–10). He entered "the greater and more perfect tent (not made with hands, that is, not of this creation)," not its earthly, human-made, derivative counterpart (9:11). He entered "not by means of the blood of goats and calves but by means of his own blood" (9:12; cf. 9:7). Finally, he obtained not provisional cleansing (9:9–10) but "eternal redemption" (9:12). Given that Hebrews explicitly details these points of discontinuity, it is highly unlikely that the simple absence of the lexeme "offering" is meant to so radically reconfigure the Yom Kippur sequence. Since our author went out of his way to describe the high priest's inner-sanctum blood manipulation as an "offering," it would take an equally loud signal to indicate that Christ made his offering before entering.

Further, three details of Heb 9:11–12 underscore continuity between Christ's sacrifice and the Levitical high priest's at precisely this focal point, the entrance to the Holy of Holies, and hence confirm that Jesus entered the Holy of Holies to make his offering there. First, like the Levitical high priest, though in a different sanctuary, Jesus passed through the tent (διὰ τῆς ... σκηνῆς) in order to enter its Holy of Holies (εἰσῆλθεν ... εἰς τὰ ἅγια). As we have seen, this course correlates with that of the Levitical high priest, who entered the Holy of Holies to make his offering there (9:7). In light of the extensive parallels between this "greater and more perfect tent" in 9:11 and the similar statements in 8:2 and 9:24, this tent can only be the tabernacle in heaven.[84] Further, we have seen that Hebrews regularly uses σκηνή to designate the whole tabernacle and

---

[83] Those who note the peculiarity of προσφέρει in 9:7 yet see its counterpart in Christ's death, not his entrance to heaven, include Young 1981:207–10; Lane 1991:2.223; Cockerill 2012:380, 394. Without reference to the lexical point, Bruce 1990:213–14 makes the same basic argument, followed by Joslin 2007:82.

[84] See Table 2.1, "Heavenly High Priest, Tabernacle, Offering (Heb 8:1–5)."

ἅγια for the Holy of Holies. In keeping with this habit, σκηνή in 9:11 denotes the heavenly tabernacle as a whole, and ἅγια its inner sanctum.[85] Therefore the διά of 9:11 is most likely local: Christ passed through the heavenly tabernacle in order to enter its Holy of Holies (cf. 6:19–20).[86] Hebrews' heavenly sanctuary is bipartite; like its earthly counterpart it has a Holy Place and a Holy of Holies. By reporting Christ's passage through the heavenly tent into its Holy of Holies, Hebrews underscores this parallel between Christ's Yom Kippur offering and that of the Levitical cult.

Second, Christ entered "once for all" (ἐφάπαξ, 9:12). This both parallels and radicalizes the singularity of the Levitical high priest's entrance: While he entered "once a year" (9:7), Christ entered "once for all." Hebrews uses ἅπαξ (9:26, 28) and ἐφάπαξ (7:27; 9:12; 10:10) to characterize Jesus' self-offering as unique, sufficient, and unrepeatable.[87] Suggestively, every other Christological use of ἅπαξ or ἐφάπαξ explicitly names Christ's offering as that which is singular. Yet here in 9:12, it is Christ's entrance to the heavenly Holy of Holies that happens ἐφάπαξ. Since 9:12 is the only Christological context in which ἅπαξ or ἐφάπαξ appears but "offering" does not, the best explanation is that Hebrews so intimately associates Christ's entrance to heaven with his self-offering that the former can fill a conceptual slot normally occupied by the latter. Hebrews can apparently say "entrance" where it would normally say "self-offering"; the same cannot be said for Jesus' death. Hence Jesus' entrance into the

---

[85] Those who identify the "tent" in 9:11 as the heavenly sanctuary as a whole include Spicq 1953:256; Hofius 1972:65–67; Loader 1981:166; Young 1981:199; Attridge 1989:246; Lane 1991:2.230; Koester 2001:409; Gäbel 2006:280, 285; Barnard 2012:112; Cockerill 2012:391; Ribbens 2016:116–17. This contrasts with those who see the referent of the tent as Christ's body: whether his human nature as instrument of salvation (Chrysostom 1994:440; Owen 1991:266–68; Cody 1960:164–65), specifically as offered in death (Calvin 1963:120); or his resurrected body as the new temple (Vanhoye 1965); or the church as his spiritual body (Westcott 1903:260); or his "Eucharistic body" (Swetnam 1966).

[86] Those in favor of the local sense include Moffatt 1924:121; Spicq 1953:256; Andriessen 1971:86; Hofius 1972:67; Attridge 1989:245–46; Löhr 1991:191–92; Weiss 1991:465; Lane 1991:2.229, 2.236–37; Gäbel 2006:285; Fuhrmann 2007:196; Mackie 2007:178–79; Telscher 2007:256 n. 694; Backhaus 2009a:318; Moffitt 2011:222 n. 10; Ribbens 2016:114–15. In favor of an instrumental reading are Vanhoye 1965; Swetnam 1966; Laub 1980:189; Koester 2001:408. Schenck 2007:164 proposes what he calls a "modal" reading. Compton 2015a:119–20 proposes three options, two local and the third instrumental or modal, citing Schenck. For critiques of Schenck see Barnard 2012:112–13; Ribbens 2016:115–16 n. 157.

[87] Gäbel 2006:288. For a valuable study of repetition and singularity in Hebrews see Moore 2015 (on this passage see 187–88).

heavenly Holy of Holies, like that of his Levitical counterpart, is not the sequel to his offering but its immediate prerequisite.

Third, like the Levitical high priest, Jesus entered the Holy of Holies (1) by means of blood, (2) which he brought with him to offer there. I argue that the διά clauses of 9:12 (IV and V above) assert the first point and imply the second. Jesus entered "not by means of the blood of goats and calves but by means of his own blood" (οὐδὲ δι᾽ αἵματος τράγων καὶ μόσχων διὰ δὲ τοῦ ἰδίου αἵματος). These clauses contrast the substance of the sacrifices offered by the Levitical high priests and Christ: animal blood versus Christ's blood.[88] Both instances of διά are clearly instrumental, the latter indicating that Christ's blood was the means by which he obtained access to the heavenly Holy of Holies. This parallels 9:7, where the high priest enters the Holy of Holies "not without blood" (οὐ χωρὶς αἵματος), and 9:25, where Levitical high priests yearly enter the Holy of Holies "by the blood of another" (ἐν αἵματι ἀλλοτρίῳ). Hebrews 9:7 indicates that the high priest entered with blood. Since the ἐν of 9:25 describes the same act, it is probably associative,[89] again implying that the high priest brought blood with him. Given these parallels, the instrumental sense of διὰ δὲ τοῦ ἰδίου αἵματος in 9:12 should not be taken to exclude the idea that Christ entered heaven with his blood. Instead, while οὐ χωρίς in 9:7 and ἐν in 9:25 explicitly indicate that the high priests entered with blood and thereby imply that they entered by means of it, the second διά in 9:12 asserts and implies the converse: because Christ entered by means of his blood, he therefore in some sense brought it with him.[90] Like his Levitical counterpart, Christ obtains access to the inner sanctum by means of his blood, and he enters *with* his blood, in order to offer it there. I will further support the idea that Christ brings blood into heaven as sacrificial material in Section 5.3, where I will also discuss what the author means by implying that Christ in some sense "offered" his blood in heaven.

When Hebrews describes Christ's entrance into the heavenly inner sanctum in 9:11–12 without using "offering," this omission does not imply that whereas the high priest entered in order to make his offering, Jesus entered having already made his offering. The mere absence of this word cannot signal such a drastic departure from the

---

[88] Ribbens 2016:117. [89] BDF §198 (2), p. 106.
[90] Similarly Andriessen 1971:90; Gäbel 2006:285–86; Moffitt 2011:223–24; Ribbens 2016:118.

author's carefully crafted Yom Kippur script.[91] Instead, in line with Hebrews' more explicit statements in 8:1–5 and 9:23–24, 9:11–12 implies that, like the earthly high priest, Christ offered his sacrifice in the Holy of Holies.

To turn to 9:13–14, what spatial referent should we discern in the assertion of 9:14 that Christ "offered himself without blemish to God"? And how should the reference to Christ's "blood" inform that judgment? Some scholars who recognize that Jesus' entry to heaven in 9:11–12 occurs at his bodily ascent there nevertheless see the frame of reference in 9:13–14 shifting to Jesus' death.[92] However, these verses provide no temporal or spatial markers to this effect. Sometimes it seems that, in somewhat circular fashion, a crucial reason scholars take "offered himself" in 9:14 as describing Jesus' death is that other references to Jesus' self-offering, none of which mention Jesus' death, are also seen as designating Jesus' death.

More substantively, many scholars of this persuasion see references to blood, here in 9:14 and elsewhere (9:12, 25; 10:19), as evidence that Jesus offers himself at his death.[93] In Chapter 5, I will argue that blood in these contexts does indeed evoke Christ's death, but this does not entail that Christ *offered himself* in death. To anticipate the later argument, blood in such contexts is what Christ offers; "blood" signifies the fact and effects of Christ's death as the material content of his heavenly offering. In offering his "blood" in heaven, Christ brings the soteriological significance of his death on earth to effective fruition in the presence of God.[94] By offering his "blood" in heaven Christ offered to God the life he gave in death. In any case, 9:13 begins with γάρ, indicating that these two verses explain or support the prior two. This γάρ renders it even less likely that the author, having reported Christ's entry to heaven in 9:11–12,

---

[91] Contra, e.g., Loader 1981:185, 189.   [92] E.g. Richardson 2012:37–38.

[93] Lane 1991:2.240; Cockerill 2012.393–94; Richardson 2012:38. Richardson offers the most elaborate recent defense of the view that Jesus' offering coincides with his death. He draws parallels between Hebrews' explicit discussions of Jesus' death and its references to his offering (and "making atonement"), comparing 2:14 with 2:17, 2:17 with 9:28, and 2:14–15 with 9:26 and 10:10, arguing that each of the latter should be interpreted in light of the former (ibid., 34–42). Yet his argument is weakened by strained parallels, a degree of the circularity mentioned earlier, and the failure to recognize that the sequence "offered then sat down" in 10:12 (cf. 1:3) can easily refer to what Jesus does *in heaven itself*, not only to the cross and exaltation. The argument of Compton 2015a:150 n. 231 also suffers from this last weakness.

[94] Similarly, though with more focus on Christ's death as "self-giving," Gäbel 2006:279, 305, 309, 315.

pivots to his death in 9:13–14. Instead, by indicating that 9:13–14 elaborates Christ's entrance in terms of what his offering accomplishes, this logical hinge strengthens the conclusion reached earlier: Christ entered the heavenly sanctuary in order to offer himself there. Eternal redemption (9:12) and the cleansing of conscience (9:14) are complementary soteriological goods that both surpass the temporally limited, external cleansing available under the old covenant (9:9–10). This thematic parallel confirms that both sentences narrate the same act. Hence, 9:14 spells out what is implicit in 9:12 – Christ did not merely enter heaven as high priest, but also, like the earthly one, offered his sacrifice there.

Self-Offering on Earth in Hebrews 9:26 and 9:28?

The most important remaining objection to my reading of these three passages (8:1–5; 9:11–14, 23–25) is that some understand Heb 9:26 and 9:28 to locate Jesus' self-offering at his death on the cross.[95] The evidence offered for this view consists in the link between Jesus' sacrifice and his suffering in 9:26, and in 9:28 both (1) the link between the human fate "death then judgment" and Jesus' act of being offered then returning and (2) the implicit identification of Jesus' "being offered" with his death as the suffering servant (Isa 53:12).

We begin with Heb 9:26. This verse denies that Jesus had to suffer repeatedly, since in his singular eschatological appearance he definitively set aside sin "by his sacrifice" (διὰ τῆς θυσίας αὐτοῦ). In this verse the singularity of Jesus' sacrifice rules out the possibility that he could have suffered repeatedly; the reference to "suffering" clearly evokes the cross. But it is an unwarranted leap from seeing Jesus' suffering as necessary to his offering to equating his suffering with his offering. As argued in Section 2.2, Christ's suffering was necessary for his perfection, which occurred at his resurrection and qualified him to offer himself once for all, as both priest and sacrifice, in the heavenly sanctuary. This reading just as much as the "self-offering on the cross" position accounts for why Christ's suffering is unrepeatable. Further, the text simply does not equate Christ's suffering with his self-offering. Instead, it would be more accurate to say that Christ's self-offering presupposes his suffering, rather than

---

[95] E.g. Young 1981:208–9; Fuhrmann 2007:220–23; Richardson 2012:39–41.

consisting in it, just as his self-offering also presupposes his resurrection and ascension.⁹⁶ Further, τῆς θυσίας αὐτοῦ ("his sacrifice") is essentially a nominal equivalent of the verbal phrase προσφέρῃ ἑαυτόν ("to offer himself") in 9:25. Just as no temporal and spatial disjunction should be inserted between 9:11–12 and 9:13–14, no such wedge can fit between 9:25 and 9:26. The sequence "enter to offer" in 9:24–25 specifies the place where, and therefore time when, the sacrifice of 9:26 is offered. Nothing in 9:26 contradicts or overrides that sequence. So 9:26b fits within the "enter to offer" paradigm that is explicit in 9:24–26a.

In 9:28 we read that Christ, "having been offered once to bear the sins of many, will appear a second time, not to deal with sin but to save those who are eagerly waiting for him." Some proponents of View 1 treat this verse as a key to identifying Jesus' death with his self-offering.⁹⁷ That is, such interpreters read Hebrews' other statements about Jesus offering himself in light of how, on their reading, 9:27–28 identifies Jesus' death as his self-offering. However, 9:28 does not say that Jesus offered himself but that he *was offered*. Two factors in 9:28 suggest that the aorist passive participle προσενεχθείς ("having been offered") not only includes a reference to Jesus' death, but actually focuses on his death. First, the passive figures Christ as *being offered* – by whom is not specified, though divine agency is likely implied – which aligns Christ's experience with that of the animal victim that was offered by another. The priest offers; the animal is offered. Given this alignment with the fate of the sacrificial animal, it is at least possible that "having been offered" includes a reference to Christ's death. Second, however, I would argue that this verse's allusion to Isa 53:12 puts a reference to Christ's death in 9:28 beyond dispute.⁹⁸ The servant of Isa 53 is led to death (53:8 LXX), assigned a grave (53:9), and has his life delivered to death (53:12). It is precisely by dying that he bears the

---

⁹⁶ Moffitt 2011:281 n. 142 rightly points out that the genitive αὐτοῦ in 9:26b is "most likely a simple possessive genitive," in contrast to the English translation tradition of interpreting it as an objective genitive and translating it "the sacrifice of himself" (RSV, NRSV, ESV, NIV). This translation, which seems to imply that Christ's "sacrifice" is his surrendering to death on the cross, both lacks grammatical warrant and contradicts the sequence presupposed in 9:24–25.
⁹⁷ E.g. Richardson 2012:39–40.
⁹⁸ In support of an allusion to Isa 53:12 LXX, see, e.g., Loader 1981:1980; Attridge 1989:266; Kraus 1991:244 n. 61; Lane 1991:2.250; Weiss 1991:484; Ellingworth 1993:487; Grässer 1993:198; Hahn 2004:433; Gäbel 2006:296, 305; Mackie 2007:97 n. 207; Ribbens 2016:222.

Locating Christ's Self-Offering in Heaven 65

sins of many (53:11–12). Just as the servant was made an offering in his death (Isa 53:10 MT), so also, says 9:28, was Jesus. Therefore, while Hebrews consistently locates Christ's high-priestly self-offering in heaven, when it figures Christ as victim here, it says he *was offered* on the cross.

As I will argue in Chapter 5, Hebrews treats "Christ as victim" and "Christ as priest" as compatible, not competing. As high priest, Jesus is appointed following his resurrection and then *offers himself* in heaven. As spotless victim he *is offered* on the cross. After his resurrection he then, as it were, takes up what his *being offered* in death achieved, and offers that to God in heaven. As 9:14 says, he offered himself without blemish – as spotless victim – to God. Christ is victim before he is high priest, but his high-priestly offering presupposes his being sacrificial victim. Even after he has become high priest, Christ remains sacrificial victim, and offers himself as such to God in heaven.

Hence, while 9:28 does use "offering" of Christ's death, it is the only passage in Hebrews to do so, and it offers a complementary conceptual framework to that of Christ offering himself as high priest. It is not that this one reference to Christ "being offered" in death controls the time and place of all of Hebrews' references to Christ "offering himself." Instead, I would argue that this lexical diversity – being offered on the cross, offering himself in heaven – is the result of Hebrews figuring Jesus as both victim and high priest.[99] And in Chapter 5 I will argue that Hebrews does not merely distinguish Jesus' act of being slaughtered on earth from his subsequent

---

[99] Kenneth Schenck notes this distinction: "Hebrews 9:25 pictures Christ offering his sacrifice in heaven; 9:28 pictures Christ being offered on earth at his death." He offers this as an example of "a situation where the most likely meanings of several verses in Hebrews conflict with each other if taken somewhat literally." Accordingly, Schenck assigns the two verses to "two slightly different metaphors of offering." One, Christ's death on the cross as a sacrificial offering, the author inherited from prior Christian tradition; the other, Christ as high priest in a heavenly sanctuary, the author created. Schenck sees the former as more fundamental, and the perceived tension between them as "a strong indication that the heavenly tabernacle in Hebrews functions primarily on a metaphorical level" (Schenck 2016:245). Contra Schenck, I argue that these different uses attest not incompatible metaphors but a deliberately deployed distinction. Far from indicating discrete, ultimately incommensurable metaphorical constructions, I will argue that this interplay of Christ-as-victim and Christ-as-priest is fundamental to Hebrews' conception of the material or substance of Christ's offering. As 8:3 affirms, just as every priest is appointed to offer gifts and sacrifices, so also Jesus needed something to offer. By being offered as victim in his death, Jesus obtained that which, as high priest, he subsequently offered to God in heaven. Making this case is the burden of Chapter 5.

self-presentation in heaven; instead, in heaven Jesus offers the outcome of his "being offered" on earth. In heaven the resurrected Jesus offers himself as that which had been slaughtered.

Summary Contra View 1

The question this entire section has addressed is, where does Christ offer himself? In our taxonomy the only position that answers this spatial question exclusively with "Jesus' death on the cross" is View 1.[100] As we saw in Section 1.2, proponents of View 1 argue that Christ offered himself in his death on the cross, and only entered the heavenly sanctuary after this offering was complete. Hence some of the more detailed defenses of View 1 argue that Hebrews deliberately reorders the sacrificial sequence of Yom Kippur in its Christological fulfillment: Unlike the high priest who entered the Holy of Holies to make his offering, Jesus entered the Holy of Holies having already made his offering. However, I have argued that Hebrews deliberately parallels the Levitical high priest and Christ at precisely this point. The author goes out of his way to describe the high priest's inner sanctum blood rite as an offering (9:7), and then he explicitly plots Christ's self-offering along the sequence "enter (the Holy of Holies) in order to offer" (9:24–25). Hebrews emphatically locates Christ's priestly activity in the heavenly sanctuary, and includes his offering in that priestly activity (8:1–5). As we saw in Section 2.2, Jesus is only qualified to be appointed high priest by virtue of his resurrection, which appointment necessarily precedes his offering a sacrifice (5:1; 8:3). Everything in the three passages this section considered is consistent with this picture. While Hebrews articulates several differences between Christ's offering and that of the Levitical high priest, both are offered in the Holy of Holies of the respective sanctuaries in which they serve. Further, that Christ offers his sacrifice in the heavenly sanctuary rather than in an earthly one is integral to its sufficiency, finality, and superiority to its Levitical precursors. Where did Christ offer himself? In the Holy of Holies in the tabernacle in heaven.

---

[100] As we will consider in Section 2.4, View 2 might be said to do this, since it treats Jesus' "entry" as a metaphorical description of his death on the cross. However, View 2 affirms that Jesus only offered himself in the heavenly sanctuary in a metaphorical sense, so I leave it to the next section.

When Did Christ Offer Himself? Upon His Bodily Ascent to Heaven

Our second question, much more briefly, is: when did Christ offer himself? By answering "where" I have already argued a position about "when," namely, upon his bodily, post-resurrection ascent to heaven. However, several of the views in my taxonomy offer subtle positions on when Christ offered himself, and are worth addressing one by one. So, here I respond to how Views 2 and 3 answer this question, with a brief word on View 4, a fuller response to which awaits the next chapter.

First, proponents of View 2 hold that at least some of Hebrews' references to Jesus entering the heavenly sanctuary are metaphorical. That is, these references do not describe an event in any sense distinct from or subsequent to Jesus' death; instead they ascribe heavenly significance to Jesus' death. The unsurmountable problem with this position is that Hebrews' references to Jesus' entry to the heavenly sanctuary weave a unified referential web that specifies where he went, where he is, and from where he will return. As we have seen, in 9:11–12, the author asserts that Christ "entered" the Holy of Holies in heaven. In 9:24, he adds a crucial detail: "For Christ has entered, not into a Holy of Holies made with hands, a copy of the true things, but into heaven itself, now to appear in the presence of God on our behalf." Christ entered the Holy of Holies and now appears before God there. As 9:28 indicates, Jesus will remain in heaven until he appears a second time to save those awaiting his return. So, in 9:24, Jesus' entry to the heavenly sanctuary is inseparable from his continuing presence there. There he went; there he remains. If Jesus' entrance to heaven is a metaphor for his suffering on the cross, per View 2, how is it that Jesus remains in heaven now?[101] This would require the contorted proposal that Jesus' entry to heaven is metaphorical but his current presence there is not. It is far simpler to hold that Jesus' entrance to heaven is an event distinct from and subsequent to his death on the cross – as it is everywhere else in the New Testament – since Jesus not only entered heaven but remains there now.

This is confirmed by 8:1–2, "Now the point in what we are saying is this: we have such a high priest, one who is seated at the right hand

---

[101] As Kibbe 2016:165 rightly asks, "How can Christ be *presently* in heaven ... if the event of his arrival there was only a metaphorical way of discussing the cross?" (emphasis original).

of the throne of the Majesty in heaven, a minister in the Holy of Holies, in the true tent that the Lord set up, not man." The heavenly tabernacle contains the throne on which Jesus now sits. So, every passage in Hebrews that attests Christ's exaltation to God's right hand also attests his entrance to the heavenly Holy of Holies, where God's throne is (1:3, 13; 10:12–13; 12:2; cf. 4:16). Accordingly, as we saw earlier, for Hebrews the heavenly tabernacle Christ enters is just as real as the throne on which he sits.[102]

Further, in 6:19–20, we read, "We have this as a sure and steadfast anchor of the soul, a hope that enters into the inner place behind the curtain, where Jesus has gone as a forerunner on our behalf, having become a high priest forever after the order of Melchizedek." While hope as an anchor passing behind a heavenly curtain is certainly a metaphor, the author speaks referentially when he says this place behind the curtain is "where Christ has gone." To treat Christ's entrance as metaphorical because hope-as-anchor is metaphorical is to lose the trail of the author's reasoning.[103] Our hope enters behind the curtain because Christ entered behind the curtain; believers' confidence is grounded on Christ's accomplishment. Further, Christ entered as "forerunner." By entering the heavenly Holy of Holies, he opened the way for others to follow (cf. 10:19–20).

Finally, Hebrews consistently narrates the sequence "humiliation then exaltation." Christ's entrance to the heavenly sanctuary is an aspect of his exaltation and hence follows, rather than coincides with, his death on the cross. We see this sequence in 2:9, where Jesus is crowned with glory and honor "because of the suffering of death"; in 2:11–13, where Jesus trusts God in trials and then proclaims God's name in the assembly; in 5:7–10, where Jesus learns obedience

---

[102] So Eric Mason: "This prominent use of Ps 110:1 in connection with Jesus' priestly sacrifice demands that any explanation of the conception of the heavenly sanctuary must also take into account the nature of the divine throne ... The author moves very comfortably in the book between discussions of Jesus in the heavenly sanctuary and at the right hand of the enthroned God" (Mason 2012:909, 912). Compare Mackie 2007:159, "As the place where Jesus' sacrifice is completed, the Heavenly Sanctuary must be as 'real' for both author and audience as the cross where Jesus' self-offering began." Cf. also Moore 2014:394–96.

[103] Those who rightly perceive a reference in 6:19 to Jesus' entry into the inner room of the bipartite heavenly sanctuary include Hofius 1972:84–94; Weiss 1991:367; Grässer 1990:384; Lane 1991:1.154; Gäbel 2006:227–28; Johnson 2006:173; Gelardini 2012:235. Contra Ellingworth 1993:349, who sees the "cosmological" language of 6:19 (as well as 9:11 and 10:20) as "an *ad hoc* and incidental way to express a soteriological reality"; and Small 2014:291, for whom "the 'veil' is a metonymy for the tabernacle or sanctuary, which in turn is a metaphor for the heavenly realm."

through suffering, and on the other side of that suffering becomes the source of salvation; and in 12:2, where Jesus endures the cross and afterward sits down at God's right hand.[104] In Hebrews, Jesus' exaltation to heaven follows his humiliation on the cross; heavenly glory follows earthly abasement.[105] The two do not coincide. In Hebrews, contra View 2, Jesus' entry to heaven took place after his death, and specifies where he is now.

View 3 offers a somewhat more complex answer to when Jesus offered himself: while begun on the cross, Christ's self-offering is completed by his entry to the heavenly sanctuary. View 3 also holds that this entry took place via Jesus' disembodied translation to heaven at the moment of his death. Yet I would argue that the only answer consistent with all of Hebrews' evidence is that Jesus entered the heavenly sanctuary after his resurrection, as a glorified, embodied human being.[106] First, 13:20 explicitly mentions Jesus' resurrection: God "brought again from the dead our Lord Jesus, the great shepherd of the sheep." Second, as discussed in Section 2.2, in 5:7 Jesus prayed to the one able to save him out of death (ἐκ θανάτου), and he was heard. This makes best sense as a reference to resurrection. Jesus' being spiritually translated to heaven at death does not amount to his being delivered "out of" death. Instead, that phrase implies that Jesus entered the condition of death and was subsequently taken out of it. Finally, again as discussed in Section 2.2, the running contrast in Heb 7 between the Levitical priests' mortality and Jesus' indestructible life (7:8, 16, 23–25) makes little sense if the author conceived of Jesus' postmortem existence in terms of a disembodied spirit alighting to heaven. Instead, the hinge between Jesus' mortality and his indestructible life is bodily resurrection (7:16).

---

[104] On 2:11–13 see Peeler 2014:84–94; Bates 2015:144–45. On 2:9, 2:11–13, and 5:7–10, see Gäbel 2006:148–58, 179–80; Easter 2014:45, 113, 154–64. On 12:2, see Croy 1998:177–88; Richardson 2012:101–5.

[105] Scholars who see Jesus' crucifixion as coincident with his exaltation in Hebrews often point to John's Gospel for parallels (e.g., John 3:14; 8:28; 12:23, 28, 32; 13:31–32). So Grässer 1993:148; Telscher 2007:255 n. 691; Rowland and Morray-Jones 2009:172. Although this is a common reading of John, Benjamin Reynolds convincingly argues that, while the cross is "clearly included in the Son of Man's glorification," this "does not mean that the crucifixion is equated with the glorification." Instead, "Jesus has two moments of glorification, one in his death, resurrection, and ascension (12.28; 13.31; 17.5) and the other following his return to the Father (12.28; 13.32; 17.5)" (Reynolds 2008:206–10, here 206, 210).

[106] For recent defenses of Jesus' bodily resurrection in Hebrews see Moffitt 2011; Easter 2014:94–99, 118–24.

Finally, a brief word on View 4, which holds that Jesus' self-offering began in his death on the cross, and was completed by his entrance to the heavenly sanctuary, which followed his resurrection. This view affirms much of what I argue in this chapter. The crucial difference is that it figures Christ's death on the cross as already an offering of himself as high priest. To consistently argue this view requires that Jesus is appointed high priest prior to his death on the cross, since Hebrews explicitly states that high priests are appointed to offer sacrifice (5:1; 8:3). Prior to his appointment as high priest Jesus is not authorized to offer sacrifice; that act is an exclusively priestly prerogative. And we have seen in Section 2.2 that Jesus is appointed high priest on the basis of his resurrection. Hebrews provides no warrant to see Jesus acting as priest before being appointed priest, or offering a sacrifice in order to become priest. Hebrews answers the question of when Jesus offered himself not only by specifying where he offered himself, but by reporting a crucial prerequisite: his appointment to priesthood on the basis of resurrection.

2.4 Conclusion

This chapter has argued that, having been qualified by the indestructible life he obtained by resurrection, Jesus was appointed high priest at his entrance to heaven; that this appointment was prerequisite to his self-offering; and that Hebrews explicitly locates Jesus' self-offering at his post-resurrection entrance to the heavenly sanctuary. Like the Levitical high priest, Jesus entered the Holy of Holies to make his offering there (9:7, 24–25). Not only does Hebrews affirm that Jesus serves as priest in the heavenly sanctuary, it includes his offering in that priestly work and denies that he could have served as priest on earth (8:1–5). Like the high priest who brought blood into the earthly Holy of Holies, Jesus entered heaven with his own blood, to offer it there (9:11–12). One of the key reasons Hebrews gives for the superiority of Christ's sacrifice compared with Levitical sacrifices is that it was offered in the heavenly sanctuary. How this heavenly self-offering relates to Jesus' death, including his *being offered* as victim in his death (9:28), will be addressed in Part II, especially Chapter 5.

I have argued that these points conclusively support View 5 against Views 1–4. In the next chapter I confirm and defend this case by examining 10:5–14, which poses certain challenges to my argument in this chapter, and by canvassing Hebrews' other cultic construals of the Christ-event.

3

CONFIRMING CHRIST'S SELF-OFFERING IN HEAVEN

3.1 Introduction

This chapter confirms and defends the thesis of Chapter 2 that, in Hebrews, Christ offers himself to God in the heavenly sanctuary after his resurrection. This will conclude my case for View 5, so in the final section I will offer a summary evaluation of Views 1–4. The chapter will proceed as follows. First, I will engage the last remaining detailed discussion of Christ's self-offering in Hebrews, 10:5–14, asking where and when Jesus offered himself. Second, I will briefly probe Hebrews' other, briefer cultic configurations of the Christ-event (1:3; 2:17; 7:27; 13:11–13), save one, arguing that all either confirm or at least cohere with Jesus offering himself in heaven. Third, I will account for 10:19–20, the last remaining passage that is sometimes cited in favor of a "metaphorical" take on Hebrews' cultic exposition of Christ's saving work, generally along the lines of View 2. Fourth, I will evaluate Views 1–4 in light of the argument of this chapter and the previous one.

3.2 The "When" and "Where" of Christ's Self-Offering in Hebrews 10:5–14

I will begin our engagement with Heb 10:5–14 by noting the challenge it seems to pose to locating Jesus' self-offering in heaven. Then I will recount two recent readings of Heb 10:5–14 from within View 5, those of Georg Gäbel and David Moffitt.[1] Despite significant similarities in their overall readings of Hebrews' cultic theology, Gäbel and Moffitt respond very differently to the pressure this passage seems to put on the idea that Jesus offered himself in heaven. After this I will argue that Heb 10:5–14 presents Christ's offering in

---

[1] Gäbel 2006:185–202; Moffitt 2011:229–256.

heaven as the goal of his incarnation. Hence, while my view of 10:5–14 overlaps with those of both Gäbel and Moffitt, it differs in key respects from each.

The Challenge of Hebrews 10:5–14 and Two Recent Responses

In 10:5–14, the first challenge to locating Jesus' self-offering in heaven comes from 10:5. According to this verse, Christ speaks the words of Ps 40:7–9 (39:7–9 LXX) when he comes into the world (εἰσερχόμενος εἰς τὸν κόσμον λέγει). Since Hebrews afterward interprets this speech with reference to the offering of Christ's body (10:10), some take 10:5 to indicate that earth, not heaven, is the theater of Christ's self-offering.[2] The second challenge is that the offering of Christ's body in 10:10 (τῆς προσφορᾶς τοῦ σώματος Ἰησοῦ Χριστοῦ; cf. 10:14) strikes many scholars as a transparent reference to the cross.[3] Read this way, these two aspects of 10:5–14 put considerable pressure on the idea that Jesus offered himself in heaven.

Georg Gäbel relieves this pressure by positing that the "offering" in 10:10 and 10:14 is Christ's earthly, non-cultic act of self-giving, which contrasts with the offering in heaven narrated in 9:11–14 and 9:24–28. Significantly, Gäbel takes 10:5 to indicate that the event in 10:10 is not a heavenly but an earthly one.[4] For Gäbel, σῶμα ("body") in 10:5 and 10:10 denotes Jesus' "lived bodily existence as a whole ... and the προσφορά of the σῶμα is to be understood as a self-giving that culminates in death, but includes the whole life lived in obedience."[5] On this reading of Hebrews' use of Ps 40:7–9, it is not that ineffective sacrifices give way to an effective sacrifice, but that the sacrificial cult is replaced "through a godly action that is not of a sacrificial, cultic nature; through confession and praise and through

---

[2] Attridge 1989:273; Isaacs 1992:202; cf. Hermann 2013:325–26.
[3] Westcott 1903:314; Spicq 1953:307; Loader 1981:186; Attridge 1989:276–77; Lane 1991:2.223, 2.266; Ellingworth 1993:505–6; Grässer 1993:224; Knöppler 2001:199–200; Koester 2001:440; Nelson 2003:254; Schenck 2003:82; Fuhrmann 2007:225; Karrer 2008:198–99; Backhaus 2009a:346; Cockerill 2012:444; Richardson 2012:41–42, 93; Eberhart 2013:141; Small 2014:224.
[4] Gäbel 2006:186–87.
[5] Ibid., 192, "... gelebte leibliche Existenz insgesamt ... und die προσφορά des σῶμα ist als Selbsthingabe zu verstehen, welche im Tode kulminiert, aber das ganze im Gehorsam gelebte Leben einschließt." Cf. Westcott 1903:314–15; Bruce 1990:243; Löhr 2005:472 (tentatively); Johnson 2006:253.

bodily obedience."[6] Further, Gäbel sees in 10:5 and 10:10 an "artistically employed equivocal use of προσφορά." In 10:5, προσφορά and σῶμα oppose each other, but in 10:10 Hebrews uses the non-cultic term σῶμα to give προσφορά a new, deepened meaning: In contrast to the cult's offerings, Christ's non-cultic "offering" of his body, his obedient self-giving, fulfills God's will.[7] Gäbel reads "offering" (προσφορᾷ) in 10:14 the same way, as denoting Christ's earthly, non-cultic self-giving.[8] Nevertheless, between these two references to Christ's earthly "offering," Gäbel sees in 10:12 a reference to Christ's heavenly sacrifice, which immediately precedes his session at God's right hand. While Gäbel sees 10:10–14 distinguishing Christ's earthly "offering" from his heavenly one, he says the passage sets these events "in close connection." Both together constitute Christ's singular saving act.[9]

In contrast, David Moffitt argues that the offering discussed throughout 10:10–14 takes place in heaven, after Jesus' resurrection. Moffitt sees 10:5 as reporting Christ's incarnation, but argues that the focus of the Psalm citation is not Christ's suffering but his deliverance from suffering in his resurrection.[10] Moffitt argues this by invoking "metalepsis," a literary trope in which the citation of a passage evokes its wider context.[11] Moffitt draws parallels between uncited portions of Ps 39 LXX and the broader context of Hebrews, as well as between Ps 39 LXX and Heb 10 in particular.[12] The former consist of a suffering individual crying out to God and being delivered (Ps 39:2; Heb 5:7), deliverance as "bringing up" (ἀνάγω, Ps 39:3; Heb 13:20), and subsequent public witness to God's salvation (Ps 39:4–6, 10; Heb 2:12).[13] The latter are a handful of terms found in Ps 39 LXX that show up in Hebrews for the first time in Heb 10; the pattern of endurance in suffering resulting in deliverance; thematic links between the author's evocation of Isa 26:20 and Hab 2:3–4 in Heb 10:36–38 on the one hand, and the treatment of

---

[6] Gäbel 2006:191, "... durch ein gottgefälliges Tun, das nicht opferkultischer Art ist; durch Bekenntnis und Lob und durch leiblichen Gehorsam."
[7] Ibid., 194, "... kunstvoll eingesetzten äquivoken Gebrauchs von προσφορά."
[8] Ibid., 198, 201.   [9] Ibid., 201 ("in engen Zusammenhang").
[10] Moffitt 2011:230–31, 238–47.
[11] Moffitt cites the influential discussion of metalepsis in Hays 1989:20.
[12] When Moffitt discusses Heb 10 in this section, he includes the whole chapter, not merely 10:5–14. In other words, Moffitt draws parallels between uncited portions of Ps 39 LXX and themes found outside Heb 10:5–14 in order to argue for a resurrection focus within 10:5–14.
[13] Moffitt 2011:238–40. Regarding the last, Moffitt puts 2:10 for 2:12.

Ps 39:7–9 LXX on the other; and the link between the psalmist's desire to have the law internalized (Ps 39:9b) and Hebrews' return to that portion of the new covenant promise (Jer 38:33 LXX) in 10:16.[14] The upshot of Moffitt's reading of Heb 10:5–10 is this: "All of this indicates that even in 10:5–10 the author has Jesus' resurrection in view just as much as Jesus' enduring the suffering of death."[15]

Moffitt offers four further lines of support for taking 10:5–14 to locate Christ's self-offering in heaven.[16] First, in 10:5–14 Jesus' death is not explicitly equated with his self-offering. Second, Moffitt earlier argues that Jesus' resurrected humanity is a necessary condition for him to assume eschatological rule at his exaltation to heaven (Heb 1:6–7, 14; 2:5–9). Since Hebrews sees Jesus entering heaven in a perfected body, it is plausible to see Jesus offering that body in heaven.[17] Third, Moffitt also argues earlier that "Jesus' resurrection stands at the heart of the author's argument for why and where Jesus is qualified to serve as a high priest." Hence Jesus is only qualified to offer himself after his resurrection, in heaven.[18] Fourth, a focus on Jesus' resurrection in 10:5–10 "aligns with the shift in Heb 10 from a discussion of what Jesus offered (see 8:3) to the parenesis of the last half of the chapter." For Moffitt, while 10:5 does highlight the incarnation, the whole passage identifies Christ's heavenly offering as the incarnation's goal. Because Jesus "lived and died with perfect faith, without sin," he received "the full and perfect inheritance of resurrected life," and "was therefore able to take his body into heaven where it was presented before God."[19]

Christ's Self-Offering in Heaven in Hebrews 10:5–14

I will now offer a reading of Heb 10:5–14 that understands Christ's self-offering in 10:10, 10:12, and 10:14 to take place in heaven (as in 8:1–5, 9:11–14, and 9:23–28), yet that also accounts for the accent on Christ's incarnation in 10:5. Like Moffitt, though by somewhat different means, I will argue that in 10:5–14 Christ's offering in heaven is the goal of his incarnation. The argument will proceed in three steps over the next three sections. First, this section will argue that locating Christ's self-offering after his resurrection, in the heavenly sanctuary, makes best sense of 10:5–14. Second, in light of this,

---

[14] Ibid., 241–43; cf. 247–52. [15] Ibid., 252. [16] Ibid., 254–55.
[17] See ibid., 45–144. [18] See ibid., 194–208. [19] Ibid., 255.

I will account for the accent on Christ's incarnation in 10:5. Third, I will conclude by offering a few further critiques of the stimulating and sophisticated readings of this passage advanced by Gäbel and Moffitt.

In support of locating Christ's self-offering in heaven in 10:5–14, we should first note, with Moffitt, that the passage nowhere identifies Christ's self-offering with his death. Nor does the passage even refer explicitly to Christ's death. Further, as Gäbel notes, 10:5 puts the Psalm citation on Christ's lips at his incarnation, not at his death.[20] Had the author wished to specify that this speech finds its telos in Christ's death, he could easily have done so. As it is, to supply the "where" and "when" of Christ's self-offering in 10:5–14 is to draw out an implication of the text; the referent should not be assumed.[21] I will argue in the next section that 10:5 highlights the incarnation because of the importance of Christ's body for both his obedience and his self-offering. Hebrews 10:5 certainly names the world as the theater of Christ's incarnation, but this does not necessarily entail that the world is the theater of his self-offering.

In order to rightly read the evidence in 10:5–14 that implies Christ offered himself in heaven, we need to recall the lexical distinctions drawn in Section 1.4. Against the common assumption that "offering" is synonymous with slaughter, which supports the conviction that Christ's self-offering is synonymous with his death, we noted that προσφορά (10:10, 14) denotes something presented to God, or the action of presenting something to God. Further, its cognate verb προσφέρω (10:12) can describe either the whole sacrificial process or the specific step of bringing to God what is offered. So, verb and noun forms of "offering" in Heb 10:10–14 do not constitute prima facie references to Christ's sacrificial slaughter on the cross. Instead, if these terms highlight any moment in the sacrificial sequence, it is typically the subsequent act of bringing sacrificial material into God's presence.[22] Hence the semantics of προσφορά and προσφέρω, rather than identifying Christ's self-offering with his death, instead support a reference to Christ's self-presentation to God in heaven.

---

[20] Gäbel 2006:193. [21] Similarly Moffitt 2011:230–31.
[22] In Hebrews, the sole exception to this is "having been offered" (προσενεχθείς) in 9:28. Yet I have argued in Section 2.3 ("Self-Offering on Earth in Hebrews 9:26 and 9:28?") that this describes not Christ offering himself as high priest, but his being offered as victim in his death. Hence, while this one instance does associate προσφέρω with Christ's death, it does not constitute a paradigm for how Hebrews describes Christ's high-priestly act of offering himself.

Further, whatever referent we assign to 10:12 we must also assign to 10:14. This is required by the γάρ ("for") in 10:14: "For by a single offering he has perfected for all time those who are being sanctified." This statement explains and grounds the claims of 10:11–13. Unlike the Levitical priests who stand daily at their service (10:11), Christ, having offered his single sacrifice, sat down at God's right hand, and now waits in kingly repose until his enemies are subdued (10:12–13). How is this radically unpriestly posture possible for Christ the high priest? Verse 14 explains: Christ's single offering accomplished all it needed to, all that the Levitical cult could not. Since the "single offering" of 10:14 explains the "single sacrifice" Christ offered in 10:12, both verses name the same act. This stands against Gäbel's bifurcation of the passage into two references to Christ's earthly, non-cultic self-offering (10:10, 10:14) and one to his high-priestly self-offering in heaven (10:12).

In Gäbel's proposal, according to Hebrews 10:10–14, Jesus presents two different "offerings," at two different times, in two different realms, with two different conceptual connotations – one cultic, and one non-cultic. But all three references to Christ's offering in 10:10–14 underscore its singularity: Christ offered his body once for all (ἐφάπαξ, 10:10), offered a single sacrifice for sins (10:12), and perfected his people by a single offering (10:14). This emphatic singularity signals that the author is spinning a single sacrificial thread, not two standing "in close connection."[23] This singularity also undermines Gäbel's assertion that the "offering" in 10:10 and 10:14 is non-cultic. Since a single sacrifice is in view, the cultic frame of reference holds throughout.

In Hebrews, the theme of singularity coordinates the Christ-event with the cult, in both continuity and contrast.[24] Every use of ἅπαξ ("once," 9:26, 28) or ἐφάπαξ ("once for all," 7:27; 9:12; 10:10) with reference to the Christ-event contrasts Christ's priestly self-offering with the repeated Levitical sacrifices. Yet the singularity of Christ's sacrifice not only contrasts with the repeated Levitical cult, but also fits with and typologically fulfills the relative singularity of Yom Kippur. As we noted in Section 2.3, the phrase ἅπαξ τοῦ ἐνιαυτοῦ ("once a year") is found in the Old and New Testaments only at Exod 30:10, Lev 16:34, and Heb 9:7, which all describe Yom

---

[23] Gäbel 2006:201.
[24] This paragraph is informed by Moore 2015:39–40, 62–66, 166–88. My thanks to the author for sharpening the present argument in personal correspondence.

Kippur. Since singularity characterizes Yom Kippur in the context of the whole Levitical cult, the author of Hebrews likely found in Yom Kippur a point of contact with early Christian convictions regarding the singularity of Christ's saving act (e.g. Rom 6:10; 1 Pet 3:18). Indeed, this may help account for Hebrews' sustained engagement with Yom Kippur, which is unique in the New Testament. The key point here is that singularity in Hebrews is not a freestanding motif but is conditioned by both its derivation from Yom Kippur and its contrast with the repeated Levitical sacrifices. Therefore the emphasis on singularity in 10:10 and 10:14 confirms that these verses are conditioned by the cultic framework of Yom Kippur.

In addition, the theme of singularity indicates that the high-priestly "offering" of 10:10 and 10:14 should be identified not only with that of 10:12 but also with the offering reported in 8:1–5, 9:11–14, and 9:23–28. As we saw in Chapter 2, 9:24–25 presupposes that Christ entered the heavenly tabernacle in order to offer himself there. If we add 10:12 to this sequence, we can say that Jesus entered the heavenly tabernacle, offered himself to God, then sat down at God's right hand. This fits with both Jesus' offering in heaven in Heb 8–9 and the sense of προσφέρω as "present" or "bring near." There is nothing jarring or inconsistent in Hebrews saying that Christ entered God's heavenly dwelling, presented himself or his body to God, and then sat down. There is certainly a sequence here, but the sequence is not that sacrifice precedes exaltation.[25] Instead, Hebrews' timeline is more refined: Jesus' presentation of his sacrifice precedes his session, and his ascent to heaven precedes both.[26]

Finally, while not decisive for my case, I would argue that the tight conjunction of sacrifice and session in 10:12 makes better sense if Christ's self-offering takes place in heaven than if it takes place on earth. On an "offering on the cross" reading, if Christ offered himself

---

[25] On the basis that sacrifice precedes session, Richardson 2012:41 (incl. n. 114) argues that "earthly humiliation and self-sacrifice precede heavenly exaltation." He further insists, rightly, that interpreters must integrate the cultic statements of 1:3 and 10:12 with the assertions about coronation and session in 2:9 and 12:2. Richardson criticizes Gäbel for a "systemic failure" on this point. But Richardson has failed to perceive the consistency of Gäbel's reading of these passages. Both recognize that death precedes coronation and sacrifice precedes session. But, contra Richardson, this furnishes no evidence for equating Jesus' death with his self-offering. Christ offers himself and then sits down. Christ's offering his sacrifice in heaven precedes his session as surely as his death does, only more immediately.

[26] Moffitt 2011:227.

and then sat down, the sequence skips Christ's resurrection.[27] This is what has led many scholars to conclude that Hebrews either "passes over" Christ's resurrection or replaces it with instantaneous disembodied translation.[28] Yet Hebrews' seamless transition from sacrifice to session makes far better sense if both follow Christ's resurrection, and if Jesus' presentation of his sacrifice immediately precedes his session. Christ offered himself and then sat down because the throne he sat on is in the place where he offered himself, the Holy of Holies in heaven.[29]

Christ's Heavenly Self-Offering as the Goal of His Incarnation

How then does the focus on incarnation in 10:5 cohere with Jesus offering himself to God in heaven? If the author does not invoke Christ's incarnation in order to identify the cross as its telos, why does he? I suggest that Hebrews spotlights Christ's incarnation in 10:5 in order to cast Christ's obedient offering of his body to God in heaven as its goal.[30] By this point Hebrews has thrice stated that

---

[27] See, for instance, the widely cited though somewhat vague comment of Hay 1973:152 on Heb 10:12, "The author comes closer here than anywhere else in his epistle to exhibiting death and heavenly session as a single theological event."

[28] See the survey in Moffitt 2011:1–41.

[29] Ribbens 2016:128; cf. Eskola 2001:208.

[30] Moffitt 2017 points out that a number of early Christian writers, in language influenced by Hebrews, construe Jesus' bodily self-offering in heaven as the goal of his incarnation. So, for instance, Hippolytus, *Noet.* 4: "There is the flesh presented (προσενεχθεῖσα) by the Word of the Father as an offering (δῶρον) – the flesh that came by the Spirit and the Virgin, demonstrated to be the perfect (τέλειος) Son of God. It is evident, therefore, that he offered himself (ἑαυτὸν προσέφερε) to the Father. But before this there was no flesh in heaven" (PG 10:809B; here *ANF* 5:225, slightly altered). Cf. the comment of Daly 1978:362 on this passage: "In heaven Jesus offered Himself – His flesh – to the Father." Similarly, in a homily on Lev 16, Origen argues that, like the earth-grown linen tunic that the Levitical high priest wore, the Son took to himself an earthly body in order, ultimately, to offer it in heaven: "It is 'a sanctified linen tunic' that Christ, the true high priest, puts on when he takes up the nature of an earthly body; for it is said about the body that 'it is earth and it will go into the earth.' Therefore, my Lord and Savior, wanting to resurrect that which had 'gone into the earth,' took an earthly body that he might carry it raised up from the earth to heaven" (*Homilies on Leviticus*, 9.2.3; Origen 1990:178–79). That Origen conceives of Christ's appearance in heaven as an atoning sacrifice is evident when he says that Christ's bringing "a pledge of our flesh" to the heavenly altar "is the real Day of Atonement when God is propitiated for men" (*Homilies on Leviticus*, 9.5.4; Origen 1990:185). And Theodoret of Cyrus offers a relevant comment on Heb 9:24: "The phrase *to appear* means, As man: now for the first time human nature went up to heaven" (PG 82:745A; Theodoret of Cyrus 2001:175).

Jesus offered himself to God (7:27; 9:14, 25). The assertion of 10:10 that Jesus offered his body is clearly a variation on this theme. And if Christ offers his body to God, then it is fitting for Hebrews to invoke a passage that contrasts a body prepared for service to God with the Levitical sacrifices that did not fulfill God's will. The Son took on a body in order, ultimately, to offer that body to God in heaven. In support of this conclusion I will trace three thematic strands from elsewhere in Hebrews that run through 10:5–14. My goal here is corroboration and confirmation, not refutation. I have argued previously that it makes best sense to locate Christ's offering in heaven in 10:5–14; here I offer a three-part material rationale for why Hebrews heads a discussion of Christ's heavenly offering with his incarnation.

First, as 10:10 indicates, the Son assumes a body prepared by God in order to offer that body back to God. Hebrews 10:5 highlights the incarnation because that is when the preexistent Son took on the human nature that would constitute the matter of his self-offering.[31] The Son's incarnation was prerequisite to his entire saving work, including his high-priestly self-offering. Since "the children" share in flesh and blood, he came to share in the same (μετέσχεν, 2:14). To become high priest, Christ had to be made like his brothers in every respect, which involved more, not less, than assuming human nature (2:17–18). So, in a context focused on Christ's offering, it is not surprising for Hebrews to shine a scriptural spotlight on the time when the Son became man. And to say that Christ became embodied in order to offer his body is not yet to say anything about when.

Corroboration that 10:5–14 figures Christ's heavenly offering as the goal of his incarnation may be found in 9:26.[32] According to 9:26, Christ "has appeared (πεφανέρωται) once for all at the end of the ages to put away sin by his sacrifice." The idea of Christ's eschatological manifestation to rescue from sin and its consequences resonates with 2 Tim 1:10, 1 Pet 1:18–20, and 1 Jn 3:5, which all use

---

[31] Some scholars have posited that the Son's preexistence in Hebrews is merely impersonal or ideal; e.g., Caird 1984; Hurst 1987; Dunn 1989:51–56, 206–9; Schenck 1997:104–15; Schenck 2001:475–76. However, each passage discussed above attests that Hebrews conceives of the Son as personally preexistent. Only a personally preexistent Son can create all things, sustain all things, outrank the angels, and come into the world of his own volition. Scholars who argue for the Son's personal preexistence in Hebrews include Meier 1985a:179–82; Parsons 1988:201–3; Grässer 1990:143–45; Grässer 1993:215; Weiss 1991:81, 93, 143–44, 321–22, 508; Gathercole 2006:33–35; Bauckham 2009; McDonough 2009:192–211; Webster 2009:80–81; Karrer 2010:129–30, 146; Peeler 2014:25–29, 41–46, 186–87.

[32] This paragraph is indebted to Gäbel 2006:295–96.

the same verb to announce Christ's end-time appearance on the world stage. This suggests that in 9:26 as well, Christ's "appearance" is his incarnation. I argued in Section 2.3 that 9:26 locates Christ's sacrifice in heaven. So, in 9:26 Christ's incarnation is oriented not merely to his earthly obedience and death, but to his subsequent presentation of his sacrifice in heaven.

Second, as argued in Section 2.2, Jesus' earthly obedience is prerequisite to his appointment to high priesthood following his resurrection. Jesus was made like his brothers in every respect – including the suffering and temptation he faithfully endured – in order to become a merciful and faithful high priest (2:17–18). Jesus is a high priest who is able to sympathize with his people's weaknesses because he was tempted in every way as they are, yet without sin (4:15). Although he is the Son, he learned obedience through what he suffered and, being perfected, became the source of eternal salvation, being designated by God high priest in the order of Melchizedek (5:8–10). In order to be appointed priest, Jesus had to faithfully fathom the darkest depths of human misery. The witness of 10:5–14 to Christ's incarnate obedience extends this trajectory. Just as Christ's obedience was necessary to his being appointed high priest, so his obedience is essential to his priestly self-offering.

Hence my third and final point: Hebrews underscores Christ's incarnation in 10:5 because Christ's earthly obedience is integral to the quality, value, and purpose of his heavenly offering.[33] According to Heb 10:7, citing Ps 40:7–8, Jesus came to earth to do God's will: The Son became incarnate to become obedient. In 10:9, Hebrews contrasts Christ's coming to do God's will (θέλημα) with the sacrifices God did not desire (οὐκ ἠθέλησας, 10:5, 8), concluding: "He abolishes the first in order to establish (ἵνα ... στήσῃ) the second." Two features of this verse recall the contrast between old and new covenants that is introduced in 8:7–13 and resurfaces in 9:1, 9:15, 9:18, and 10:15–18 (cf. 7:22; 8:6; 12:24). First, that Christ "establishes (στήσῃ) the second" echoes the reference in 9:8 to the first tent, which belonged to the first covenant (9:1) and had normative status or legal standing (στάσιν).[34] The first tent and its covenant had standing, but now Christ's sacrifice has established the second covenant. Second, the terms "first"

---

[33] Moore 2015:175–76 rightly notes that the willing obedience enacted in Jesus' self-offering, which imparts to it a different quality from the Levitical sacrifices, is a central concern in 10:5–10.

[34] On στάσιν in 9:8 see Hofius 1972:62–63; Attridge 1989:240; Lane 1991:2.216.

(πρῶτον) and "second" (δεύτερον) suggest not merely items ordered in the Psalm, but a covenantal sequence: The first has a cult whose sacrifices fail to please God; the second is founded on the fulfillment of God's will.[35]

When Hebrews again invokes the new covenant promise of Jer 31:33 in 10:15–17, in contrast to its citation in 8:8–12 the quote begins, "This is the covenant I will make with them after those days, declares the Lord: I will put my laws on their hearts, and write them on their minds." The tailoring of this citation fits the focus on obedience from the heart that is embodied, literally, in the citation and discussion of Ps 40:7–9 in 10:5–14. Hebrews reads Ps 40:7–9 and Jer 31:31–34 in light of each other. The new covenant that writes God's law on the heart is founded by a willing self-offering that fulfills God's will. Christ's obedience is crucial for his offering because his whole earthly life embodies the commitment to God that characterizes the new covenant that his offering inaugurates.[36] That Christ's whole course of obedience is integral to his heavenly self-offering is evident in 10:10, "by whose will we have been sanctified through the offering of the body of Jesus Christ once for all." Believers are sanctified by the will Christ came to carry out, through the instrumentality of his self-offering. Christ's self-offering sanctifies because it presents to God the body in which he fulfilled God's will. In Heb 10:10 Christ's body becomes as it were a living transcript of his obedience to God.

By announcing the incarnation, Heb 10:5 sets the world as the stage not of Christ's offering but of his obedience. The preexistent Son embraced the body prepared for him in order to offer that body back to God in heaven after obeying, suffering, dying, and rising again. Christ's incarnation sets in motion a sequence that leads through faithful endurance of suffering, to the cross, and then, through his appointment as high priest at his arrival in heaven, into God's innermost presence in the heavenly Holy of Holies. And Christ's incarnate obedience is integral to his heavenly self-offering in that his offering consummates the lived commitment to God that defines the new covenant, whose promises Christ's offering brought to fruition. Hence there is no tension between a focus on Jesus'

---

[35] Gäbel 2006:185, 195. Others who note the covenantal, epochal contrast of 10:9 include Lane 1991:2.264–65; Grässer 1993:222–23; Karrer 2008:197; Backhaus 2009a:347.

[36] Moffitt 2011:246–47.

incarnation and his bodily self-offering in heaven; the two themes are tightly bound together.

Concluding Synopsis

I will conclude this treatment of the location of Jesus' self-offering in Heb 10:5–14 by summarizing my reading, contrasting it with those of Gäbel and Moffitt, and offering a few final critiques of theirs. I have argued that Heb 10:5–14 treats Christ's bodily self-offering in heaven as a goal of his incarnation. Hebrews 10:5 announces Christ's incarnation in order to highlight Christ's earthly obedience as a crucial condition for his eventual heavenly self-offering. Christ's willing obedience, consummated in his in-person self-offering to the Father, provides one more reason why Hebrews considers this sacrifice superior to those of the Levitical cult.

Hence, with Gäbel and Moffitt, I recognize that 10:5 assigns Christ's speaking of Ps 40:7–9 to his incarnation. With Moffitt and against Gäbel, I read all three subsequent references to Christ's offering as describing Christ's presentation of himself to God in the heavenly tabernacle (10:10, 12, 14). According to Gäbel, Christ's "offering" in 10:10 and 10:14 is earthly, non-cultic self-giving. I have criticized this view on the grounds that the same offering is described in 10:10, 12, and 14. All three verses fit within the same cultic frame, and all three describe the same sacrifice as Hebrews' earlier treatment of Christ's heavenly self-offering (8:3–4; 9:11–14, 23–28). Further, the sequence of 10:12 – offering sacrifice then sitting at God's right hand – makes best sense as narrating what Jesus does after entering the heavenly sanctuary (cf. 9:24–25), not his death-then-exaltation.

Thus I agree with Moffitt's conclusion, but not with the primary arguments by which he supports it.[37] Moffitt's metaleptic argument lacks plausibility for at least three reasons. First, many of the resonances he perceives between the broader contexts of Ps 39 LXX and Heb 10 are drawn from statements occurring after the major transition at 10:19–25. There may be thematic links that stretch from 10:5 to 10:38.[38] But the shifts at 10:19–25 in genre (exposition to exhortation) and topic (Christ's offering to believers' perseverance) send

---

[37] Though, as the discussion above indicates, I agree with the first three of the four supporting arguments in ibid., 254–55.
[38] See, e.g., Ellis 1978:155; Guthrie 1994:141.

even stronger signals, and weigh against taking allusive resonances from after 10:18 to determine the focus of 10:5–10. Second, the resonances Moffitt detects between the uncited portions of Ps 39:7–9 LXX and Heb 10 are too faint to establish that the author intended to invoke these passages, much less to warrant the decisive role Moffitt gives them in framing the focus of the citation. Third, Moffitt's metaleptic reading requires the Son to speak at the incarnation from the vantage point of his resurrection, but Moffitt does not provide sufficient warrant for or explanation of this prospective stance. By contrast, on my view the Son speaks at the incarnation about the incarnation. However, I concur with Moffitt not only about 10:10–14 describing Jesus' offering in heaven, and about how this fits with Heb 8–9, but also that this passage figures Jesus' heavenly self-offering as the goal of his incarnation. That the Son assumed a body at his incarnation and remains embodied after his resurrection is crucial to Hebrews' entire cultic construal of the Christ-event.[39]

3.3 Locating Hebrews' Other Cultic Configurations of the Christ-Event

Now that we have discerned when and where Hebrews' most elaborate cultic configurations of the Christ-event locate his self-offering, we consider whether its briefer statements cohere with the conclusion that Christ offered himself in heaven after his resurrection. In 1:3 we read, "After making purification for sins, he sat down at the right hand of the Majesty on high." As many scholars recognize, 1:3 is elaborated in 10:12.[40] In both, the aorist indicative ἐκάθισεν follows an aorist participle. Both verses cast Christ's saving work in cultic terms and place his priestly sacrifice immediately before his kingly session. Regarding the former, 10:12 names the act, 1:3 its result.[41] On first read, 1:3 does not specify either earth or heaven as the place where Christ effected purification.[42] Yet, in light of the more explicit

---

[39] Moffitt 2011:255–56.
[40] E.g. Attridge 1989:279; Lane 1991:2.267; Gäbel 2006:201.
[41] For brief discussion of 1:3, see Section 2.3, "Yom Kippur in Hebrews."
[42] This helps explain why, as Barnard 2012:133 recognizes, most fail to ask whether 1:3 refers to an event on earth or in heaven, "and/or assume that it is a reference to the crucifixion." For the cross as assumed referent see, e.g., Spicq 1953:10; Laub 1980:19–20; Loader 1981:186; Attridge 1989:45–46; Grässer 1990:64; Lane 1991:1.15; Ellingworth 1993:73; Koester 2001:178–79; Mackie 2007:169–70.

sequence in 10:12, we should see the latter verse's heavenly referent as specifying that of the former.[43]

In 2:17, Christ had to be made like his brothers in every respect "so as to become a merciful and faithful high priest in the service of God, in order to atone for (εἰς τὸ ἱλάσκεσθαι) the sins of the people." Most scholars take ἱλάσκεσθαι to articulate the goal of Christ's priestly self-offering.[44] Some, however, argue for a reference to Christ's ongoing priestly intercession in heaven (cf. 7:25), which follows his singular offering.[45] I find the majority view more persuasive.[46] On this reading, the only temporal or spatial clue in the verse is that Christ's making atonement is a function of his high priesthood, and he became priest by virtue of having become like his brothers in every respect. As we discussed in Section 2.2, mention in 2:18 of Christ's suffering in temptation indicates that "being made like his brothers" includes not only his incarnation but also his endurance of hardship. With 2:10 and 5:9–10, 2:17–18 presents Christ's earthly endurance as prerequisite to his becoming high priest, which followed his resurrection. Therefore 2:17 not only fits with but corroborates the contention that Christ offers himself in heaven. Christ persevered through suffering in order to become high priest, in order then to make atonement by offering himself to God.

Hebrews 7:27 requires only brief comment on the last phrase: "he offered himself (ἑαυτὸν ἀνενέγκας) once for all." Bearing no marks of where and when this self-offering takes place, 7:27 should be read, in light of Hebrews' fuller discussions elsewhere, as describing Christ's self-offering in heaven.[47] After all, given the explicit sequence "enter in order to offer" that Hebrews plots in 9:24–25, it would take equally explicit signals here to plot Christ's offering on a different, contradictory sequence.

---

[43] Gäbel 2006:291; Moffitt 2011:227; and Ribbens 2016:99 also take Hebrews' later discussion of Christ's sacrifice to specify heaven as the location of 1:3. Moore 2015:185–86 sees 1:3 as "entirely consistent with Hebrews' view of Christ's entrance into heaven occurring *before* purification and session" (emphasis original).

[44] Braun 1984:70–71; Attridge 1989:96; Bénétreau 1989b:134; Grässer 1990:153–54; Lane 1991:1.65–66; Weiss 1991:224–25; Koester 2001:240–41; Richardson 2012:28–45; Ribbens 2016:206–11.

[45] Spicq 1953:48; Vanhoye 1969:380–82; Ellingworth 1993:186, 188; Gäbel 2006:213–27; Fuhrmann 2007:18–30.

[46] If the minority view is adopted, the passage does not refer to Christ's offering and so does not concern us here.

[47] Gäbel 2006:253, 279.

Finally, 13:11–13 presents a more complex picture. Here, the author recalls Lev 16:27 LXX with a near-verbatim paraphrase, "For the bodies of those animals whose blood is brought into the Holy of Holies by the high priest as a sin offering are burned outside the camp" (13:11). This gestures to one of the final stages in the Yom Kippur ritual, the postrequisite disposal of the sin-offering corpses,[48] and Hebrews plugs Jesus' death into this sequence in a way that we might not expect. Hebrews 13:12 infers, "For this reason Jesus also suffered outside the gate in order to sanctify the people through his own blood." This verse juxtaposes the area outside the gate of Jerusalem with the area outside the Israelites' wilderness camp in order to characterize the former with the profanity and impurity of the latter.[49] This transfer of cultic evaluation undergirds the following exhortation: "Therefore let us go to him outside the camp, bearing his reproach" (13:13). The point of this creative cultic recasting of Christ's crucifixion is to summon the hearers to embrace the particular form of profanity Christ endured: shame.[50]

In asking what 13:11–13 tells us about the time and place of Christ's self-offering, it is crucial to keep the passage's hortatory purpose in mind. The author draws a narrow, pointed parallel – between Christ's suffering in a profane place and corpse burning in a profane place – in order to exhort the hearers to follow Christ into that same "place." In saying that Christ suffered outside the gate, his crucifixion is clearly in view, which means this is the only place in Hebrews where Christ's death is explicitly set within a Yom Kippur framework. But does this locate Christ's self-offering at his death?

It is important to note that Christ's suffering is not designated an "offering" in this passage. The only probable reference to "offering" is in 13:11, where περὶ ἁμαρτίας likely means "as a sin offering."[51] However, here it is not Jesus' death that is designated a "sin offering," but the animal blood that the high priest brings into the inner sanctum (cf. 9:7). Further, as Hebrews repeatedly clarifies, it is not Jesus' death that corresponds to this act, but his post-resurrection entrance to the Holy of Holies in heaven (9:11–12,

---

[48] On which see Milgrom 1991:1052–53; Gane 2005:239–40.

[49] Wright 1987:243–47 points out that in the Levitical legislation the area outside the Israelite camp is neutral; it can be either pure or impure. Thus, "The activities carried out there such as the disposal of sacrifices ... will determine the quality of a particular locale outside the camp" (244 n. 35).

[50] Gäbel 2006:461–62; Filtvedt 2015b:231.

[51] See Section 2.3, "Yom Kippur in Hebrews."

24–25). Therefore, when Hebrews says Jesus suffered in order to sanctify the people, it does not thereby identify Jesus' death as the event that accomplishes the people's sanctification. Instead, just as it is the blood brought into the Holy of Holies that constitutes a sin offering, and atones for the sins-in-ignorance of the people (9:7; 13:11), so also Jesus' entry into the heavenly Holy of Holies with and by means of his blood is what sanctifies the people (cf. 9:12).

Hebrews 13:11–13 is indeed a notable exception to Hebrews' typically tight, consistent correlation of Christ's entry to heaven with the high priest's entry to the holy of Holies. Here Christ's entry simply is not mentioned. Hebrews implies that Christ's blood is "brought in," but does not say by whom. However, the crucial point for our purposes is that, in narrating this slice of the Yom Kippur script in 13:11–13, Hebrews does not conflate blood presentation with the moment of slaughter. Christ's death does not map onto the "blood-brought-in" moment of the sequence: his entry into the heavenly inner sanctum already fills that slot.[52] And 13:11–13 does not script the entire sequence of Christ's saving act, but locates Christ's suffering in the profane realm in order to draw the hearers toward him there.[53] Therefore, none of the texts surveyed here challenge the conclusion that Christ's offering takes place in heaven; instead, what time and space cues they offer tend rather to confirm it. Even 13:11–13 offers no support for View 1, since it does not conflate blood presentation with the moment of slaughter. At minimum, all these passages cohere with the contention that Hebrews locates Christ's self-offering in the heavenly sanctuary after his resurrection.

3.4 What about the Veil and Christ's Flesh in Hebrews 10:20?

The last remaining passage to address is 10:20, which appears to equate Christ's flesh with the veil in front of the Holy of Holies in

---

[52] Contra many scholars who see 13:12 correlating Jesus' death with the blood manipulation and/or see 13:12 as locating Christ's self-offering on the cross, e.g., Knöppler 2001:200; Löhr 2005:472; Mackie 2007:95, 169–70; Richardson 2012:44. Moffitt 2011:276–77 hits the mark: "Remarkably, in the one passage where Jesus' suffering/death is plainly identified with a specific element of Yom Kippur (13:12), the author focuses on exactly the wrong moment. Wrong, that is, if the traditional understanding of how he maps Jesus' death and exaltation onto Yom Kippur were correct ... A careful mapping of Jesus' suffering onto the moment of the slaughter of Yom Kippur is simply not what the author is about here."
[53] Cf. Filtvedt 2015b:229, who rightly notes that in 13:11–13 "the Yom Kippur typology is used in a significantly different way than has been the case previously."

heaven. This is why a number of scholars have exhibited it as evidence for a broader metaphorical construal of Hebrews' language regarding Christ's priestly work in the heavenly tabernacle. For instance, Schenck argues that in 10:20, "the author explicitly makes a metaphor out of the sanctuary when he compares Christ's flesh to the tabernacle's veil." This signals to Schenck that Hebrews' treatment of the heavenly sanctuary is consistently metaphorical: "The reason these images break down is because they are primarily metaphorical in nature" (cf. 8:5; 9:11–12, 23–24).[54] In other words, if Hebrews equates Christ's flesh with the veil in 10:20, then other references to the heavenly sanctuary must not be describing a structure Christ entered. Instead, Christ's entrance to the Holy of Holies in heaven is an elaborate metaphorical interpretation of his death on the cross. Those who make this argument tend to align with View 2, though there are exceptions.

Hebrews 10:20 is a notorious crux. The key issue is how the phrase τοῦτ' ἔστιν τῆς σαρκὸς αὐτοῦ relates to what precedes. There are three popular options, and a fourth combines elements of the first and third. First, many treat the phrase as appositional to the immediately preceding phrase, διὰ τοῦ καταπετάσματος ("through the veil").[55] Most exponents of this grammatical solution see the phrase as somehow equating Christ's flesh with the veil ("through the veil, that is, his flesh"). As noted earlier, many therefore draw the conclusion that Hebrews "allegorizes the veil."[56] Second, a number of scholars treat τοῦτ' ἔστιν τῆς σαρκὸς αὐτοῦ as an attributive genitive dependent on ὁδόν earlier in 10:20.[57] On this reading, for Hebrews to say "the way ... of his flesh" is to say that this "new and living way" consists in Christ's flesh, which is typically held to designate either his incarnate obedience or his self-offering in death. Third, following

---

[54] Schenck 2003:81; cf. Schenck 2007:176–77. See also Laub 1991:78, who argues, "Bemerkenswert und ein wesentlicher Schlüssel zum Verständnis der Hohepriesteranschauung ist die Gleichsetzung von καταπέτασμα und σάρξ Jesu." Johnsson 1978:107 notes the possibility that Hebrews equates Christ's flesh with the veil in 10:20, which "would supply unambiguous evidence of a 'spiritualizing' intent on the part of the author," and suggests such a move could "provide the clue to the writer's purpose in his extensive use of the cultic language." But, contra Schenck 2007:177, Johnsson does not commit himself to either conclusion.
[55] Moffatt 1924:143; Dahl 1951:404–5; Michel 1966:345; Thompson 1982:147–48; Braun 1984:307–8; Bénétreau 1990:110–11; Laub 1991:78–81; Isaacs 1992:57; Schenck 2003:81.
[56] Moffatt 1924:143.
[57] Westcott 1903:321–23; Spicq 1953:316; Andriessen 1971:78–81; Loader 1981:175–78; Löhr 1991:195–97; Gäbel 2006:203–7.

Otfried Hofius, some argue that another διά is implied before τῆς σαρκός αὐτοῦ, and, unlike its local sense earlier in 10:20, the implied διά has an instrumental sense.[58] Although I have not seen it labelled such, this reading takes Heb 10:20 to be an instance of the rhetorical figure "syllepsis" or "complicated zeugma," where "the word to be understood must be modified in meaning or syntax in order to suit the remaining phrases."[59] On this reading, Christ "inaugurated a new and living way through the veil, that is, by means of his flesh." Hence this view takes τοῦτ' ἔστιν to further specify the whole phrase, not merely the noun "veil." Within this camp, scholars divide over the referent of "flesh": Hofius argues for the incarnation, Jeremias for Jesus' death, and Moffitt for Christ's offering in heaven. Fourth, Norman Young argues for the first, appositional reading but concludes that τῆς σαρκός αὐτοῦ bears an instrumental sense, because the "ambiguity of διά" was "close to mind as he added the appositional phrase."[60] So he arrives at substantially the same conclusion as the third view.

My primary goal is to demonstrate, contra the first view, that it is exceedingly improbable that Heb 10:20 equates Christ's flesh with the veil of the sanctuary in heaven. First, in 6:19–20 Hebrews asserts that Christ passed behind the veil, which is precisely the act that 10:19–20 elaborates.[61] In 6:20, believers' hope enters behind the curtain in heaven because that is where Jesus went as forerunner. Jesus himself trod the path into the heavenly Holy of Holies in order to open the way for his followers. In 10:19, believers have freedom to enter the Holy of Holies in heaven by the blood of Jesus.[62] This "entrance" (εἴσοδον) is further characterized in 10:20 as a "new and living way" that passes "through the curtain." In other words, the role 6:20 describes as "forerunner" is expounded in 10:20 as Jesus inaugurating (ἐνεκαίνισεν) a way into the Holy of Holies in heaven. While the verb ἐγκαινίζω in 10:20 does not by itself indicate that Jesus inaugurated this way by traveling it himself, the parallel with 6:20

---

[58] Hofius 1970a; Hofius 1972:81–83; Jeremias 1971; Lane 1991:2.275–76, 2.284; Weiss 1991:523–26; Ellingworth 1993:519–21; Koester 2001:443–44; Moffitt 2010; Filtvedt 2015b:152–53 n. 51.

[59] Rowe 1997:135; cf. Lausberg 1998:311–15. Hofius 1970a:136 calls this usage a "Brachylogie" or ellipsis, of which syllepsis is a specific type.

[60] Young 1973:100–4, here 104; followed by Attridge 1989:286–87; Schreiner 2015:316–17.

[61] Similarly Hofius 1970a:134, 136; Andriessen 1971:79; Lane 1991:2.275.

[62] On the objective sense of παρρησία and the instrumental sense of ἐν in 10:19, see Lane 1991:2.274, 2.283.

implies it. Jesus made a way for believers to enter the Holy of Holies in heaven by his own entrance there. Believers have confidence to pass behind the curtain because Christ did so first, making a way for them to follow. Therefore, it is acutely implausible to see 10:20b as collapsing the distinction between Christ and the curtain through which he opened a way.

Second, the other spatial language in 10:19–20a consistently refers to the heavenly tabernacle as a structure in heaven. Believers have confidence to enter the Holy of Holies in heaven (εἰς τὴν εἴσοδον τῶν ἁγίων, 10:19). The way by which they enter leads through the veil (10:20a): διά here is clearly local, and the veil, as in 6:19, lies before the Holy of Holies in heaven.[63] Prior to the phrase τοῦτ' ἔστιν τῆς σαρκὸς αὐτοῦ in 10:20b, Hebrews nowhere treats the heavenly tabernacle as a symbol for something else.

Third, Hebrews consistently portrays the veil as hindering access to God (9:3; cf. 9:8). Even when Christ is said to have passed behind the veil in 6:19, the veil is not rendered a positive means of access, such as Christ's blood is elsewhere (9:12); the veil remains a barrier through which Christ passed. If the way into the heavenly inner sanctum passes through Christ's flesh, then Christ's flesh itself is figured, in part, as a hindrance to fellowship with God. As Hurst puts it, this "requires the grotesque corollary that Christ's flesh *is a barrier which he himself had to penetrate, and which he helps others to penetrate.*"[64]

Therefore the possibility that Hebrews here equates the veil with Christ's flesh should be ruled out as clashing with the sense of 10:19–20 as a whole and as out of keeping with Hebrews' consistent treatment of the heavenly tabernacle. Further, it is not coherent to argue for grammatical apposition yet give the phrase in question (τῆς σαρκὸς αὐτοῦ) an instrumental sense, as does the fourth view. If the phrase is appositive, it re-describes the previous noun phrase and stands in the same relationship to its governing preposition. Those who argue for apposition with an instrumental sense either fail to reckon with the implications of their grammatical analysis or depend in the end on Hofius's solution, an implied instrumental διά. Finally, to say that the veil that is Christ's flesh affords access to God is, again, to reverse the symbolic significance of the veil.[65] Thus, every

---

[63] Hofius 1970a:136.
[64] Hurst 1990:29, emphasis original; cf. Hofius 1970a:134.
[65] Gäbel 2006:205.

appositional reading should be rejected: Heb 10:20 does not "allegorize" the veil. This removes the last potential support for construing Hebrews' description of Christ's priestly offering in the heavenly tabernacle as an elaborate metaphor for his death on the cross. For Hebrews, the heavenly tabernacle is a place. It is where Christ went, where he offered himself, and where he remains.

Where then does this leave our problematic phrase? For present purposes, it is not strictly necessary to decide between the second and third options, the dependent attributive genitive and the implied instrumental διά. The greatest difficulty with the second, attributive option is that throughout Hebrews, τοῦτ' ἔστιν introduces a phrase in the same case as what it qualifies.[66] Gäbel dismisses this difficulty by pointing out that in no other instance in Hebrews does τοῦτ' ἔστιν introduce an attributive genitive.[67] Yet, given how far back this reading requires τοῦτ' ἔστιν to reach, the lack of concord is conspicuous. If the author had wished to modify the distant ὁδόν with the genitive phrase, he could have clarified by re-supplying the head noun, as Paul does in a similar situation (Rom 10:8).[68]

So, as Churchill once said of democracy, Hofius's grammatical solution seems to me the worst except for all the others. Its weakest point is that there appear to be no other attested instances, in classical or Hellenistic Greek, of an implied preposition used in a sense different from its explicit counterpart.[69] However, if this particular prepositional use is unattested, the figure of omitting a word that must be resupplied with a different sense is well attested in classical rhetoric.[70] Further, supplying an instrumental διά fits seamlessly with the apparent conceptual structure of 10:19–20. As Jeremias points out, on this reading the two verses each name the new way into God's presence (εἴσοδον / ὁδόν), its direction or goal (τῶν ἁγίων / διὰ τοῦ καταπετάσματος), and the means by which it is opened (ἐν τῷ αἵματι Ἰησοῦ / [διὰ] τῆς σαρκὸς αὐτοῦ).[71] Moffitt plausibly argues that Hebrews more or less interchangeably designates Christ's blood,

---

[66] Attridge 1989:286; Hurst 1990:28. [67] Gäbel 2006:206; cf. Löhr 1991:197.
[68] Young 1973:103.
[69] Hofius 1970a:136 finds a parallel in Justin, *Dial.* 118.3, which lauds Christians as superior to Jews in wisdom and worship διὰ τῆς κλήσεως τῆς καινῆς καὶ αἰωνίου διαθήκης, τοῦτ' ἔστιν τοῦ Χριστοῦ. But Young 1973:102 n. 1 rightly points out that the genitive phrase in τοῦτ' ἔστιν τοῦ Χριστοῦ is probably dependent on διαθήκης instead of being governed by an implied διά.
[70] As the discussions cited in Note 59 indicate.   [71] Jeremias 1971:131.

body, and self as what he offers to God in heaven.[72] Therefore, the assertion that Christ opens this way into the inner sanctum by means of his flesh – that is, by offering his body to God in heaven – is a fitting precis of Hebrews' entire cultic construal of the Christ-event. Given the difficulties of all the other readings, I suggest that the conceptual plausibility of the "implied διά" reading outweighs its relative grammatical implausibility.

However, if one adopts the attributive genitive reading, a virtually identical sense is possible. Most proponents of this reading assign some earthly referent to the "way of his flesh." For instance, Westcott sees the "way of his flesh" as designating the whole course of Christ's incarnate obedience and earthly self-offering as the route by which he ultimately came to pass behind the veil in heaven.[73] Gäbel similarly sees "flesh" as denoting the "way" of Jesus' earthly obedience, in line with his reading of σῶμα ("body") in 10:10.[74] However, Hebrews figures access to the heavenly Holy of Holies as an effect of Jesus' self-offering there, by which he presented the effect of his death to God.[75] Unlike the Levitical high priest who alone entered the earthly inner sanctum (9:7), Jesus entered the true Holy of Holies in order to enable his people to join him there. Therefore, if the phrase does modify ὁδόν, the attributive genitive, contra Westcott and Gäbel, should amount to something like "the way opened by his flesh," referring to Jesus' heavenly offering of his body, not "the way consisting in his flesh." On this reading the "way" is not identified with but rather produced by Christ's flesh, that is, the body he presented to God in heaven. While uncommon, this is a possible sense of the genitive.[76] Thus, while I favor the "implied διά" reading, either alternative to the appositional reading can furnish a sense that makes sense of 10:19–20 as a whole and offers a plausible summary of Hebrews' entire sacrificial soteriology. In any case, what is least plausible is any reading of 10:20 that sees Hebrews, contrary to its consistent practice elsewhere, treating the heavenly tabernacle as a symbol for something else.

---

[72] Moffitt 2011:229, 278–81. We will discuss this further in Section 5.3, "Blood as Material Offered."
[73] Westcott 1903:322.   [74] Gäbel 2006:206–7.   [75] See Chapter 5.
[76] Cf. discussion of the "genitive of product/producer" in Wallace 1996:104–6.

3.5 Concluding the Broad Conversation

We have now addressed every passage in Hebrews that construes the Christ-event in cultic terms. These include not only passages that explicitly use language of "offering," but also passages that speak of purification, sanctification, and so on. This chapter has confirmed the conclusion of Chapter 2, in support of View 5, that Hebrews consistently locates Christ's self-offering in heaven. Christ's incarnation, obedience, and death are crucial for his heavenly offering, in ways explored here and to be explored in Part II. Yet when Hebrews uses the language of "self-offering" it refers to Christ's presentation of his blood, body, and self to God in the heavenly sanctuary. Nowhere does Hebrews identify Jesus' death on the cross as his offering of himself to God. Some passages we have read in this chapter confirm the heavenly location of Jesus' self-offering; all cohere with it.

All that remains for Part I, therefore, is to conclude the "broad conversation" with Views 1–5. This will reiterate elements of Section 2.3, but these points are worth repeating in light of the fuller coverage this chapter has provided. First, regarding View 1: The most decisive evidence against its contention that Christ's self-offering begins and ends on the cross is the presupposition evident in 9:23–25 that Jesus entered the Holy of Holies in heaven in order to offer himself there. This presupposition makes sense of why Hebrews goes out of its way to describe the Levitical high priest's inner sanctum blood manipulation as an "offering" (9:7). And this "enter in order to offer" sequence also explains Hebrews' consistent focus on Christ's entry to heaven as the decisive moment in his eschatological Yom Kippur rite (6:20; 9:12, 24; cf. 10:20). Like the Levitical high priest, Christ entered the Holy of Holies in order to present his offering there.

Regarding View 2, we should underscore that throughout Hebrews, the heavenly sanctuary is a place where Christ goes, not a metaphor for something else. Christ went there, remains there, and from there will return (6:19–20; 8:1–5; 9:11–12, 24, 28; 10:12–13; cf. 1:3; 12:2). Any reading of the sequence of Christ's sacrifice that makes "metaphor" programmatic founders on the intractably referential quality of Hebrews' assertions that Jesus entered heaven. Jesus' entry to the heavenly sanctuary not only explains how he obtained redemption but specifies his present location (8:1; 9:24). As Moffitt has recently argued, Hebrews' application of the role of high priest to Jesus involves not metaphor but analogy.[77] Specifically, in Janet Soskice's terms, Hebrews' rendering of Jesus as high priest is not a "paramorphic" model but a "homeomorphic" one, "whose subject is also its source."[78] That is, Hebrews develops a structural analogy between the Levitical high priest's Yom Kippur offering and that of Jesus. There are explicit points of discontinuity: animal blood versus Jesus' blood, yearly versus once for all, earthly sanctuary versus heavenly, and temporary purification versus eternal redemption. Yet all these differences rest atop extensive, point-by-point parallels: For Hebrews, Jesus is really a high priest, who really offers a sacrifice, in a real sanctuary. The differences derive from the uniqueness of Christ's self-offering, not from metaphorical deployment of Levitical categories to describe the cross.

Over against View 3, I have argued that Hebrews attests Christ's bodily resurrection. While View 3 embodies a crucial insight about the constitutive role of Christ's exaltation for his self-offering, its proponents diminish this insight by disembodying Christ's entrance there.

My critiques of View 4 are more subtle. As noted in Section 1.2, in principle View 4 can say that Christ "offered himself" both on the cross and in heaven. For example, Richard Nelson rightly recognizes that Christ's "decisive act of purification" occurs at his entrance to the heavenly inner sanctum.[79] Nevertheless, citing 10:5 and 10:10, Nelson says, "His death was an offering of his body."[80] While Nelson skillfully sketches many aspects of Hebrews' appropriation of Yom Kippur, the exegesis offered in this chapter and the previous weighs against designating Christ's death as his self-offering, since at his death Jesus was not yet appointed high priest, and he entered heaven in order to offer himself there.

Further, proponents of View 4 sometimes argue that Christ's self-offering in Hebrews is a process that begins on earth and culminates in heaven.[81] On one hand, I agree that Hebrews treats Christ's incarnation, obedience, and death as integral to his heavenly

---

[77] Moffitt 2016b.
[78] Ibid., 261–67, here 261; citing Soskice 1985:49–53, 64–66, 102–3.
[79] Nelson 2003:255, cf. 256.
[80] Ibid., 254; cf. Koester 2001:440. Other proponents of View 4 who argue similarly include deSilva 2000:313, who reads 13:12 as indicating that Christ cleanses the people by his passion; and Moore 2015:198, who identifies the "altar" of 13:10 with Christ's death on the cross.
[81] Koester 2001:411, 415; Mackie 2007:95–96, 158–59, 169–70.

offering. In one sense Hebrews construes Christ's entire saving mission in cultic terms, and shorthand such as "a single sacrificial script"[82] can gesture toward this unity. Further, as I will argue in Chapter 5, Hebrews' use of "blood" aligns Christ's death with sacrificial slaughter and the material that is offered. Nevertheless, while Christ's death is an integral component in Hebrews' "single sacrificial script," it is not the time and place of his self-offering. When Hebrews says Jesus offered himself to God it makes not merely an intentional claim but a spatial one: Jesus entered God's heavenly throne room and presented himself to God there.

While it may be helpful to speak of a single sequence spanning heaven and earth as a second-order description, Hebrews does not say that Christ's "self-offering" itself spans heaven and earth. The Son became incarnate, endured suffering, died on the cross, was resurrected and perfected – and only thereafter appointed priest, thereby becoming qualified to make his offering. Upon his ascent to heaven, he offered himself to God in the heavenly Holy of Holies. Heaven is the place, and Christ's ascent there is the time, when he offered himself to God. The question this naturally raises for many is: What role then does Jesus' death play in Hebrews' soteriology, specifically in Jesus' self-offering? We have addressed this question occasionally in Part I; in Part II it takes center stage.

---

[82] Nelson 2003:255; followed by Mackie 2007:159.

Part II

The Material Question

4

WHAT CHRIST'S DEATH ACHIEVED

4.1 Questioning a Conclusion

If Hebrews locates Christ's self-offering in heaven, what did his death itself achieve? As we saw in Section 1.3, some answer, "not atonement." For instance, Walter Brooks argues, "In the light of the book of Leviticus, it is inconceivable how the author could think that death atoned."[1] Also Timo Eskola: "It is naturally important to note that atonement was obtained only in the Holy of Holies, and not at the moment when the sacrifice was slaughtered."[2] Hence Eskola denies that "the atonement is attached to the moment of Christ's death."[3] More recently, David Moffitt has argued that, because Christ offers himself in heaven, Jesus' death is not "the agent that effects redemption." In a passage such as 9:15–18, Hebrews "is not conflating Jesus' death and the atonement." Again, "he does not conflate that event with the atoning moment. Rather, he locates Jesus' death at the front end of a process that culminates in the atoning moment." According to Moffitt's monograph, while Jesus' death is "part of a larger sacrificial act," it is apparently not "atoning" in any objective sense. Instead, Jesus' death "serves as *the* paradigm of righteous suffering" and "stands as the event *sine qua non* for initiating the new covenant and in Jesus' *preparation* for his high-priestly ministry and atoning offering."[4]

All these statements share a common premise and conclusion. The premise is that Hebrews' predominant, Yom Kippur-stamped construal of the Christ-event locates Jesus' self-offering in heaven. Within that frame of reference, the decisive atoning "moment" is Jesus' entry into the heavenly Holy of Holies. Part I of this work

---

[1] Brooks 1970:210. [2] Eskola 2001:267. [3] Ibid., 267 n. 55.
[4] Moffitt 2011:290, 293, 292, 285, emphasis original.

essentially endorses this premise. And the conclusion these scholars draw from this premise is that, in Hebrews' account, Jesus' death does not in any objective sense achieve atonement.

This conclusion is questionable on at least two grounds. The first is whether these scholars are correct that within Hebrews' cultic construal of the Christ-event, Christ's death, as the moment equivalent to the slaughter of the animal, serves only to set the sacrificial sequence in motion. We will engage this issue in Chapter 5, which considers the role of Christ's death within Hebrews' appropriation of Levitical sacrifice, chiefly Yom Kippur. The second liability of the conclusion that Christ's death is not atoning in Hebrews is a hidden middle premise. If the stated premise is that Christ's self-offering takes place in heaven, and the conclusion is that his death does not effect atonement, the unstated premise is that what Hebrews says about "atonement" is coextensive with its Levitical framework. In other words, all that Hebrews says about Jesus' death fits within Levitical sacrificial categories.

The goal of this chapter is to demonstrate that this is not the case: sacrificial categories are prominent but not exclusive. In at least three passages – 2:9, 2:14–15, and 9:15–17 – Hebrews uses other conceptual frameworks to ascribe objective soteriological significance to the death of Christ. The primary task of this chapter will be to read these passages, asking what each sees as wrong with the human condition, and how Christ's death itself rights these wrongs. In order to analyze these passages where Hebrews seems explicitly to ascribe soteriological significance to Jesus' death itself I will use the categories of "plight" and "solution." What does Hebrews assert or presuppose about the human predicament, and how does Jesus' death address it? Where available, I will draw on other discussions in Hebrews of the relevant aspects of humanity's plight in order to provide an appropriately thick context in which to read each soteriological assertion. This heuristic use of "plight" and "solution" does not necessarily imply that Hebrews reasons "from plight to solution." Instead, this analysis merely presupposes a basic fit between what Hebrews sees as wrong with the world and how Christ's death sets things right.

In other words, this chapter offers a wide-angle view of the soteriological significance of Christ's death in Hebrews. In it I will confirm and extend the observations of scholars who have noted that, in addition to the predominant Levitical framework, Hebrews expounds Christ's death in light of other conceptual resources that have their own shape and substance.⁵ In the course of reading these passages, I will roughly sketch their place within the broader sweep of New Testament reflection on the saving significance of Christ's death. What is at stake in this chapter and the next is whether Hebrews' cultic construal of the Christ-event develops or departs from the early Christian kerygma. The saving significance of Jesus' crucifixion is widely emphasized in early Christian proclamation. Does Hebrews then deliberately, and somewhat anomalously, avoid ascribing atoning significance to Christ's death? Does the author, as it were, pan the camera away from Christ's death to his resurrection and ascension? Or does he instead zoom out, ascribing atoning significance to Christ's ascension while preserving and elaborating an atoning role for Christ's death?

4.2   Hebrews 2:9: Jesus Tasted Death for All

Regarding Heb 2:9, our focus is the concluding assertion that Jesus "tasted death for all" (ὑπὲρ παντός γεύσηται θανάτου). This assertion names the purpose (ὅπως) of Jesus having been made lower than the angels in his death and crowned with glory and honor following his resurrection. This purposeful sequence of humiliation-then-exaltation, in turn, explains how humanity's dominion over creation, lost almost as soon as given, has been regained (2:5–9). I will first trace the conception of humanity's plight that unfolds in Hebrews' reading of Ps 8:5–7 LXX in 2:5–9, then discuss Hebrews' broader treatment of the themes of death, judgment, and postmortem retribution, all of which impinge on 2:9. Finally, against this backdrop, I will display the soteriological effects Heb 2:9 ascribes to Jesus' death.

Plight: Fallen Present, Future Death and Judgment

What does Heb 2:5–9 assert or imply about the plight of humanity? I argue that the way the passage introduces, cites, and expounds

---

⁵ E.g. Löhr 2005:459, commenting on the passages we will discuss in this chapter, "Auf dieser allein am Lexem θάνατος orientierten Übersicht wird bereits deutlich, dass der Hebr die Bedeutung des Todes Jesu unter verschiedenen Aspekten wahrgenommen hat und beschreiben kann." See also Gäbel 2006:181; Marshall 2009:261; Small 2014:228.

Ps 8:5–7 LXX points to humanity's primeval "fall" into sin as the source of the cosmic disorder that presently harasses human life. The opening statement in 2:5 hangs an eschatological frame: "Now it was not to angels that he subjected the world to come, of which we are speaking." The verb "subjected" (ὑπέταξεν) anticipates its occurrence in Ps 8:7, cited in 2:8. That the "world to come" is the object of subjection indicates that the author has in view not merely the past or present but the future. The world to come is still to come, though God has already subjected it to someone. But to whom? The negative form of 2:5 raises this question; the following citation and exposition answer it.

Hebrews 2:6–7 cites Ps 8:5–7 LXX, omitting 8:7a: "What is man, that you are mindful of him, or the son of man, that you care for him? You made him for a little while lower than the angels; you have crowned him with glory and honor, putting everything in subjection under his feet." In 2:8b, he underscores the scope of what God subjected: "Now in subjecting all things to him he left nothing unsubjected to him." However, 2:8c adds, "But now we do not yet see everything subjected to him." We must now supplement our question about 2:5: who is the referent of "man" and "son of man" (2:6), as well as the string of personal pronouns (2:7–8)? To whom, on Hebrews' reading of Ps 8, did God subject all things, and whom did he make for a little while lower than the angels?

The predominant scholarly answers to these questions are often designated "anthropological" and "Christological"; there are also "both-and" readings, some of which are nearly indistinguishable from the "anthropological." However, these terms may mislead. Virtually all interpreters recognize that 2:9 portrays Jesus as fulfilling the psalm: "But we see him who for a little while was made lower than the angels, namely Jesus, crowned with glory and honor because of the suffering of death." In 2:9 at least, Hebrews offers a transparently "Christological" reading of Ps 8:5–7. Nevertheless, if we restrict our focus to the implied question of 2:5, the referent of "man" and "son of man" in 2:6, and the personal pronouns in 2:7–8, these terms offer serviceable shorthand. Understood as answering these questions with "humankind," "Christ," or "both" (or "deliberate ambiguity"), we can identify "anthropological," "Christological," and "both-and" readings of Heb 2:5–8.[6]

---

[6] For representative anthropological readings, see Westcott 1903:41–45; Hurst 1987:153–54; Grässer 1992a; Kinzer 1995:256–74; Gäbel 2006:134–48; Blomberg

Both anthropological and "both-and" readings see the exposition of Ps 8 in Heb 2:5–8 as alluding to the effects of humanity's fall into sin; the Christological reading may or may not. At least three factors favor the anthropological reading.[7] First, in the context of the whole psalm, whether Hebrew or Greek, these verses clearly refer to humankind.[8] Second, many early Jewish readings of Psalm 8 take the passage to describe the dominion granted to humankind at creation.[9]

A third reason to see humanity in general as the referent of Ps 8:5–7 in Heb 2:5–8 is the transition from 2:8c to 2:9: "Now we do not yet see everything subjected to him (αὐτῷ), but we do see ... Jesus crowned." As Jared Compton points out, if the author took Jesus to be the referent of the psalm, as the Christological reading argues, we would expect the "him" of 2:8c and the "Jesus" of 2:9 to occur in reverse order.[10] In other words, the delayed, emphatic introduction of the name "Jesus" is difficult to account for if Jesus is already the referent of the pronoun "him" in 2:8c. Instead, it is far more natural to understand the "him ... namely Jesus" of 2:9 as introducing a different referent from the previous pronoun. The "him" who does not presently possess dominion is humanity as a whole; the "him"

2008; Easter 2014:35–45; Compton 2015a:38–51. For "both-and" readings see Grogan 1969:58; Leschert 1994:98–115; März 1996; deSilva 2000:108–11; Koester 2005:364; Schenck 2007:54–59 (though Schenck's reading has strong affinities with the anthropological); De Wet 2010; Moffitt 2011:121–29. For Christological readings see Loader 1981:29–38; Attridge 1989:69–77; Löhr 1997:176–77; Guthrie and Quinn 2006; Backhaus 2009b:204.

[7] For fuller accounts to which mine is indebted, see Easter 2014:35–45; Compton 2015a:38–51.

[8] See, e.g., Maré 2010.

[9] Philo, *Creation* 84; 4 Ezra 6:53–54, 59; 2 Bar 14:17–19; 15:7–8; 2 En. 30:11–12, 31:1–6, 58:1–3; possibly 1QS 3:17–18a; also t. Naš. Soṭah 6:5; b. Sanh. 38b. For discussion see Kinzer 1995:40–208; Anderson 2000:89–90; Gäbel 2006:137–44; Filtvedt 2015a:286–87. 2 Enoch 31:1–6 is a particularly close parallel (cf. Heb 2:5), since v. 3 says God intended to create "another world" in order that everything could be subjected to Adam on the earth. Another close parallel is 2 Bar 14:17–19; 15:7–8, where we encounter both rueful reflection on humanity's current lack of dominion and expectation that the world to come will be for the glory of the righteous: "And you said that you would make a man for your world as a guardian of your works, so that it might be known that he was not created for the world, but the world for him. And now I see that the world which was made for us, behold, it endures, but we, for whom it was made, depart" (14:18–19); "And concerning what you said pertaining to the righteous, that because of them this world has come, so also shall that which is to come, come on their account. For this world is to them a struggle and a labor with much trouble; but that which is to come (will be) a crown with great glory" (15:7–8; translation from Gurtner 2009:49).

[10] Compton 2015a:43.

who does is Jesus. The passage portrays Jesus as the one human being who presently possesses the dominion declared in Ps 8.

In contrast to the exalted Jesus, for humanity as a whole God's creation purposes remain unfulfilled. Psalm 8 proclaims humanity's dominion, but present experience testifies otherwise. Since Ps 8 invokes the creation account of Genesis, especially Gen 1:26–28, Hebrews here seems to presuppose humanity's subsequent fall into sin.[11] If humanity's original dominion over creation is Point A, and present lack of dominion is Point C, Hebrews' train of thought seems to run through the fall as Point B.[12] The idea that death entered the world as the result of Adam's sin (cf. Gen 2:17; 3:9) is evident in Paul, well-attested in early Judaism, and makes good sense of Hebrews' reading of Ps 8 here.[13]

Confirmation that Hebrews presupposes humanity's fall into sin is found just a few verses later in 2:14–15. These verses describe the devil as "the one having the power of death" and humanity as "subject through fear of death to lifelong slavery." This state of servitude is the precise opposite of the glorious dominion announced in Ps 8.[14] Of course, in the narrative of Gen 3, it is through Satan's deceit that Adam and Eve sin and are punished by death. This renders the fall a likely explanation of how the devil came to possess the "power of death" described in 2:14–15, corroborating its relevance for 2:5–8. According to Hebrews' reading of Ps 8:5–7 in light of present experience, humanity lives amid cosmic disorder that includes, though is not limited to, the specter of death.

Also relevant to the assertion of Heb 2:9 that Jesus "tasted death for all" is Hebrews' treatment of death, judgment, and postmortem retribution as the default outcome of human life apart from Christ.[15]

---

[11] I take Hebrews' most likely scriptural source for this to be Gen 3.

[12] Übelacker 2010:238–39 rightly argues that, in view of Hebrews' reliance on Old Testament creation theology, "Die Unvollkommenheit des Menschen wird jedoch weniger auf das Geschaffensein des Menschen zurückgeführt als auf das bewusste Nicht-Tun des vom Schöpfer Gewollten." In addition to Übelacker, those who regard Heb 2:5–9 as presupposing the fall include Grässer 1992a:162; Kinzer 1995:265–67; Gäbel 2006:132–33, 144–45; Blomberg 2008:95. Contra Schenck 2007:59, 109, 132.

[13] Rom 5:12; 1 Cor 15:25–27 (which also alludes to Ps 8:6); 4 Ezra 3:7, 7:118; 2 Bar. 17:2–3, 23:4, 54:15; Apoc. Mos. 24; Philo, *QG* 1:45.

[14] So, e.g., Lane 1991:1.61. Kinzer 1995:265 n. 95 rightly compares δουλεία in 2:15 with δουλεία τῆς φθορᾶς in Rom 8:21. This is a fitting parallel since Rom 8:20 describes God's act of subjecting creation to futility in the wake of Adam's sin, a state δουλεία τῆς φθορᾶς names from another angle.

[15] I adapt this language from Easter 2014:45–77, who says "the default human story" has death and postmortem retribution as its "assured conclusion."

For Hebrews, death is a problem for humanity not only in its own right, but also because it leads inexorably to judgment and retribution: "It is appointed for people to die once, and after that is judgment" (9:27). While mortality is a distinguishing, universal characteristic of humanity (7:8; cf. 7:23), it is not a "natural" feature of human life, since God originally destined humanity for glory. Yet God's creation purpose is presently frustrated; death encloses life.[16] And, as 9:27 indicates, death and judgment are inseparable. The author treats everlasting judgment as an elementary teaching with which even his immature hearers were well acquainted (6:2). This was a safe assumption given how widespread teaching on final judgment is in early Jewish and Christian literature.[17] Hebrews names God "the judge of all" in 12:23; from his judgment none are exempt (10:30).[18] Further, as Walter Übelacker observes, Hebrews' paraenetic sections regularly conclude with warnings of judgment (4:12–13, 6:7–8, 10:26–31, 12:25–29).[19]

Finally, for all who lack Christ, the outcome of this judgment is postmortem retribution. Hebrews' axiomatic statements about God's retributive action, while primarily serving to warn against apostasy, nevertheless illumine the character of the one who will judge all (6:8; 10:31, 39; 12:29). Since Christ's sacrifice is the only effective remedy for sin, when apostates reject that sacrifice they return to the default human state of liability for sin and fearful expectation of judgment (10:26–29), now with even greater liability.[20] Because all have sinned, all are due sin's just penalty.[21] This postmortem repayment of evil is characterized as a curse and

---

[16] On how Hebrews accents mortality in its depiction of the human condition, see Löhr 2005:457; Reinmuth 2006:275, 279; Reinmuth 2012:376. The comments of Gray 2003:113 on death in Hebrews are worth citing in full: "It is something to be suffered (5:7–8; 11:37a) and not eagerly anticipated as a peaceful slumber or as a way of escaping the troublesome realities of bodily existence as in some intellectual traditions. Faith may make it possible to overcome death or to nullify some of its effects (11:4, 5, 12, 13, 19, 21, 29, 31, 35) but not to prevent its occurrence in the first place."

[17] See, e.g., Wis 4:20–5:23; T. Levi 3:2–3; 4 Ezra 7:33–44; 8:38; 9:10–12; 14:35; 2 Bar. 51:1–6; Matt 10:15; 11:22–24; 25:31–46; John 5:22–29; Acts 10:42; 17:31; 24:25; Rom 2:1–11, 16; 3:6; 14:10–12; 1 Cor 4:4–5; 5:5; 11:32; 2 Cor 5:10; 2 Thess 1:5–10; 2 Tim 4:1, 14; James 5:9; 1 Pet 1:17; 2:23; 4:5; 2 Pet 2:4; 3:7; 1 John 4:17; Jude 6; Rev 11:18; 20:11–13.

[18] As Löhr 1991:201 rightly observes, the context of 12:23 describes salvation but this descriptor inserts a note of warning.

[19] Übelacker 2007:248.

[20] Reinmuth 2012:387, "Der Abschnitt 10,19–39 macht deutlich, dass das Schicksal der Abtrünnigen dem der Ungläubigen gleichen wird."

[21] Übelacker 2007:256.

burning (6:8),[22] punishment (10:29), vengeance (10:30), and destruction (10:39). Postmortem retribution is the personal response of God the judge to what contradicts his will. As sin is a universal human condition, so also the expectation of retribution. As Matthew Easter observes, "The default human story concludes without any hope of a happy life after death."[23] Hence the human plight presupposed in Heb 2:5–9 consists in the ongoing effects of humanity's primeval fall into sin: lost dominion over creation, universal mortality, and the threat of retribution after death.

Solution: Activated by His Exaltation, Jesus' Death Averts Death

This picture of humanity's plight proves relevant for reading the crucial concluding assertion of Heb 2:9: "... so that by the grace of God he might taste death for everyone." We can visually arrange the whole verse as follows:

τὸν δὲ βραχύ τι παρ' ἀγγέλους ἠλαττωμένον βλέπομεν Ἰησοῦν
διὰ τὸ πάθημα τοῦ θανάτου
δόξῃ καὶ τιμῇ ἐστεφανωμένον,
ὅπως χάριτι θεοῦ ὑπὲρ παντὸς γεύσηται θανάτου.

Two syntactical issues deserve comment. First, which participle does διὰ τὸ πάθημα τοῦ θανάτου modify? A few scholars argue that it attaches to the preceding one (ἠλαττωμένον), indicating that Jesus was made lower than the angels for the sake of suffering death.[24] That is, he became incarnate in order to be crucified. This thought is evident in 2:14–15 and possible here. However, since the διά clause is closer to the latter participial phrase, and the main verb comes between it and the earlier participle, it is much more plausible to attach the διά clause to what follows, as do most scholars.[25] Hence Jesus was crowned with glory and honor *because* he suffered death (cf. Phil 2:8–9). On either reading, but especially the latter, the verse

---

[22] For eternal damnation as the fate of apostates in 6:4–8, see McKnight 1992:35–36; Nongbri 2003:266, 269, 278–79.
[23] Easter 2014:77; see further 70–77.
[24] E.g., Johnson 2006:91–92; Rascher 2007:62–63.
[25] E.g., Vanhoye 1969:288; Loader 1981:194; Attridge 1989:73 n. 35; Lane 1991:1.49; Weiss 1991:196; Ellingworth 1993:155; Koester 2001:217; Gäbel 2006:148–49; Small 2014:274 n. 59.

articulates the programmatic pattern of humiliation-then-exaltation that recurs at key junctures (5:7–10; 12:2).

Second, how does the ὅπως clause relate to the rest of the sentence? Among answers that have been advanced, four are worth engaging here.[26] First, some link ὅπως to the first participial phrase (τὸν ... ἠλαττωμένον).[27] This makes conceptual sense ("Jesus was made lower ... in order to taste death for all"), but is syntactically unlikely, since it requires the reader or hearer to refer so far back. Second, some take ὅπως with the prepositional phrase διὰ τὸ πάθημα τοῦ θανάτου. This is also conceptually plausible but grammatically improbable; while πάθημα is a verbal noun, the subordinate purpose clause introduced by ὅπως more likely depends on a verbal element.[28] Third, some see the clause connecting specifically to the predicate participle (ἐστεφανωμένον) that it immediately follows.[29] Or, fourth, one could attach the ὅπως clause to the entire preceding sentence.[30] In terms of sense, options three and four amount to virtually the same thing, since, as we will see, the predicate participle receives the emphasis of the whole sentence.

However, in terms of formal analysis, it is better, with the third view, to take ὅπως to depend specifically on the immediately preceding predicate participle. The first reason for this is proximity: ὅπως immediately follows ἐστεφανωμένον. Second, the emphasis of the preceding sentence falls on the predicate participle. The basic structure of the sentence is subject–verb–object–object complement. That is, "We see him crowned." The direct object is "the one made lower," with "Jesus" in apposition, and the prepositional phrase indicating Christ's death modifies the predicate participle "crowned." Hence, while conceptually significant, Jesus' abasement and death are not the emphasis of the sentence. Instead, its weight falls on the predicate participle. What is said *about* the "one who was made for a little while lower than the angels" is that he was "crowned with glory and honor." In other words, even if one took ὅπως to modify the whole sentence, the weight of it, and hence the point of departure for further development, falls at the end. Third, Jesus' exaltation is what

---

[26] Cf. the overview in Small 2014:275 n. 60. For each view I list scholars who support the position; critiques are my own.
[27] Michel 1966:139; Lane 1991:1.43, 1.49.
[28] Moffatt 1924:25; Thompson 2008:71.
[29] Delitzsch 1886:112–13; Hegermann 1988:68–69; Gäbel 2006:149.
[30] Loader 1981:195; Attridge 1989:76; Weiss 1991:199–200; Ellingworth 1993:155; Small 2014:275 n. 60.

renders him the solution to Hebrews' exegetical dilemma with regard to Ps 8. The problem the author perceives in 2:8c is that all things are not yet subjected to humanity. However, in his exaltation Jesus has been granted universal dominion. It is because Jesus has been exalted that Ps 8 is finally coming true.[31] Hebrews' argument in these verses pivots on Christ's exaltation to glory. Hence it is most probable that, rather than reaching farther back to some other element or depending on the sentence as a whole, the ὅπως clause specifies a purpose or goal of Christ's exaltation in particular.

The sense is, "Jesus was crowned with glory and honor *so that* by God's grace he might taste death for everyone." Jesus was exalted *in order to* taste death for everyone. The purpose of Jesus' exaltation is not limited to the dominion it enacts; that dominion also imparts soteriological significance to his death. In other words, Jesus' exaltation to God's right hand is a decisive factor in what makes his death a saving event for all. Hebrews 2:9 therefore maps two-way traffic between Jesus' death and exaltation.[32] On the one hand, Jesus' death is the basis for his exaltation: He was crowned with glory and honor "because of the suffering of death." Likely implicit here is the idea that Jesus' obedient endurance of death is the ground of his exaltation (5:7–10; 12:2; cf. Phil 2:9).[33] Jesus' death precedes and warrants his exaltation. On the other hand, Jesus' exaltation retrospectively qualifies his death as that which delivers others from death. The phrase γεύσηται θανάτου ("that he might taste death") vividly underscores Jesus' anguished experience of death,[34] and ὑπὲρ παντός ("for everyone") characterizes Jesus' death as vicariously effective for others. Finally, the ὅπως clause indicates that one purpose of Jesus' exaltation was to render his death just such a saving event.[35]

---

[31] Hegermann 1988:69, "Die eigenartige Nachstellung des ὅπως-Satzes hängt mit der pescherartigen Interpretationsweise im vorausgehenden Text zusammen; mit dem ὅπως-Satz wird der springende Punkt der Kommentierung des Psalmtextes noch einmal hervorgehoben und zugleich der anschließenden Entfaltung der Soteriologie das Thema gegeben."
[32] On this two-way traffic see especially Delitzsch 1886:112–16; Hegermann 1988:68–69; Weiss 1991:198–200; Gäbel 2006:148–51.
[33] Hegermann 1988:68.
[34] E.g., Attridge 1989:77; Gäbel 2006:148, 158–59 n. 122.
[35] So Hegermann 1988:69, "Die Inthronisation ist das Mittel der Inmachtsetzung des Todes Jesu als Heilsgeschehen." Similarly Weiss 1991:199, "Erhöhung ist hier im Hebr in der Tat verstanden als Bestätigung und Inkraftsetzung des 'Todesleidens' Jesu hinsichtlich seiner universalen Geltung." And Gäbel 2006:149–50, "Die χάρις-Aussage bezeichnet nicht das Todesleiden Christi als solches als Gnade Gottes, sondern sie will

This reading of 2:9 is confirmed and sharpened by how 2:9 concludes 2:5–9, and by how 2:10 elaborates 2:9. Regarding the former, as noted earlier, 2:9 presents Jesus as the solution to the tension between Psalm 8 and present experience introduced in 2:8c: "At present, we do not yet see everything in subjection to him. But we see him who for a little while was made lower than the angels, namely Jesus, crowned with glory and honor because of the suffering of death, so that by the grace of God he might taste death for everyone." This is the climax of the author's exegesis of Ps 8:5–7. He introduces and comments on this passage so as to uncover tension between its claims and present experience, in order to announce that Jesus is the one in whom the human destiny of Ps 8 is fulfilled. Jesus representatively embodies the entire human condition and its solution, opening the way for others to follow.[36] Jesus was made for a little while lower than the angels not merely in being made human, but in suffering a vile, excruciating death (cf. 12:2; 13:12–13). And Jesus was crowned with glory and honor after and because he suffered death, being then exalted above the angels (cf. 1:4, 5–14), thereby regaining Adam's lost dominion and inaugurating humanity's rule over the world to come (2:5). In Ps 8 the author finds hidden, as it were, not a state but a trajectory: Jesus was humiliated then exalted, made lower than angels then awarded universal dominion. Precisely because Jesus himself passed through the nadir of humiliation to reach the apex of exaltation, his death became that which wrests people out of the former and delivers them to the latter.[37] Insofar as death epitomizes the plight Hebrews sets in tension with Ps 8, Jesus' crucifixion, transfigured by his exaltation, becomes that which averts death for others.[38] Because Jesus arrived at humanity's final, divinely

---

sagen, dass es durch Christi von Gott gewährte Erhöhung aus dem Tode gnadenhaft 'für einen jeden' zur Geltung kommt."

[36] On the way Jesus' representative solidarity with humanity undergirds 2:8–9 (as it does all of 2:5–18), see especially Kögel 1904:22–23, 43–44; Hegermann 1988:68; Lane 1991:1.48–49; Weiss 1991:198–99; Compton 2015a:51.

[37] Cf. Delitzsch 1886:113, "The sacred writer would state for what end Jesus, not without mortal suffering – nay, in consequence of that suffering – has been thus exalted. That end is this: that He, through divine grace, should be found to have tasted death for the good of all and each of us, and that He should thus have entered into the lowliness of our death-subjected humanity, in order to exalt that lowliness to the high estate which the eighth Psalm declares to be our ultimate destination, and into which He is already entered Himself."

[38] I borrow the language of transfiguration from a comment of Francis Watson on Paul's Christology: "The resurrection transfigures the crucifixion, but it does not cancel it out; the risen Jesus does not cease to be the crucified one" (Watson 2000:116).

ordained dominion, his death is not a problem for his followers but his solution to their problem.[39]

Further, this soteriological assertion of 2:9, that Jesus' exaltation renders his death an event of universal saving efficacy, is developed in 2:10. The γάρ of 2:10 indicates that, even as 2:10 introduces a new line of thought that develops through 2:18, it elaborates the assertion with which 2:9 closes.[40] The following three parallels between 2:9 and 2:10 are telling.[41] First, in both Jesus saves people as the representative human. In 2:9 he is the one in whom their destiny is attained; in 2:10 he is the "pioneer" or "founder" (ἀρχηγόν) of the many sons' salvation (cf. 12:2). Hebrews' use of this term indicates not merely that Jesus guarantees his people's glory, but that he does so by first traveling the path of suffering-then-exaltation on which "many sons" will follow (cf. πρόδρομος, 6:20).[42] The solidarity between Jesus and humanity that is presupposed in 2:5–9 is made explicit in 2:10 and elaborated throughout 2:10–18.

Second, just as 2:9 invokes the pattern of suffering then exaltation, 2:10 says Jesus was made perfect through suffering. Here a logic similar to the ὅπως clause of 2:9 is evident: As the one who passed through suffering to perfection, Jesus is the founder of salvation. As discussed in Section 2.2, 5:7–10 develops this theme: Jesus faithfully endured the anguish of death, learning obedience through what he suffered, and then, having been perfected by resurrection, became the source of eternal salvation.

A third parallel between 2:9 and 2:10 is that Jesus' tasting death for everyone by God's grace mirrors his being God's means of leading many sons to glory. Since death is the dramatic foe of the glory announced in Ps 8, Jesus' tasting death for others in 2:9 implies that he brings them into the glory he entered, such that Ps 8 becomes true for them and humankind will indeed rule the world to come (2:5). The positive statement of 2:10, "leading many sons to glory," likewise describes humanity's new destination in Christ in terms colored by Ps 8. Even as 2:10 begins a new line of thought, it continues to comment indirectly on Ps 8. "Taste death" in 2:9 implies the plight from which Jesus rescues; "leading many sons to glory" in

---

[39] Cf. Weiss 1991:199, "Unter der Voraussetzung, daß dem Erhöhten nunmehr 'alles' unterworfen ist (V. 8), gewinnt sein 'Todesleiden' (V. 9a) seine Heilsbedeutung ὑπὲρ παντός."

[40] For how 2:10–18 develops 2:5–9 see ibid., 200, 203; Guthrie 1994:102; Compton 2015a:53, 64.

[41] Cf. Section 2.2.   [42] Easter 2014:113–14; cf. 146–49.

2:10 describes the destiny to which he delivers. These three parallels confirm that it is precisely as the one who has passed through suffering and is now glorified – or "perfected" – that Jesus is able to save. As in 5:9, Jesus' perfection is both a result of his suffering and a qualification to save. In a complementary way to 2:9, in 2:10 Jesus' exaltation gives new meaning to his sufferings.[43]

Finally, how does Heb 2:9 fit within the broader tapestry of early Christian reflection on the saving significance of Jesus' death? That Christ tasted death "for everyone" (ὑπέρ παντός) likely has both a representative and a substitutionary nuance. Regarding the former, the broader context highlights Christ's solidarity with his people, and narrates how he first treads the path on which they will follow. From this vantage point, Jesus saves humanity by sharing and transforming their fate. In support of a substitutionary sense, in the context of 2:5–9 death not only precedes glory but it also epitomizes humanity's plight. In this plight, death, judgment, and postmortem retribution form an indissoluble unity. Death is not merely physical expiration but a segue to condemnation. Hence in 2:9 death is both plight and solution: The problem is that humanity is subject to death, and Jesus' death rescues from death. Though believers still die (9:27), for them death is, so to speak, no longer death. All this supports a substitutionary nuance for ὑπέρ in 2:9. Jesus suffers death not only in solidarity with people but also instead of them. By dying Jesus averts death.

Hence Heb 2:9 shares much with Paul's assertions that Christ died for – that is, in place of – "the ungodly" (ὑπὲρ ἀσεβῶν, Rom 5:6), "us" (ὑπὲρ ἡμῶν, Rom 5:8; cf. 14:15; 1 Thess 5:10), and especially "all" (ὑπὲρ πάντων, 2 Cor 5:14–15). Also closely related are the assertion of 1 Pet 2:21 that Christ suffered "for you" (ὑπὲρ ὑμῶν) and 1 John 3:16 that he laid down his life "for us" (ὑπὲρ ἡμῶν).[44] In common with these Pauline and other texts, in 2:9 Jesus' death is vicariously effective as a saving act for others.[45]

---

[43] Weiss 1991:200, "Gerade aus der äußersten Erniedrigung, daraus also, daß der Erniedrigte die Bitternis des Todes 'geschmeckt' hat, erwächst die Heilsbedeutung dieser Erniedrigung und kann nunmehr der Erhöhte der 'Anführer' und der 'Uhreber des Heils' sein (2,10; 5,9)."

[44] In support of a substitutionary reading of Rom 5:6, 8, see Gathercole 2015:85–107. Harris 2012:216 sees in all of the passages in the main-text paragraph above a use of ὑπέρ that involves both substitution and representation.

[45] Grässer 1992b:182 and Weiss 1991:200 n. 25 root 2:9 in an "urchristliche Sterbeformel." Cf. more broadly Johnson 2006:92.

4.3 Hebrews 2:14–15: He Destroyed the Devil, Defeating Death

Our second passage follows closely on the heels of the first, occurring within 2:5–18. In 2:14–15, Hebrews presents humanity as in thrall to the devil through fear of death, and asserts that Christ's death delivers humanity from this bondage by destroying the devil's power. Here, as in 2:9, plight and solution are closely intertwined; to gain purchase on the passage we will pry them apart and consider the latter in light of the former. After considering the plight and solution set forth in 2:14–15, we will consider how the soteriology of 2:5–18 furnishes a backdrop for Christ's high-priestly self-offering.

Plight: Slavery under the Devil's Dominion through Fear of Death

Hebrews 2:14–15 describes all of humanity as in thrall to the devil (τὸν διάβολον). Specifically, these verses characterize the devil as "the one having the power of death" (2:14) and humanity as "through fear of death subject to lifelong slavery" (2:15). Verse 14 narrates how Christ came to share the universal condition of "blood and flesh" in order to destroy Satan and deliver people from his sway. The context says nothing to limit the scope of this predicament: subjection to Satan's power and servitude through fear of death are, outside of Christ, universal human conditions.[46]

The precise sense of "the power of death" is difficult to determine. Given that 2:5–9 presupposes the fall of humanity into sin (cf. Gen 3), the link between Satan and death likewise seems to presuppose that the devil "did not possess control over death inherently but gained his power when he seduced humankind to rebel against God."[47] Hebrews' thought here seems reasonably similar to Paul's portrayal of death as a power that entered the world through sin and thereafter reigned over humanity (Rom 5:12, 14, 17, 20; 6:9–10).[48] Also similar is the concept, widespread in the New Testament, of

---

[46] So, e.g., Weiss 1991:217; Johnson 2006:99. Gray 2003:114 aptly comments, "The use of the imperfect (ἦσαν) and the modifying phrase 'lifelong' ... distinguish this fear as an enduring characteristic of humans as such from periodic outbreaks of fear such as occur in dangerous situations."

[47] Lane 1991:1.61.

[48] Cf. Westcott 1903:53, "The devil, as the author of sin, has the power over death its consequence (Rom. v. 12), not as though he could inflict it at his pleasure; but death is his realm: he makes it subservient to his end."

Satan as ruler of the present world (John 12:31; Acts 26:18; Eph 2:2, 6:12; Col 1:13). Further, Wis 2:23–24 is perhaps the closest, certainly most frequently cited, early Jewish parallel to Hebrews' depiction of the devil here: "[F]or God created man for incorruption, and made him in the image of his own eternity, but through the devil's envy death entered the world, and those who belong to his party experience it" (RSV).[49] Hence, I tentatively take the phrase to describe death as an indirect effect of Satan's spiritual dominion over the present age, and a consequence of his original corruption of the human race.[50]

Further, some light is shed by the assertion of 2:15 that people are subject to slavery through lifelong fear of death.[51] In any case, Satan's power of death results in chronic fear and servitude. There is some debate over whether δουλείας attaches to ἔνοχοι or ἀπαλλάξῃ, and whether φόβῳ θανάτου is an instrumental dative or the complement of ἔνοχοι. Most scholars and translations prefer both former options, though Moffatt argues for the latter.[52] In favor of the majority, when ἔνοχος means "subject to" it can in fact take a genitive complement, as in v. 13 of the prologue to Sirach.[53] Further, both the proximity of δουλείας to ἔνοχοι and the distance between

---

[49] See, e.g., ibid.; Moffatt 1924:34; Attridge 1989:92; Lane 1991:1.61; Weiss 1991:219; Koester 2001:231; Johnson 2006:100.

[50] I take the more elaborate comments of Delitzsch 1886:132–33 to basically hit the mark: "The devil is here styled ὁ [sic] κράτος ἔχων τοῦ θανάτου, not as an angel of death appointed as God's messenger in all instances, nor as an arbitrary lord of death, placed in this respect especially over man; but as being one whose dominion is the hidden cause of all dying, having the power of death not immediately, but mediately, through sin, through which he delivers men over to the judicial punishment of death. For death is as much a judicial exercise of God's power as it is a God-hostile exercise of the devil's power by means of sin transmitted from him to men but cherished by them."

[51] As is frequently noted, the fear of death is a common motif in classical authors. See, e.g., Xenophon, *Cyropaedia*, 3.1.23–25; Lucretius, *De rer. nat.*, 1.102–26, 3.59–93; Lucian, *Peregr.* 23, 33; Cicero, *Tusc.* 1; Epictetus, *Diatr.* 1,17,25, 1,27,7–10, 2.18.30, 3.26.38–39; Dio Chrysostom, *Or.* 6:42. As Lucretius' discussion attests, the fear of death is a particular target of Epicurean philosophy; on Epicurus' view see Rosenbaum 1986. Those who describe fear of death as slavery include Euripides, *Orest.* 1520–24; Seneca, *Ep.* 24:4; Plutarch, *Mor.* 34B, 106D; Cicero, *Letters to Atticus* 9.2a; Epictetus, *Diatr.* 4.7.17–18. Greco-Roman authors who comment, albeit critically, on how Christians overcome the fear of death include Epictetus, *Diatr.* 4.7.6; Lucian, *Peregr.* 13; Marcus Aurelius, *Meditations* 11.3. For early Jewish discussions of the fear of death see Sir 40:1–7; 41:1–4; Philo, *Good Person* 22.

[52] Moffatt 1924:35; followed by Fuhrmann 2010:91 and, in part, by Peeler 2014:99 n. 105.

[53] Contra Fuhrmann 2010:91 n. 28; Peeler 2014:99 n. 105.

δουλείας and ἀπαλλάξῃ favor the majority view.⁵⁴ The sense is that, through fear of death, humankind is subject to lifelong servitude. The one to whom humanity is enslaved is not explicitly stated. However, since Jesus defeated the devil in order to deliver humanity (ἵνα ... ἀπαλλάξῃ), the devil seems to be the implied master. These verses present humanity's plight as more than merely anthropological; Satan's power plays its own fearsome part.

Solution: Jesus' Death Disarms and Delivers

In this section we consider just the soteriology of Heb 2:14–15; in the next we examine what the soteriological assertions of 2:9 and 2:14–15 contribute to the exposition that stretches from 2:5–18, and how this section prepares for Hebrews' cultic construal of the Christ-event. Hebrews 2:14–15 consists of two indicative verbal clauses, the first grounding the second, followed by a purpose clause with two verbal predicates. Since the children share in (κεκοινώνηκεν) blood and flesh, Jesus likewise came to share in the same (μετέσχεν τῶν αὐτῶν), in order (1) to disarm the devil through death and (2) to deliver those who were in lifelong bondage through fear of death (ἵνα ... καταργήσῃ ... καὶ ἀπαλλάξῃ). In light of the purpose clause, the assertion that Christ shared in "blood and flesh" names the ontological conditions necessary for Christ's saving work: He had to enter fully into the human condition in order to transform it from within. As Otfried Hofius comments, "To 'share in flesh and blood' is therefore the path that Jesus had to take in order to enter the devil's prison himself and, as it were, burst it open from within."⁵⁵ And the ἵνα clause states the purpose for which Christ assumed human nature: to defeat the devil and deliver people from his dominion.

What does it mean that Christ became incarnate and died in order to disarm the devil? The meaning of καταργέω here is probably not "destroy" in the sense of "to cause something to come to an end or to be no longer in existence,"⁵⁶ since it is unlikely that the verse envisions the devil's extinction. Instead, here the verb means "to cause

---

⁵⁴ So, e.g., Ellingworth 1993:174.
⁵⁵ Hofius 1972:62, "Das μετέχειν αἵματος καὶ σαρκός ist demnach der Weg, den Jesus nehmen mußte, um selbst in Gefängnis des διάβολος zu gelangen und es gleichsam von innen her aufzusprengen."
⁵⁶ Contra BDAG 525 §3.

something to lose its power or effectiveness."⁵⁷ Whatever the devil's power of death consists in, Jesus' death strips him of it. Here again, as in 2:9, Hebrews sees death as more than physical. If the devil's fear-provoking power of death has been abolished, then death itself has been changed, even though it remains humanity's immediate fate. Also as in 2:9, in 2:14 death is a central aspect of the plight to which Jesus' death is the solution. The focus in 2:14 is on the ironic means of deliverance: Through death Jesus disables the devil's power of death. To adapt a point from Craig Koester, Jesus was not only death's victim but also its assailant.⁵⁸

As many have pointed out, Hebrews' assertion that Jesus' death destroys the devil's power resonates with many Old Testament and early Jewish texts that look forward to an end-time defeat of the forces of evil.⁵⁹ Particularly relevant for our purposes, however, are New Testament texts in which Jesus' saving work destroys death and overcomes the devil and other evil powers. With the hour of Jesus' death came the time for "this world's ruler" to be "cast out" (John 12:31); Jesus came to destroy the works of the devil (ἵνα λύσῃ, 1 John 3:8); by his death he disarmed the heavenly rulers (Col 2:15); by Jesus' "appearance" on earth he abolished death (2 Tim 1:10). In asserting that Jesus destroyed the devil as the one holding the power of death, Heb 2:14 weaves these traditional threads together.

The second purpose of Christ's incarnation that 2:14–15 articulates is that he would deliver those who through fear of death were subject to lifelong slavery. Here that by which people are enslaved is fear of death, which clearly corresponds to the devil's possession of the power of death in the previous clause. So, while the devil is not named as slave-master, his ownership is clearly implied. Jesus not only destroys the devil; he wrests people from his grip. And the act by which Jesus frees people from Satan's tyranny is his death. Erich Grässer describes this deliverance as a "repatriation" ("Heimholung"): Jesus' death itself liberates from the world of fallen mortality and fear of death, and delivers "the children" into their "unshakeable kingdom" (cf. 12:28).⁶⁰

---

⁵⁷ As in BDAG 525 §2.
⁵⁸ Koester 2005:366, "Jesus encountered death as an assailant rather than a victim." Also Söding 2005:70, "Paradoxerweise triumphiert aber in seinem Sterben nicht der Tod über Jesus, sondern Jesus über den Tod."
⁵⁹ E.g. Loader 1981:112–13; Attridge 1989:92; Backhaus 2009b:200 n. 9; Gäbel 2006:159–61.
⁶⁰ Grässer 1992b:184.

A number of scholars comment that Heb 2:14–15 does not name the precise mechanism by which Jesus' death defeats the devil and delivers people from his dominion.[61] By contrast, Gäbel suggests that Christ overcomes the devil by faithfully resisting temptation throughout his entire life, succeeding where the "first Adam" failed.[62] Since the context alludes to Christ's faithful life (ἔσομαι πεποιθὼς ἐπ' αὐτῷ, 2:13) against the backdrop of humanity's fall, this is possible, though nothing in my case depends on it. From another angle, Paul Andriessen argues that all of 2:14–3:2 is informed by exodus typology, and that 2:14–15 in particular figures Jesus' triumph over the devil as recapitulating Moses' triumph over Pharaoh.[63] This reading provides soteriological specification of a sort, but to see Jesus' defeat of Satan paralleling Moses' defeat of Pharaoh is a stretch, since it is not Moses but God who triumphs over the Egyptian tyrant (Exod 14:4, 17–18; 15:1, 21). Moses did bring out the people (Exod 3:12, 16–17), but it was God who struck down the firstborn, army, and gods of Egypt (Exod 12:12; 15:1–12). Hence, in the main I concur with those who see Hebrews as forbearing to further specify the means by which Christ's death defeats the devil. Hebrews focuses on the "that," not the "how." These verses simply assert that, by dying on the cross, Christ achieved the decisive eschatological victory over Satan.

Hebrews 2:5–18 as Theological Backdrop to Christ's Self-Offering

I now suggest that the author places these images of humanity's universal plight, and its solution in Christ's death, as a theological backdrop for the subsequent exposition of his self-offering. We have seen something of how both 2:9 and 2:14–15 ascribe soteriological significance to Jesus' death itself. In 2:9, by dying Jesus delivers others from death; in 2:14–15 Jesus' death destroys Satan and defeats death's power. Both passages treat Jesus' death as effecting a decisive change in the human condition. The former presupposes and the latter articulates the incarnate Christ's representative solidarity with humanity. Finally, both passages make best sense against the backdrop of humanity's fall into sin and death. This is why all things are

---

[61] Moffatt 1924:34; Attridge 1989:93; Long 1998:65; Peeler 2014:101; Small 2014:232.
[62] Gäbel 2006:133, 160–61.   [63] Andriessen 1976:304–13, esp. 306–8.

not subject to humankind; this is why the devil holds the power of death. These parallels are unsurprising, though no less significant, in light of the fact that 2:5–18 is widely regarded as a coherent expository unit.[64] In relation to the striking focus on Christ's exaltation in 1:1–14, 2:5–18 unfolds both how and why the one now exalted above the angels became for a little while lower than the angels, how the one who now shares God's throne came to share humanity's abasement. And not only share but transform: Christ entered the human condition in order to remake it. Thus, in the context of 2:5–18 the two soteriological passages we have examined serve to set Christ's saving achievement in the context of humanity's universal plight. In 2:5–18 Hebrews frames the largest possible canvas on which to render the salvation Christ has accomplished, and gives Christ's death itself a decisive role in achieving that salvation.[65]

But Heb 2:5–18 also both prepares for and introduces the letter's central theological contribution, Christ's self-offering as Melchizedekian high priest. At the culmination of this section, in 2:17, Hebrews introduces the concept of Christ as high priest who makes atonement for the people that will dominate its central expository section (5:1–10:18, with 4:14–16 and 10:19–25): "Therefore he had to be made like his brothers in every respect, so that he might become a merciful and faithful high priest in the service of God, to make atonement for the sins of the people."[66] Hence in 2:5–18 the characterization of humanity's plight under sin and death, and brief statements of how Christ's death saves from this plight, serve not only to announce believers' great salvation (cf. 2:3), but also to pave the way for Hebrews' elaborate cultic construal of the Christ-event. The universal problems of sin, death, and the devil's dominion form the

---

[64] Spicq 1953:29–30; Vanhoye 1963:77–84; Michel 1966:133–36; Braun 1984:52; Grässer 1990:111–13; Weiss 1991:190–91; Ellingworth 1993:143–44.

[65] So Compton 2015a:51, on 2:5–9, "The argument to this point probably indicates that before the author introduces the Levitical cult or Melchizedek, he wants to establish the larger context in which these items find their place. Priests, covenants, sacrifices and sacred spaces were established with a larger story in mind. They were intended to solve – or at least, prepare for the solution of – the Adam-problem (cf. 7.11–12, 18–19; 8.8; 10.1; et al.). They were introduced for the purpose of regaining protological 'glory' (2.10) or 'perfection' (7.11; cf. 2.10–11; 9.14; 10.14). Thus, before Jesus is the better priest, the author wants us to see that he is first the better or true Adam." Cf. p. 64, on 2:10–18, "Once again, Jesus' mediation, which is first described as priestly in this paragraph, is placed in the largest context possible."

[66] Cf. Gäbel 2006:132, who calls 2:5–16 the "Zugang zur Hohepriester-Christologie des Hebr."

backdrop to Christ's high-priestly work.[67] It is sometimes remarked that Hebrews progresses from what it holds in common with the early Christian kerygma, which is prominent in chapters 1–2, to its own distinct development of that kerygma, which is elaborated especially in the central expository section.[68] Our discussion of Heb 2:9 and 2:14–15 confirms this observation. Given what we have argued in Part I regarding the saving significance of Christ's ascension to heaven, it is striking to note that, apart from the briefest of hints in 1:3, Hebrews' first significant soteriological statements focus squarely on Jesus' death. Before elaborating the soteriological impact of Christ's exaltation in a manner unparalleled in the New Testament, the author asserts that in his death Christ tasted death for all and defeated the devil.

This in turn suggests that the saving significance of Christ's death is not merely preliminary to but a presupposition of Hebrews' exposition of Jesus' work as high priest in the heavenly sanctuary. For instance, we have seen that the ὅπως clause of 2:9 not only ascribes saving efficacy to both Christ's death and his exaltation, but specifies that the saving force of Christ's death in some sense derives from his exaltation. At least in 2:9, Christ's death and exaltation do not merely sit side by side, but instead are intimately intertwined. And so we arrive at a partial, provisional answer to the thematic question framing Part II. In developing its unique, ascension-focused account of Christ's priestly work in the heavenly sanctuary, Hebrews does not depart from the saving significance of Christ's death but instead develops it.

4.4 Hebrews 9:15–17: Jesus' Death Bears the Old Covenant Curse and Inaugurates New Covenant Blessing

Our third passage, 9:15–17, articulates the saving significance of Christ's death from yet another angle: the redemptive enaction of

---

[67] With a view to Hebrews' hortatory agenda, Löhr 1997:179–80 asks whether 2:14–16 is a theological gaffe ("theologischer Ausrutscher"), and replies that Heb 2 presents an anthropological perspective that clearly correlates with the letter's eschatological statements, and is significant for the text's hortatory theology as a whole. Thus, "Der Abschnitt wäre dann nicht zufälliges Rudiment einer mythischen Anschauung, sondern bewußt zu Beginn des Textes plazierte Verknüpfung anthropologischer, soteriologischer und eschatologischer Aussagen im Hinblick auf die Adressaten."

[68] Lindars 1991:27, 29; Bauckham 2004:169–70.

covenant sanctions. I will argue that 9:15 itself attests the plight of retributive sanctions for the broken Mosaic covenant, and presents Christ's death as the representative, redemptive execution of those sanctions. Further, I take διαθήκη in 9:16–17 also to mean "covenant," and to refer specifically to the broken Mosaic covenant; hence I also take these verses to elaborate the covenantal significance of Christ's death.[69] Nevertheless, 9:16–17 does not assert something qualitatively new over against 9:15. Instead, on my view, those verses elaborate the prior one's assertion of what Christ's death achieved, and strengthen the impression that, via the logic of covenant initiation and enforcement, the author is developing a conceptual resource that is distinct from, though by no means incommensurable with, the Levitical framework that is so prominent in the epistle. Thematically speaking, the bud in 9:15 blossoms briefly in 9:16–17.

[69] The meaning of διαθήκη in 9:16–17 is a longstanding crux. The two primary options for its English translation are "testament" and "covenant," the former describing contemporary Hellenistic practice regarding disposition of property by a will, the latter the biblical institution most commonly called a ברית in the Hebrew Bible and διαθήκη in the LXX. Throughout the twentieth century, "testament" was the clear majority position. (See, e.g., Vos 1915:614–15; Moffatt 1924:125–29; Spicq 1953:260–63; Swetnam 1965; Michel 1966:315–18; Attridge 1989:255–56; Bruce 1990:221–24; Ellingworth 1993:462–65. For advocates of "covenant" prior to Hughes 1979, see Westcott 1903:300–304; Nairne 1913:364–66; Kilpatrick 1977.) Against this reading Hughes 1979 advanced strong arguments that have perhaps not received the scholarly attention they deserve. Hahn 2004 summarized Hughes' arguments against the testamentary reading and attempted to improve upon problems he perceives with Hughes' covenantal solution. In the wake of Hughes and especially Hahn, the "covenant" reading is gaining ground, though proponents of "testament" still abound. (Among post-Hughes advocates of the "testament" reading, Attridge 1989:255–56 and Moffitt 2011:291 do not mention Hughes. Ellingworth 1993:462–65 refers to Hughes but does not engage his arguments. By contrast, Koester 2001:417–18 responds to several key points.) I find the arguments of Hughes and Hahn against "testament" and for "covenant" decisive. Further, I take Hahn's argument that the verses presuppose a broken covenant and specify the execution of its sanctions to be more convincing than Hughes' reading, which takes the implied referent to be covenant inauguration exclusively. Advocates of "covenant" who have been influenced by Hughes and/or Hahn include Lane 1991:2.231, 2.242–43; Williamson 2007:203–6; Cockerill 2012:403–7; Moret 2014:49–51; Compton 2015a:128–32. Post-Hughes supporters of "testament" include, in addition to those mentioned earlier, Wiid 1992; Gheorghita 2003:117–23; Johnson 2006:240–41; Thompson 2008:189–90; Vanhoye 2011:291–92; Small 2014:298; Filtvedt 2015b:118–20; Schreiner 2015:275–77. In recent German scholarship, "testament" is the consensus. So Braun 1984:273–75; Weiss 1991:477–79; Grässer 1993:172–75; Frey 1996:288; Gäbel 2006:181–84; Fuhrmann 2007:209–14; Karrer 2008:161–62; Backhaus 2009a:329–30; Kraus 2014:79–80. Also worth mentioning is the attempt to account for strong points of both readings with something like "testamentary covenant," which is sometimes identified with a particular variety of Ancient Near Eastern covenant. See Kline 1963:41; Campbell 1972; Allen 2008:174–81.

However, readers who disagree with my perspective on διαθήκη in 9:16–17 can still agree with the main point of this section, though they will disagree about the extent to which Hebrews elaborates this point.

Plight: The Consequences of a Broken Covenant

The plight that 9:15 presents is a broken covenant and its consequences. We read, "Therefore he is the mediator of a new covenant, so that those who are called may receive the promised eternal inheritance, since a death has occurred that redeems them from the transgressions committed under the first covenant." In this verse the transgressions for which Jesus' death obtains redemption are those committed "under" or "against the first covenant" (ἐπὶ τῇ πρώτῃ διαθήκῃ).[70] The covenant God made with Israel at Sinai was meant to govern their lives, but they consistently threw off God's rule of law. Hence in 8:7 the author infers that the only reason God would introduce a "second" covenant is that there was something lacking in the first. In 8:8 he clarifies that the fault is not so much with the covenant itself as with the people (μεμφόμενος γὰρ αὐτούς). This is confirmed by the citation of Jer 31:31–34 that follows (8:8–12). The problem with that first covenant was that the people did not remain in it (Heb 8:9 // Jer 31:32); they turned their backs on the God who rescued them from Egypt.

Hebrews 9:15 presupposes at least two consequences of this broken covenant: (1) the judicial liability of sins committed against the Mosaic covenant still rested on the people; and (2) the paradigmatic penal sanction owed them for covenant violation is death. When 9:15 speaks of "redemption for transgressions" (ἀπολύτρωσιν τῶν ... παραβάσεων), it characterizes transgressions against the covenant as generating a state of liability that can be likened to bondage from which one requires release. In 2:2 the author paints a similar picture: The message delivered through angels – that is, the Mosaic covenant – "was in force" (ἐγένετο βέβαιος), and "every transgression (παράβασις) and disobedience received a just retribution." The shared terminology between 2:2 and 9:15–17 is striking (παραβάσεων, 9:15; βεβαία, 9:17). Further, 10:28 states, "Anyone who has

---

[70] Whether ἐπί specifies the basis on which transgressions are reckoned (BDAG 364 §6) or the time during which they were committed (BDAG 367 §18) makes little difference.

set aside (ἀθετήσας) the law of Moses dies without mercy on the evidence of two or three witnesses." This verse alludes to Deut 17:6, whose context specifies that the crime in view is idolatry, which in itself constitutes "transgressing his covenant" (παρελθεῖν τὴν διαθήκην αὐτοῦ, Deut 17:2 LXX). This renders it likely that the sin Hebrews calls "setting aside the law of Moses," whose death sentence the author endorses, is covenantal apostasy. And if the author treats death as the sentence for breaking the covenant in 10:28, this confirms that in 9:15 he presupposes that death is the paradigmatic penal sanction for covenant violation.[71] As we have just glimpsed, this appeal to death as the judicial consequence of violating the Mosaic covenant has deep roots in the Old Testament. The covenant curses of Lev 26:14–39 and Deut 28:15–68 threaten death by many means, interwoven with exile.[72] God warns the people that if they forsake the covenant they will be not merely banished from the land, but will be left "few in number" in the lands to which they are scattered (Deut 4:27); they will "perish among the nations" to which God banishes them (Lev 28:38).

The idea that Hebrews sees the curse of the Sinai covenant hanging over the people prior to the death of Jesus is rendered more plausible by the range of roughly contemporary Jewish sources that express the same point.[73] Drawing on Deut 28–30 as well as Ezek 11:17 and 36:24, Jub 1:15–23 promises Israel's restoration from exile, in which "they will become a blessing and not a curse" (1:16).[74] As

---

[71] Compton 2015a:131 criticizes this line of reasoning on the grounds that the beneficiaries of redemption in 9:15 are οἱ κεκλημένοι ("the called"), a subset of whom were the "old covenant elect." Compton argues that these "elect/faithful ... needed to be redeemed not because they were covenant breakers ... but because their sacrifices were inadequate." He also adduces the positive portrayal of such figures in Heb 11, and suggests that their "problem, if we can call it that, was not their lack of faith but, rather, their place in redemptive history: their perfection required something available only in the present era (11.40; cf. 12.23)." However, to say that the covenant curse remained in force does not necessarily imply that the "old covenant elect" were covenantal apostates. Instead, it implies that the Sinai covenant kept a record of wrongs, and that every transgression of it, not only wholesale apostasy, merited commensurate retribution (cf. 2:2). Further, according to Hebrews the Levitical sacrifices were inadequate because the people kept sinning, and the sacrifices themselves were unable fully to eradicate sin's consequences (10:1–4). To say that the sacrifices themselves were the problem is to come short of Hebrews' diagnosis of the people's plight under the old covenant.
[72] See especially Lev 26:17, 22, 25, 33; Deut 28:20–22, 24, 26, 45, 48, 51, 61; cf. Josh 7:11–15; 23:15–16; Jer 22:8–12; 34:17–22. Cf. Hahn 2004:428.
[73] For general discussion see VanderKam 1997:94–104.
[74] Translation from VanderKam 1989.

Rodrigo Morales comments, "Although we cannot say for certain at what point in the eschatological framework the writer of *Jubilees* saw himself, the fact that the work takes up the language of the prophets and still portrays it as a reality yet to be accomplished suggests an as yet unfulfilled expectation on the part of the writer."[75] In other words, Jubilees forecasts the reversal of the covenant curse because, from its author's perspective, this has not yet occurred.

Similarly, in Baruch the "evil and curse" that Moses warned of "have clung to us, as they still do today" (1:20).[76] In 2:13 Baruch prays for God's wrath to depart from the people, since "we are left as a few among the nations to which you have banished us." In 2:26 the author recounts God's making the temple desolate, "as it still is today." In 3:8 the people "are at this day an object of reproach, curse and repugnance because of all the iniquities of our ancestors" (echoing Dan 9:7, 11; cf. T. Levi 16:5). Finally, in 4:24–25, Baruch exhorts the people to "endure with patience the wrath that God has brought upon you," because God will soon restore their fortunes. Tobit 13:1–18 similarly exhorts Israel to bless God and seek him in their present captivity (13:3–4, 10, 13), because he will soon repeal the covenant curse and restore the fortunes of his people (13:5–6, 9, 13–14, 16–18).[77]

Another witness to this sense of continuing exile, and the contemporary enaction of the covenant curse, is 4Q504 (4Q Words of the Luminaries[a]).[78] In 4Q504 1–2 III, 8–13, "illness, famine, thirst, plague, [and] the sword" are apparently manifestations of God avenging his covenant, of which Moses and the prophets warned. Even though at least one petition in this text regards the restoration of the people from the covenant curse as in some sense a completed event (4Q504 1–2 V, 9–16), a later petition nevertheless asks, "O Lord ... may, then, your wrath and rage withdraw from us," and elaborates this request in terms of restoration from dispersion among the nations (4Q504 1–2 VI, 10–13). What all these early Jewish texts have in common is that the covenant penalties of death and exile are regarded not as having been exhausted in exile and then lifted in the

---

[75] Morales 2010:45–46, cf. 95–96. See also Knibb 1976:266–67; VanderKam 1997:104.

[76] Translation from Tov 1975. For discussion of Baruch along these lines see Scott 1993:202–3.

[77] Cf. Scott 1993:212.

[78] See Morales 2010:52–55; translations that follow are from García Martínez and Tigchelaar 1998.

people's fifth-century return to Judea, but instead as present realities that provide a theological rationale for their current plight. As such they furnish close analogies to Hebrews' presupposition that the curse of the covenant was still a live problem for God's people, a problem our author sees as decisively addressed in the death of Christ.

Before treating Hebrews' exposition of this solution in 9:15, it is worth comparing the problem Hebrews here perceives with the Mosaic covenant to its other characterizations of this "first" or "old" covenant. Hebrews 7:19 declares that "the law made nothing perfect." However broadly or narrowly one construes "the law," it is closely associated with the Mosaic covenant and its Levitical priesthood, which is here said to have proven unable to usher the people into God's presence, as the contrast with the "better promise through which we draw near to God" indicates. In 7:22, the covenant Jesus mediates is "better" because its priesthood, unlike that of the Mosaic covenant, is not hampered by mortality (7:23–25). In 8:8, as noted previously, the author introduces the new covenant promise with God's finding fault with the people; this is unpacked in the citation of Jer 31:31–34 in terms of the people forsaking the covenant God made with them at Sinai (8:9). In 9:6–10, Hebrews reads the entire Levitical system as a parable attesting its own inability to grant access to God's presence in the Holy of Holies. This is confirmed by the fact that the descriptors "first" and "second" (9:2, 3, 6, 7, 8), which refer first to the two compartments of the tabernacle (or possibly the first tent as a whole in 9:8), are the same terms used in 8:7, 8:13, and 9:1 for the two covenants. By the time we arrive at 9:15, the old covenant has been characterized from many different angles as unable to realize God's purpose of dwelling in intimate fellowship with his people. In 9:15, the author pivots to the judicial aspects of the covenant, and considers the failure of the first covenant from the standpoint of the retributive sanctions its breaking entails. This juridical characterization of the covenant people's plight adds another dimension to the critique of the Mosaic covenant that runs through the epistle's central expository section.

Solution: Redemption from Transgressions, for an Eternal Inheritance

This juridical problem is what 9:15 says Jesus' death solves. Here we will briefly address three features of this solution: the role of Jesus' death as the hinge between the covenants, the significance of "redemption" (ἀπολύτρωσιν), and the fact that it is Jesus' death per se to which Hebrews ascribes these saving effects.

Our first observation is that Jesus' death is the hinge between the old and new covenants.[79] The primary assertion of 9:15 is that Jesus is mediator of the new covenant. The subsequent purpose clause (ὅπως) specifies that Jesus' new covenant mediation enables "the called" to obtain their promised eternal inheritance. And the genitive absolute (θανάτου γενομένου) describes the basis on which Christ mediates this inheritance-guaranteeing covenant: A death has occurred for redemption of transgressions against the first covenant. Jesus' death at once satisfies the sanctions of the old covenant and ushers in the blessings of the new.[80] As Hahn puts it, "The death of Christ becomes a soteriological 'Janus': it is simultaneously the experience and expiation of the curse of death of the Old Covenant, and the inaugural sacrifice that ratifies the new."[81]

Jesus' death therefore has both retrospective and prospective effects. Retrospectively, his death enacts the old covenant's curse of death. Jesus dies the death the people of Israel deserved for their covenant defection. Prospectively, Jesus' death secures his people's permanent inheritance. Jesus is the heir of all things (1:2), so he is able to bestow a permanent inheritance on his people (cf. 1:14). Elsewhere in Hebrews this inheritance is closely associated with Abraham, who was promised the land of Canaan as an inheritance (11:8), but who looked ahead to something greater and more permanent (11:10, 13–16). In 6:12 the author exhorts his hearers to imitate those who, like Abraham, through faith and patience inherited the promises (6:12, cf. 6:13–15). And the oath by which God confirmed his promise to Abraham served also to confirm the unchangeable character of his purpose to "the heirs of the promise" (6:17). The sworn promise by which God granted Abraham and his offspring an everlasting inheritance could not be realized through the

---

[79] So Hegermann 1988:183, commenting on 9:15, "Vielmehr lenkt der Autor hier den Blick speziell auf die heilbringende Wende vom alten zum neuen Bund. Das Sterben Jesu brachte den grundlegenden Durchbruch durch den Bann, der in der ersten Ordnung über den sündigen Gottesvolk lag und den Heilswillen Gottes unheilvoll aufhielt (vgl. Hebr. 8,9)."

[80] There is no warrant, therefore, to pit these two against each other and affirm that only the latter is in view, as does, e.g., Filtvedt 2015b:119.

[81] Hahn 2009:319; cf. Hughes 1979:47–48.

ministry of the Mosaic covenant. But this, says 9:15, Christ's death has now brought to pass.[82]

And it is no coincidence that Hebrews names an everlasting inheritance as a blessing secured by the "new covenant," since many passages in the prophets foretell both the inner transformation of God's people and their permanent restoration to the land of their inheritance. For instance, Jer 30:3, opening the literary cycle that includes the new covenant promise, foretells that the people of Israel and Judah will again "take possession" of their land. In Jer 32:37–41, God promises to regather the people (32:37), give them "one heart and one way" (32:39), make with them an everlasting covenant (32:40), and "plant them in this land in faithfulness" (32:40).[83] As do such passages, Hebrews figures this restoration as the flip side of the covenant curse, the promised result of satisfied sanctions. Not only is Hebrews' characterization of the people's plight deeply embedded in the logic of Old Testament covenantal traditions, but its Christological solution is as well. Jesus' death bestows an eternal inheritance because, in inaugurating the new covenant, it initiates the people's eschatological restoration.

Second, we need to address the sense and significance of ἀπολύτρωσιν, "redemption" (9:15). Much ink has been spilled debating whether ἀπολύτρωσις (or simple λύτρωσις) merely means "deliverance" or has the more specific sense of "setting free by means of a payment or cost" (cf. Rom 3:24; Eph 1:7; Col 1:14).[84] In my judgment, the solution to this lexical question is not entirely transparent in Heb 9:15, though it is possible that the idea of a "price" is operative in the redemptive enaction of covenant sanctions.[85] In any case, the usage here does seem to include a substitutionary nuance, in which something given in someone else's stead effects deliverance. Here the deliverance consists in release from judicial liability. Jesus releases the heirs of the new covenant from the old covenant's overhanging sentence of death by suffering that sentence on the cross.

---

[82] Cf. the broader thematic analysis of Hahn 2009:319–24, on Heb 9:15 in relation to the old and new covenants, as well as to God's promises to Abraham and David. I find Hahn's analysis of these connections largely helpful, though sometimes overly specific.
[83] See also Ezek 11:16–20; 36:22–36; 37:15–28; 39:25–29.
[84] For a survey of the issue and detailed discussion of this passage see Ribbens 2016:178–84.
[85] We might compare the "ransom for many" of Mark 10:45. Pitre 2005:399–417, for instance, argues that this phrase figures Christ's death as releasing Israel from its exile among the nations, repealing the covenantal curse.

It is critical to construe the sense of ἀπολύτρωσις within the conceptual frame of covenant sanctions. Again, this holds whether or not one reads διαθήκη as "covenant" in 9:16–17, since, as we have seen, 9:15 itself specifies that this redemption pertains to "transgressions committed against the first covenant." Thus Moffitt is not entirely right to say,

> The language of redemption here, particularly in view of the comment in 9:12 that Jesus obtained λύτρωσις by means of his own blood, must bear a sacrificial connotation. The redemption, in other words, is the kind of redemption one receives because blood was offered (and, given the context, on account of the Yom Kippur offerings in particular).[86]

This reading fails to reckon with the distinct conceptual contribution of the intertwined themes of covenant sanction and covenant inauguration. We have shown that 9:15 reads Jesus' death in light of biblical traditions regarding covenant sanctions. That is, the sense of "redemption" here should not be restricted to conceptual categories offered by the Levitical cult in general or Yom Kippur in particular.[87] In Hebrews, the cult mediates the covenant. While covenant and cult are tightly interwoven, they are not identical. And here in 9:15 it is the judicial framework of covenant sanctions that clarifies the sense of "redemption." Though Hebrews does not use the word "curse," to rule out its relevance here would be to succumb to the word-concept fallacy. In his death on the cross, says 9:15, Jesus redeemed his people from the curse of the covenant by suffering that curse himself. The covenant was not enforced while covenant-breakers lived (9:17); its full force fell, finally, on Christ.

Third, it is worth underscoring that 9:15 ascribes these salvific ends to Jesus' death itself. This, again, stands against Moffitt's reading: "I suggest, though, that it is not necessary to assume that the death itself – presumably of Jesus – is identified here as the agent that effects the redemption."[88] Moffitt observes that the preposition εἰς in 9:15 might signify either purpose or result: "In either case the death is not itself unambiguously identified with the *means* of redemption."[89]

---

[86] Moffitt 2011:289.

[87] So Löhr 1994:43, "Es ist nicht mehr eine Sühne- oder Reinigungsvorstellung, welche die Soteriologie von V. 15 bestimmt."

[88] Moffitt 2011:290. Presumably, what Moffitt means by "agent" might be more precisely described as, e.g., an "instrumental cause." Subsequent citations of Moffitt's discussion of Heb 9:15 are also from this page.

[89] Emphasis original.

Ultimately, Moffitt decides in favor of "the resultative sense of εἰς" since the author "is careful to highlight the presentation of the blood within the process of blood offering as the atoning moment." On this reading, Jesus' death resulted in redemption in the sense that without his death, "none of the other events follow in the argument ... In short, Jesus could not make any atoning offering if he had not died." Hence, "If this larger understanding of how sacrifice works is in play, then, while the author here slides from one part of the sacrificial process to another – specifically the initiating event and the final result – he is not conflating Jesus' death and the atonement."

While I agree with much of Moffitt's overall construal of Hebrews' appropriation of Levitical sacrifice, I would suggest that he fails to perceive the unique contribution that the logic of covenant inauguration and enforcement makes to Hebrews' soteriology. A covenant is ratified by an oath sworn on pain of death, and its violation is enforced by death.[90] Hebrews discusses Jesus' death here not to interpret it by analogy with the slaughter of an animal in the Levitical cultus, but to identify it as God's final execution of the sanctions of the Mosaic covenant. What the ritual enaction of covenant curses upon slaughtered animals forebodingly pictured, God made real in Christ's death.[91] Within the cultural encyclopedia of Heb 9:15 there are sacrificial animals close at hand, but their significance centers on death, as we will see in Chapter 5.

Finally, to connect this section's contribution to our broader question of Hebrews' relationship to the rest of the New Testament, I note that Heb 9:15 (and, in my view, 9:16–17) bears striking similarities to both Rom 3:24–26 and Gal 3:10–14, as well as to the Last Supper narratives. In the former, God passed over sins previously committed until he enacted their judgment, and thereby his people's justification, on the cross. And the soteriological good resulting from this act is, as in Heb 9:15, "redemption" (ἀπολυτρώσεως, Rom 3:24).[92] The connections to Gal 3:10–14 are even closer.[93] In Gal 3:10 Paul invokes the curse of the law on those

---

[90] Cf. Hahn 2004:427–29.

[91] Mackie 2011:110–11, "This eschatological Yom Kippur sacrifice is then refracted through another interpretive lens: the bloody inauguration of the Sinai covenant (9:15–22). With fine detail the community is transported back to this ancient event, and led to believe that through his sacrificial self-offering Jesus received the penalty the blood-spattered Israelites were threatened with."

[92] For further discussion see Ribbens 2012:556–65. On the eschatological enactment of divine judgment on the cross in Rom 3:24–26, see Linebaugh 2013:145–49.

[93] For a reading of Gal 3:10–14 that I find generally convincing, see Morales 2010:86–114.

who are under the law, because they do not keep the law. In 3:13 he confesses that Christ "redeemed (ἐξηγόρασεν) us from the curse of the law by becoming a curse for us." And he assigns to this redemption a twofold result: the blessing of Abraham is extended to the Gentiles, and "we" receive the promised Spirit through faith (3:14). Just as in Heb 9:15, Christ's suffering the curse of the covenant enables the Abrahamic promises to find fruition, and this in terms characteristic of promised restoration from exile.[94] Finally, the parallels between Heb 9:15–17 and the Last Supper narratives might be set out as follows: (1) Jesus' death is a covenant sacrifice that consummates the old and ushers in the new (Mark 14:24; Luke 22:20; cf. Exod 24:8); (2) Jesus' death is representative and substitutionary (Matt 26:26, 28; Mark 14:22, 24; Luke 22:19–20); (3) Jesus' death – interpreted through the Passover meal which the Last Supper transforms – ushers in a new exodus, which is of a piece with the prophetic hopes for restoration to which Jeremiah's new covenant belongs.[95]

4.5 Conclusion

Each of the three passages this chapter has surveyed contributes something distinct to Hebrews' soteriological exposition of Jesus' death. And each, as we have seen, has close points of contact with other New Testament treatments of Jesus' death. Humanity's primeval fall into sin forms the backdrop for the first two, and the broken Sinai covenant for the third. While each passage's exposition of Christ's death is brief, each has its own logic, each ascribes salvific goods to Jesus' death per se, and each intersects other early Christian elaborations of Jesus' death. At the very least, the soteriological significance of Jesus' death occupies its own wing of Hebrews' theological floorplan. But it remains to ask whether – and, if so, how – the saving significance of Jesus' death is integrated into the central feature of Hebrews' theological edifice: the cultic construal of the Christ-event that rises to its full height in Hebrews' ninth and tenth chapters. This question sets the agenda for Chapter 5.

---

[94] Cf. the broader comment of Witherington 1991:148, "Though the author of the Homily to the Hebrews is no slavish imitator of anyone, having in fact one of the most creative and original minds amongst the NT writers, one cannot but be struck at how many points his discussion of the relationship of Abrahamic promises, Mosaic covenant, and the new covenant parallels Paul's discussion of the same especially in Galatians."

[95] Adapted from Hahn 2009:329–30, who summarizes Hughes 1979:55–57.

5

DEATH AND BLOOD IN CHRIST'S HEAVENLY OFFERING

5.1 Coming Full Circle

It is time to come full circle. The argument of this thesis began in Chapter 2 with the proposal that in Hebrews, the cross is not where and when Jesus offers himself. Instead, Jesus offers himself in the Holy of Holies in heaven, after his resurrection and ascension. Hebrews says once that Jesus "was offered" (9:28) – implying God as the one offering. Yet when Hebrews explicitly configures Jesus' saving act as a high-priestly *self*-offering, it locates that offering in heaven (e.g. 9:24–25). Jesus' death is therefore formally distinct from his self-offering. They are not identical; the latter presupposes and follows the former. Following this, Chapter 3 argued for the consistency of this formal assertion with the rest of Hebrews' cultic configurations of the Christ event, especially 10:5–14.

In Chapter 4, we examined the material significance of Jesus' death per se in Hebrews' soteriology. Invoking Jesus' death as the solution to humanity's fall into sin and its effects (2:9), defeat of death and the devil (2:14–15), and redemption from covenant sanctions (9:15), Hebrews ascribes a rich variety of saving effects to Jesus' death itself. So we should not conclude that because Hebrews locates Jesus' self-offering in heaven, his death is merely the first step in a sequence culminating in atonement. To use "atonement" in a broad sense, Hebrews figures Christ's death as accomplishing various objectively atoning effects. Yet Chapter 4 snapped a wide-angle picture that deliberately left a key conceptual field out of the frame.

We now pan the camera and zoom in, returning to the conceptual field where we began: Hebrews' Christological appropriation of the Levitical cult, especially Yom Kippur. Only now our interest in the relationship between Christ's death and his self-offering is not formal but material. What substantive role does Christ's death play in his self-giving to God in heaven? Is Christ's death merely the initial step

127

in the sequence, the domino that sets the others falling? Within Hebrews' cultic framework is Jesus' death only, as Christian Eberhart puts it, the "precondition for the availability of his blood"?[1] Or does Jesus' death feature materially in his heavenly offering?

This chapter seeks to demonstrate that the latter is indeed the case. I will argue a three-part thesis, each part the focus of its own section: (1) in a variety of cultic contexts, Hebrews conceptually equates blood with death, including Jesus' death; (2) "blood" is one term for what Jesus offers in heaven; (3) in some sense Jesus' death, as a soteriological achievement, is what he offers to God in heaven. Jesus' death is not when and where he offers himself, but it is what he offers.[2] To make this case, I will chart three sets of conceptual connections in Hebrews' cultic construal of the Christ-event: those between Jesus' death and blood, his blood and offering, and his death and offering.

5.2 Death and Blood

The first question this chapter seeks to answer is: in Hebrews what, if anything, does Jesus' "blood" have to do with his death? "Blood" in Hebrews clearly has a number of conceptual associations.[3] This section does not aim to be comprehensive but instead asks whether, and how, Christ's blood signifies his life, death, or some synthesis of the two. Proponents of View 1 often treat blood as a metonymy for Jesus' death; Gäbel argues that blood signifies Christ's whole earthly course of self-giving, culminating in death; Moffitt sees resurrection life as the exclusive conceptual connotation of Christ's blood.[4] Which, if any, are right?

The thesis of this section is that at key points Hebrews conceptually equates blood, including Christ's blood, with death. Blood is

---

[1] Eberhart 2005:52. However, more recently Eberhart has argued that Hebrews deliberately shifts the weight of "sacrificial metaphors" to the death of Jesus. See Eberhart 2013:131–56.
[2] A concise statement of this chapter's thesis can be found in Walter 1997:159, "... so hat er ... in seinem Tode zugleich ein Opfer erworben, das weit besser ist als jeder Opfertier des irdischen Kultus (vgl. 9,12 u.ö.) und das er nun in die himmlische Opferdarbringung mit einbringt: sich selbst (9,14)."
[3] See, e.g., Kuma 2012:118, 170, 349.
[4] Gäbel 2006:279, 290, 305, 315, 464–65; Moffitt 2011:271–77; Moffitt 2012:218–22. For View 1 see Lane 1991:2.238, 2.240; Weiss 1991:467; Cockerill 2012:394; Richardson 2012:40 n. 110. I will engage each position in detail in Section 6.2 in light of this chapter.

indeed a metonym for Christ's death. As we will see, this does not rule out a conceptual equation between blood and life. But instead of resurrection life à la Moffitt, or Jesus' entire life of self-giving à la Gäbel, I will argue that blood in Hebrews signifies Christ's life given in death as a life-for-life exchange. I will make this case by examining three passages in which Hebrews draws some kind of conceptual equation between Christ's blood and his death: 9:18, 9:22, and 13:20.

Blood as Ritually Enacted Death in Hebrews 9:18

Hebrews 9:18 draws an inference from the three preceding verses (9:15–17): "Therefore (ὅθεν) not even the first covenant was inaugurated without blood." As often in Hebrews, here ὅθεν has a strong inferential sense.[5] The logic runs as follows: the exposition of the role of death in a διαθήκη in 9:15–17 provides a reason why the Sinai covenant (ἡ πρώτη) was inaugurated by means of blood sacrifices, which 9:19–21 describes. As discussed in Section 4.4, 9:15 asserts that Jesus mediates the new covenant because his death redeemed people from the transgressions committed against the first covenant. Then, in 9:16–17, the author elaborates the crucial role of death in a διαθήκη. Whether one reads διαθήκη as testament or covenant – and, if covenant, whether the focus is inauguration or the execution of sanctions – death remains the focus of 9:16–17. If there is a διαθήκη, the death of its maker must be "borne" (9:16); a διαθήκη is secured "over dead ones" (ἐπὶ νεκροῖς), and is not in force while its maker lives (9:17). Even if one sees διαθήκη as "testament" in 9:16–17, these verses elaborate the statement about Christ undergoing the sanctions of the Sinai covenant in 9:15 (γάρ, 9:16) and inform the inference about the inauguration of the Sinai covenant in 9:18. Whatever else the author is doing in 9:16–17, he sees the necessity of death for a διαθήκη as integral to both the inauguration of the Sinai covenant (9:18–22) and the execution of its sanctions (9:15). As noted in Section 4.4, I regard a covenantal reading of διαθήκη with a focus on covenant sanctions to be the most plausible reading of 9:16–17. As before, this reading will inform the following analysis, though the main lines of argument do not depend on it.

Why then the switch from death in 9:15–17 to blood in 9:18? Is this an abrupt, perhaps even incoherent, shift from the legal-judicial realm back to the cultic? Christian Eberhart draws this conclusion: "Here

[5] Cf. 2:17; 3:1; 7:25; 8:3.

conceptual horizons are interconnected that are actually incongruent."[6] But γάρ in 9:16 and ὅθεν in 9:18 indicate that the author did not see himself as stitching together incompatible conceptual fabrics. Instead, the assertions about death throughout 9:15–17 fund the inference about blood in 9:18. How then might we explain this logical connection?

I would suggest that the author sees the application of blood in the covenant-inaugurating sacrifices at Sinai as ritually enacting death. Specifically, the author figures the blood rite of Exod 24:3–8 as a self-maledictory oath-sign, forecasting that if the people disobey the covenant, they will die. The spilled blood sprinkled on the people signifies that their blood will be spilled if they transgress the covenant.[7] That the covenant-inaugurating sacrifices of Exod 24:3–8 enacted self-maledictory symbolism is, of course, a conclusion that not all modern scholars would draw.[8] Nevertheless this reading of Exod 24:3–8 has both premodern and modern supporters, which supports the plausibility of seeing Hebrews reading the passage this way. For instance, Ibn Ezra, though he regards this reading as midrashic, reports that Saadia "takes [the blood rite] as an allusion, as if to say, 'Your blood may be spilled with impunity, just as this blood is, if you do not keep the covenant.'"[9] Among modern commentators William Propp argues that this blood rite "represents the sanguinary fate that awaits the traitor to the pact."[10] He concludes, "The people hence are implicitly equated with the slain victims."[11]

Also supporting the plausibility of this reading of Hebrews' engagement with Exod 24:3–8 is the fact that already in 9:15, Hebrews implies that death is the ultimate sanction for breaking the Sinai covenant. Only in 9:15 it is not the people who suffer death, but Jesus their representative. On the reading of 9:18 argued here, the inference attests a homology between the inauguration of the covenant and the execution of its sanctions. Because the penalty for covenant violation is death, that death is ritually enacted in the covenant's birth. Another piece of evidence that might favor this reading is the change in 9:20 from the likely LXX *Vorlage* of διέθετο ("made" or "covenanted") to

---

[6] Eberhart 2013:150, "Hier werden Vorstellungshorizonte miteinander verbunden, die eigentlich inkongruent sind." Cf. the similar opinion in Gäbel 2006:406.
[7] Lane 1991:2.243; Hahn 2004:434–35; Cockerill 2012:407.
[8] Gilders 2004:39, for instance, argues against it.
[9] Caraski 2005:209. See also Leviticus Rabbah 6:5, in Freedman and Simon 1939:82–83.
[10] Propp 2006:308.
[11] Ibid., 309. See also Scharbert 1970:78; Vervenne 1993:470.

ἐνετείλατο ("commanded"). Hebrews thereby seems intentionally to underscore the obligation Israel incurred when the Sinai covenant was inaugurated. The covenant laid on the people a solemn obligation. It is a small step from this textual highlight to the conclusion that Hebrews sees the Sinai covenant's inaugural sacrifices as ritually foreboding the sanctions attending the failure to keep the covenant.

If this is indeed the logic undergirding Hebrews' inference at 9:18, then it follows that here, in a cultic context, Hebrews treats the cultic manipulation of blood as symbolically enacting death.[12] Arguably, in its treatment of Exod 24:3–8, Hebrews also invokes analogous rites such as tabernacle inauguration and priestly ordination (Exod 29; 40; Lev 8; Num 7) in order to figure the Sinai inauguration as a rite of purification.[13] Hence Hebrews deliberately assimilates covenant inauguration to cultic purification. While 9:18 focuses on covenant inauguration, 9:19–22 draws tight connections between the inauguration of the covenant and its maintenance through the cult. Therefore it is not the case that Hebrews here uses "blood" as shorthand for death in a discussion that is somehow insulated from the author's appropriation of the Levitical cult.[14] Instead, Hebrews treats the ritual manipulation of blood as symbolically enacting death in a context intimately associated with Levitical purification rites. A conceptual equation between blood and death is integral to how Hebrews "reads" the Levitical cult.

---

[12] Here I attempt to state more precisely what a number of scholars have put more generally. For instance, Loader 1981:191, "In 9,15ff wird noch deutlich, daß 'Blut' mit 'Tod' fast synonym ist"; Weiss 1991:480 n. 21, "Der Übergang von θάνατος in den VV. 15 und 16 zu αἷμα in V. 18 weist wiederum darauf hin, daß αἷμα im Hebr den Tod bezeichnet"; Grässer 1993:176, "Aber αἷμα und θάνατος sind im Hebr 'wesentlich identische Begriffe'" (citing Riggenbach 1987:277); Allen 2008:179, "Hebrews 9:18–22 explicates the establishment of the Sinai covenant, treating death and blood interchangeably." Apart from these scholars who identify an equation between blood and death in the inference of 9:18, the only other comments on the issue I have encountered suggest a degree of conceptual tension between (what is taken to be) the testamentary framework of 9:15–17 and the cultic one of 9·18ff, as in the works of Eberhart and Gäbel cited in Note 6.
[13] For details see Jamieson 2016:574–77.
[14] Moffitt 2011:291 comments on 9:18 that "here, in a context where the ritual manipulation of blood is close to hand (9:15, 22), blood language is apparently used as a shorthand for death." Moffitt goes on to argue that the "concept of death" overlaps with those of "blood offering and atonement," yet he fails to observe that it is precisely the ritual manipulation of blood in the Sinai inauguration that ritually enacts death. In 9:18, blood does not leave its death-symbolism behind when it is used to inaugurate covenant and cult. But on Moffitt's account, ritually manipulated blood signifies only life, not death. Hence his legitimate insight into 9:18 stands in tension with his broader account of Hebrews' appropriation of Levitical sacrifice.

Blood as Medium of Life-for-Life Exchange in Hebrews 9:22b

Hebrews 9:18–21 narrates the bloody inauguration of the Sinai covenant, figuring it as a rite of purification. The author will explicitly apply this paradigm of cleansing to Christ's self-offering in 9:23–28, which again contrasts Christ's sacrifice with Levitical ones. Before this Christological exposition, 9:22 offers a generalizing gloss on the sacrificial logic of the Levitical cult as a whole: "And according to the law almost everything is purified with blood, and without the shedding of blood (αἱματεκχυσίας) there is no forgiveness (ἄφεσις)." The following argument focuses primarily on the cultic maxim of 9:22b and the passage to which it alludes, Lev 17:11. After a few introductory comments on the verse, I will discuss the disputed sense of ἄφεσις, arguing for "forgiveness." Next I will argue that Heb 9:22b, drawing on Lev 17:11, construes blood as a cultic medium of life-for-life exchange. With this reading of the whole clause in place, I will argue that the much-discussed term αἱματεκχυσία does indeed refer to ritual slaughter. Finally, in response to the objection that αἱματεκχυσία must have to do with ritual manipulation of blood instead of slaughter (since the former, not the latter, is when atonement is obtained), I will discuss life-for-life exchange and the timing of atonement in Heb 9:22b, arguing that this phrase does not specify when blood effects atonement, whether the moment of slaughter or subsequent application. Hebrews 9:22b does not say that slaughter is sufficient for atonement, merely that it is necessary, and why.

Hebrews 9:22 articulates a generalization based, in part, on the preceding exposition of the Sinai covenant's inauguration. Verse 19 reports that Moses took blood and other cleansing agents and sprinkled both "the book" and "all the people." Verse 20 reports that Moses identified this blood as "the blood of the covenant," and 9:21, conflating this event with the inaugurations of the tabernacle and priesthood, reports that Moses "likewise" sprinkled both the tent and all its vessels with blood. Verse 22 then adds (καί) that according to the law almost everything is purified with blood.[15] Hebrews 9:22a states a principle at work in the covenant inauguration that holds for the Levitical cult as a whole: blood effects purification. Just as tent

---

[15] The adverb σχεδόν qualifies πάντα, indicating the author's awareness of sacrificial rites in which media other than blood cleanse or atone, as in Lev 5:11–13; 14:7–8; 15:5–12; 16:26, 28; 22:6; Num 31:19–24. See, e.g., Attridge 1989:258.

and people were purified via blood sprinkling when the covenant and its cult were inaugurated, so also is purity regularly restored through blood application. Verse 22b then underscores the necessity of blood by saying that there is no forgiveness without it. The aphoristic character of the statement suggests that, while the author derives the point from the Mosaic law, he formulates it here with a view to Christ's saving act. "No forgiveness without bloodshed" interprets cult and Christ-event alike.[16]

The Meaning of ἄφεσις in Hebrews 9:22b

However, does 9:22b actually speak of forgiveness? Interpreters are divided.[17] The noun ἄφεσις has a general, profane sense of "release," whereas in the New Testament it typically means "forgiveness (of sins)." Some interpreters argue for the former, general sense; similarly, some argue that "release" here obtains a cultic nuance such as "definitive putting away (of defilement)" or "decisive purgation."[18] Both versions of this position deny that the term here has its common New Testament meaning, "forgiveness." Others, however, hold that ἄφεσις in 9:22b denotes forgiveness.[19] The two primary arguments against "forgiveness" are that ἄφεσις is used absolutely here, without "of sins" or an equivalent, and that the concept of forgiveness is foreign to the cultic framework of Hebrews and the Levitical material on which it draws. However, ἄφεσις is used absolutely with the meaning "forgiveness" in Mark 3:29, where the following clause specifies that forgiveness of sins is meant. Further, in all of its other New Testament occurrences save two, ἄφεσις means "forgiveness."[20] The only exceptions occur in the citation of Isa 61:1–2 in Luke 4:18, which proclaims liberty to the captive and oppressed.

---

[16] So, e.g., Weiss 1991:481–82.
[17] The following both depends on and develops Ribbens 2016:156–58.
[18] For general "release" see Westcott 1903:271. For specifically cultic purgation or cleansing see Johnsson 1973:325–28; Braun 1984:280; Lane 1991:1.232–33; Ellingworth 1993:474.
[19] So Moffatt 1924:130; Attridge 1989:259; Weiss 1991:482; Gordon 2000:105; Gäbel 2006:418; Johnson 2006:242; Moffitt 2011:269; Ribbens 2016:210–12. Additionally, Spicq 1953:265 and Cockerill 2012:410–11 argue for a comprehensive sense that includes forgiveness. Finally, Grässer 1993:185 and Koester 2001:420 treat forgiveness and cleansing as effectively interchangeable.
[20] Matt 26:28; Mark 1:4; 3:29; Luke 1:77; 24:47; Acts 2:38; 5:31; 10:43; 13:38; 26:18; Eph 1:7; Col 1:14; Heb 10:18.

Regarding the second argument against "forgiveness," that it is foreign to the cultic context of Heb 9:22b, attention should first be drawn to Heb 10:18, which reflects on Jeremiah's new covenant promise: "Where there is forgiveness of these (ἄφεσις τούτων), there is no longer any offering for sin." Hebrews 9:22b asserts the necessity of sacrificial blood for ἄφεσις; Heb 10:18 asserts that once the kind of ἄφεσις proclaimed in the new covenant obtains, there is no need for animal sacrifices. The two assertions mirror one another. It is from the premise of forgiveness that Heb 10:18 draws its cultic – in some sense, cult-critical – conclusion. What Heb 9:22b asserts, 10:18 assumes. Hence, contrary to those who see the lack of "sins" in 9:22b as evidence for a sense of ἄφεσις in 9:22b different from that in 10:18, the logical fit between these passages requires that the same end is in view.

Further, far from being foreign to the Levitical cult on which Hebrews draws, forgiveness is an explicit goal of blood sacrifice. For instance, in the prescriptions for the sin offering in Lev 4–5 and Num 15, and for the reparation offering in Lev 5 and 19, the formula "and he/they shall be forgiven" (typically וְנִסְלַח לוֹ or וְנִסְלַח לָהֶם) repeatedly identifies forgiveness as the goal of the entire process of cultic כפר.[21] The LXX translates each of the uses of niphal סלח with ἀφεθήσεται, which is cognate with ἄφεσις. So, Hebrews saying that the sacrificial use of blood is necessary for forgiveness fits perfectly not only with the sense of these repeated statements in the Hebrew texts, but with the terms with which they were rendered in Greek. That forgiveness was a goal of sacrificial blood rites in the Levitical cult indicates a role for blood that is distinguishable from, though certainly compatible with, its role as a means of purification. That Heb 9:22b uses ἄφεσις to mean "forgiveness" suggests that the author was aware of the manner in which the Levitical cult treated sin not merely as a quasi-biological substance to be removed, but also as an interpersonal reality that threatened one's relationship with God. Levitical sacrifices did not remove the interpersonal effects of sin mechanically; forgiveness was God's to grant or withhold.[22]

---

[21] Lev 4:20, 26, 31, 35; 5:10, 13, 16, 18, 26; 19:22; Num 15:25, 26, 28.
[22] See Gane 2005:51–52. Gane contrasts "the purity that inevitably results from acceptable (i.e., properly performed) rites provided for by Yhwh to remedy physical ritual impurities" with "forgiveness for moral faults," which "did not automatically result from the priest's activities."

Blood as Medium of Life-for-Life Exchange in Leviticus 17:11

In this section I argue that Heb 9:22b alludes to Lev 17:11, and that Lev 17:11 figures sacrificial blood as a medium of life-for-life exchange. I also begin an argument, which the following two sections will complete, that Heb 9:22b appropriates from Lev 17:11 this logic of life-for-life exchange. Many scholars perceive an allusion to Lev 17:11 in Heb 9:22b.[23] Many simply do not raise the issue; none, as far as I am aware, argue against it.

Leviticus 17:11 LXX reads, "For the life of all flesh is its blood, and I have given it to you upon the altar to make atonement for your lives (ἐξιλάσκεσθαι περὶ τῶν ψυχῶν ὑμῶν), for it is its blood that makes atonement in place of the life (τὸ γὰρ αἷμα αὐτοῦ ἀντὶ τῆς ψυχῆς ἐξιλάσεται)." Leviticus 17:11 specifies that blood is what makes atonement; Heb 9:22b says that without sacrificial blood there is no forgiveness. In support of a conscious allusion to the former in the latter, we should note the striking functional parallels between the two verses. Leviticus 17:11 is the only passage in the Levitical legislation that provides a generalizing rationale for the atoning function of blood. It is the only passage that offers anything like an explanation of why and how blood effects atonement.[24] Similarly, Heb 9:22 first refers to the general function of blood throughout the cult: "Indeed, under the law almost everything is purified with blood." From this systemic use of blood it draws an inference: "and without the shedding of blood there is no forgiveness of sins." Hebrews 9:22, like Lev 17:11, supplies a theological rationale for the atoning use of blood in the cult as a whole. Hence, if our author obtained this idea from scripture, this passage is the only realistic candidate.[25]

But did our author get this idea from scripture? A clue that he has Lev 17:11 in mind is the phrase "according to the law" (κατὰ τὸν

---

[23] See Delitzsch 1887:121; Michel 1966:322; Lane 1991:2.246; Grässer 1993:129; Koester 2001:421; Karrer 2008:164; Ribbens 2016:155.

[24] Milgrom 2000:1474–78 has argued that Lev 17:11 applies only to the well-being offering, but as Nihan 2007:422 n. 114 points out, Milgrom's thesis "has been almost unanimously rejected, and is unlikely." In addition to Nihan's capable critique, see Gorman 1990:184–89; Gilders 2004:168; Gane 2005:171; Sklar 2005:174–81.

[25] As we will see, Num 35:33 comments on blood's atoning function in terms similar to Lev 17:11. However, since its context is judicial retribution for murder rather than the operation of the Levitical cult, it is unlikely that our author has Num 35:33 directly in view.

νόμον) in 9:22a: "Indeed, under the law almost everything is purified with blood." This statement broadens the focus from covenant inauguration (9:18–21) to the entire Levitical cult, which stipulates blood as the nearly exclusive medium of purification.[26] That the first half of the verse comments on the law's whole system of cultic prescriptions renders it more likely that the second half reflects on the most explicit rationale for such practice that the law itself offers. As Otto Michel notes, the verse's second half strengthens and explains the first half.[27]

Further, it is often noted that Heb 9:22b has close parallels in several rabbinic sources. In fact, precisely the same phrase appears repeatedly: אין כפרה אלא בדם, "There is no atonement except by blood" (b. Yoma 5a (2x); b. Zebaḥ. 6a; b. Menaḥ. 93b (2x)).[28] In each of these instances, this maxim is immediately supported by a citation of the final, explanatory clause of Lev 17:11. Hence, in its rabbinic form, this maxim is not a freestanding comment on blood atonement but a summary of Lev 17:11. It is also worth underscoring the close syntactic parallels between the rabbinic version of this axiom and that of Hebrews. The statements categorically deny the possibility of cultic atonement or one of its chief effects, with the proper use of blood as sole exception.[29] Given the apparently fixed form of this rabbinic maxim, it is plausible that it was already current in the second half of the first century. Given its nearly verbatim expression in Hebrews' Greek, I think it likely that our author was acquainted with a version of this maxim, and here explicitly reproduces it.[30] Given that in rabbinic sources this maxim is always underwritten by

---

[26] So, e.g., Ellingworth 1993:471; Gäbel 2006:418.   [27] Michel 1966:320.

[28] My translation, with thanks to Kim Phillips and David Instone-Brewer for help navigating Talmudic sources and their Hebrew. A nearly identical version of the saying, including subsequent citation of Lev 17:11, is attributed to the second-century R. Judah in t. Zebaḥ. 8:17, "You have nothing which effects atonement except for the blood of life alone" (אין לך שמכפר אלא דם הנפש בלבד). (For Hebrew and English see, respectively, Zuckermandel 1937:492; Neusner 1979:38.) This version adds "of life" (הנפש) after "blood," specifying that only blood lost in the giving of life atones, not blood exuded after death. The saying also occurs in Sifra 4:10, "Since we find that there is no atonement except by blood" (ומצינו שאין כפרה אלא בדם), which introduces a question about hand-laying. While this version does not cite Lev 17:11, "we find," indicating that the principle is found in scripture, implies the source. (For Hebrew and English see Ginsberg 1999:72, though the translation here is mine.)

[29] The precision of this parallel is obscured by the periphrastic English translation in, e.g., Epstein 1974, though preserved in the German of Strack and Billerbeck 1926:742.

[30] Scholars who see Hebrews as making essentially the same point as the rabbinic maxim, even if not drawing on an earlier oral version of it, include Delitzsch 1887:121;

Lev 17:11, I take this to heighten the probability of a conscious allusion to the passage in Heb 9:22b.[31] More specifically, I think David deSilva is right to conclude that Heb 9:22b offers a "negative restatement" of Lev 17:11.[32] One might say the author draws what he regarded as a necessary inference from Lev 17:11, asserting an implication of the verse's rationale for blood's atoning function. Since it is blood that makes atonement, the result of atonement – forgiveness – can be obtained in no other way.

Now for this section's second point: Lev 17:11 figures sacrificial blood as a medium of life-for-life exchange. A number of recent works on Levitical sacrifice argue that the Hebrew text of Lev 17:11 features blood as a medium of life-for-life exchange. I give the text and a translation below:

כִּי נֶפֶשׁ הַבָּשָׂר בַּדָּם הִוא וַאֲנִי נְתַתִּיו לָכֶם עַל־הַמִּזְבֵּחַ לְכַפֵּר עַל־נַפְשֹׁתֵיכֶם:
כִּי־הַדָּם הוּא בַּנֶּפֶשׁ יְכַפֵּר

For the life of the flesh is in the blood, and I have given it to you on the altar to ransom your lives, for it is the blood that ransoms by means of the life.[33]

Two details in the verse underscore the role of blood as medium of life-for-life exchange. The first is that, while debate continues apace about senses of כִּפֶּר throughout the Levitical legislation, here in Lev 17:11 the verb denotes "ransom," and is denominative of כֹּפֶר. This is a point of broad scholarly consensus.[34] In support of this consensus one can point out that the phrase לְכַפֵּר עַל־נַפְשֹׁתֵיכֶם occurs in only two other places in the Hebrew Bible, Exod 30:15–16 and Num 31:50. Each describes a census in which individuals pay a monetary cost in order to "ransom" their lives. Jacob Milgrom points out that the parallel of Lev 17:11 with Exod 30:15–16 is particularly close, since the verbal action in the latter is described in Exod 30:12 with the noun phrase כֹּפֶר נַפְשׁוֹ, "a ransom for his life."[35] Since only these three

---

Westcott 1903:271; Attridge 1989:258; Bruce 1990:227 n. 144; Weiss 1991:482; Ellingworth 1993:473; Grässer 1993:184; Gäbel 2006:410 n. 35.

[31] That Hebrews does not cite the passage but alludes to it is in keeping with its consistently allusive handling of the Levitical texts, in contrast to its frequent citations of other portions of scripture.

[32] deSilva 2006:308.   [33] Translation adapted from Sklar 2005:173.

[34] Levine 1989:115; Milgrom 1991:707–8; Schwartz 1991:55–56; Jürgens 2001:166–68; Gilders 2004:170–76; Sklar 2005:168; Nihan 2007:420–21; Feder 2011:203–6.

[35] Milgrom 1991:707–8; cf. Sklar 2005:168.

passages speak of enacting כפר for one's life, it seems best to understand לְכַפֵּר עַל־נַפְשֹׁתֵיכֶם in Lev 17:11 as "to ransom your lives." That is, the blood given by YHWH on the altar enacts a life-for-life exchange.[36]

A second detail in Lev 17:11 that underscores the role of blood as a medium of life-for-life exchange is the meaning of its third verbal clause: כִּי־הַדָּם הוּא בַּנֶּפֶשׁ יְכַפֵּר, "for the blood ransoms by means of the life." In order to understand this clause we need to consider the logic of the whole verse. Leviticus 17:11 stands in the midst of a chapter detailing how the people of Israel should deal with the blood of animals.[37] In its immediate context of 17:10–12, 17:11 grounds a prohibition in 17:10 against "eating blood" – that is, consuming meat with blood in it – that is reiterated in 17:12. In its first two clauses, 17:11 gives two reasons for the prohibition of consuming blood. The first clause states that the life of an animal is in its blood. The second clause says that God has given blood upon the altar for the Israelites in order to ransom their lives. That is, the sole legitimate use of blood is sacrificial atonement. Finally, the third clause combines the first two, asserting that blood "ransoms by means of the life" (בַּנֶּפֶשׁ יְכַפֵּר). As Baruch Schwartz points out, "The third clause does more than merely summarize. It provides the logical connection between clause 1 and clause 2; it says that clause 2 is true *because of* clause 1. How does blood מכפר? בנפש."[38] The third clause explains that it is the life of the animal, offered as blood, that ransoms the life of the offerer.[39] Leviticus 17:11 presupposes, but does not specify exactly why, the life of the one offering sacrifice is forfeit through sin. With this in mind it is worth quoting Schwartz's reflections on the verse:

> Consider the paradox in this: on the one hand, this is a clear expression of the idea of measure for measure embodied in

---

[36] Sklar 2005:60 offers a nuanced definition of כֹּפֶר, that is, ransom: "Positively, a כֹּפֶר is a legally or ethically legitimate payment that delivers a guilty party from a just punishment that is the right of the offended party to execute or to have executed. The acceptance of this payment is entirely dependent upon the choice of the offended party [,] is a lesser punishment than was originally expected, and its acceptance serves both to rescue the life of the guilty and to appease the offended party, thus restoring peace to the relationship."

[37] For careful analysis of the structure and content of the whole chapter, see Schwartz 1991.

[38] Ibid., 47, emphasis original.

[39] For a defense of the instrumental reading of בְּ presupposed here, see Sklar 2005:168–74.

the talionic demand, expressed by Priestly law in the phrase
נפש תחת נפש – 'life for life' (Lev. 24.18). Man has somehow
incurred a debt of his life, his נפש, and this is what he gives –
a נפש. On the other hand it is a rejection, or at least an
alleviation, of the very same talionic demand, since the נפש
that man offers here is not his own ... but merely a כֹּפֶר – a
substitute, an exchange which God is willing to receive in
place of the real thing. It is merely the symbolic representation of the life of an animal, a bit of its blood – an appropriate symbol, to be sure, since blood embodies life, but a symbol nonetheless.[40]

In other words, the ransom offered in sacrificial blood redeems the offerer from liability to death. This exchange of life is a divinely gifted means of averting the judicial threat of death. In a manner similar to Schwartz, both William Gilders and Yitzhaq Feder affirm not only that the blood ransoms the life of the offerer, but that this constitutes a substitutionary exchange.[41] Gilders argues,

On its own, *kipper* does not refer to substitution because there is no necessity of actual equivalency for a ransom to work. That is, a payment in precious metal is not the equivalent of a human life ... In contrast, since human life and animal life are both designated as *nepeš*, it is possible to identify animal life as equivalent to human life, at least for the purpose of having the former act as a ransom price for the latter.[42]

Like Schwartz, Feder also affirms that "the logic of ransom expounded by Lev 17:11 is based on the talionic formula 'a life for a life.'"[43] Like Gilders, Feder argues, "Since blood contains the spirit (נפש) of the animal, it can be viewed as being of the same currency as the life (נפש) of the offerer, and thus the former can be given as a substitute for the latter."[44] Feder's use of the economic term "currency" is apt. Because of its association with life, blood serves in Lev 17:11 as a medium of exchange, an exchange of a life given in place

---

[40] Schwartz 1991:56–57; see also Sklar 2005:171–72 n. 33.
[41] Compare the way Schwartz 1991:57 criticizes the reticence of many scholars to see "vicarious sacrifice" at work in Lev 17:11.
[42] Gilders 2004:175–76.   [43] Feder 2011:204.
[44] Ibid., 203–4. Though Feder's gloss "spirit" is somewhat wide of the mark.

of a life owed. Sacrificial blood exchanges a life given in death for a life liable to death.

But how likely is it that the author of Hebrews would have discerned such a logic of life-for-life exchange in Greek Leviticus, his scriptural source for the axiom of 9:22b?[45] I would suggest that this is very likely indeed. The LXX of Lev 17:11 reads,

ἡ γὰρ ψυχὴ πάσης σαρκὸς αἷμα αὐτοῦ ἐστιν καὶ ἐγὼ δέδωκα αὐτὸ ὑμῖν ἐπὶ τοῦ θυσιαστηρίου ἐξιλάσκεσθαι περὶ τῶν ψυχῶν ὑμῶν· τὸ γὰρ αἷμα αὐτοῦ ἀντὶ τῆς ψυχῆς ἐξιλάσεται.

Despite relatively minor divergences from the MT, I would argue that the idea of blood as medium of life-for-life exchange is evident in the Greek version also. First, we should note that ψυχή, as a calque for נפש, is present in all three clauses. Second, whatever one makes of debates surrounding non-Jewish usage of ἐξιλάσκομαι and its appropriation in the LXX, in its use in Greek Leviticus it should be seen as a calque for כפר. That is, by using ἐξιλάσκομαι, the translator of Greek Leviticus intended to transfer what he took to be the Hebrew sense into Greek, not alter or adapt it.[46] So the use of ἐξιλάσκομαι itself should not be taken as evidence for or against the sense of "ransom" or "redeem" in either the Hebrew or Greek texts. Third, in the third clause, the LXX renders בַּנֶּפֶשׁ as ἀντὶ τῆς ψυχῆς. This reflects a reading of the pronoun בְּ as *beth pretii*, that is, the blood ransoms "for" or "in place of" the life, and the life in question is that of the human offerer, not the animal being sacrificed. This reading of the Hebrew is adopted by a minority of modern scholars,

---

[45] For the likelihood that Hebrews' Greek text of Leviticus was substantially identical to that engaged here, see Section 2.3, "Yom Kippur in Leviticus 16 in Light of Hebrews."

[46] Büchner 2010b offers a valuable study of the issue, though I disagree with his contention that ἐξιλάσκομαι in Greek Leviticus means "appease" or "propitiate." Given how the syntax of Hebrew clauses with Piel כפר is "mechanically imitated" in over 90 percent of instances (ibid., 249), I think it far more likely that the translator of Greek Leviticus intended to map ἐξιλάσκομαι onto the semantic range of כפר, whatever he understood that to be. For instance, Büchner requires Lev 16:16 LXX to mean "He shall reverence the altar because of the uncleannesses of the people of Israel," taking ἀπό in a causal sense. However, since the Hebrew has the sense "He shall purge the altar of the impurities of the people of Israel," the preposition מן indicating removal, it is far more natural to see ἐξιλάσκομαι, embedded as it is in a phrase mirroring the Hebrew syntax, as meaning "purge" or "cleanse." For a more convincing analysis of this passage see Wevers 1997:249. In any case, my point with regard to the Greek of Lev 17:11 is simply that it is best to take the verb there as a deliberately formulaic equivalent for the Hebrew.

though I think an instrumental meaning more likely.[47] Whatever one makes of the exegetical merits of this translation, it clearly conveys the idea that blood enacts a life-for-life exchange. According to the LXX, the ψυχή of all flesh is its blood, and God has given it to the Israelites on the altar in order to make atonement περὶ τῶν ψυχῶν ὑμῶν, "for your lives." For it is the animal's blood, the third clause concludes, that makes atonement "in place of" the human offerer's life. As John William Wevers puts it, "What ἀντί contributes is a notion of exchange; what 'its blood,' i.e. the blood of the sacrificial animal, does is to substitute atonement for the life."[48] Thus, whatever the author of Hebrews may have brought with him to the text, I suggest that he found in Lev 17:11 LXX the concept of sacrificial blood enacting a life-for-life exchange.

The Meaning of αἱματεκχυσία in Hebrews 9:22b

With all this in view, we now consider the sense of αἱματεκχυσία in 9:22b, on which the foregoing affords a fresh vantage point. The term is first attested in Hebrews; whether it was coined by our author or current in Greek-speaking Judaism need not concern us here. There are two predominant views on what αἱματεκχυσία refers to: ritual manipulation of blood and ritual slaughter.[49] I will argue for the latter. The strongest case for taking αἱματεκχυσία to denote blood application is a lexical one. Here I will summarize and respond to this case before addressing another, broader counterargument in the following section.

The noun αἱματεκχυσία is a compound of αἷμα and ἔκχυσις, which is cognate with ἐκχέω.[50] The verb's basic meaning is "pour out"; hence the noun's meaning "pouring out." One could establish a lexical fit

---

[47] For evaluation of the *beth pretii* reading see Sklar 2005:169–71.
[48] Wevers 1997:268. Though instead of "substitute atonement for the life," I might say "enact atonement for the offerer's life in a substitutionary, life-for-life exchange."
[49] Ritual manipulation: Spicq 1953:265; Thornton 1964; Braun 1984:279–80; Attridge 1989:259; Lane 1991:2.232; Weiss 1991:482; Ellingworth 1993:474; Gordon 2000:105; Koester 2001:420; Gäbel 2006:418; Moffitt 2011:291–92 n. 157; Ribbens 2016:155–56. Slaughter: Delitzsch 1887:121–22; Moffatt 1924:130; Behm 1964; Michel 1966:321; Young 1979; Hegermann 1988:186; Grässer 1993:185; Cockerill 2012:410. Among those who argue for ritual manipulation, some (e.g., Lane) speak specifically of pouring out blood on or near the altar, whereas others (e.g., Attridge) identify blood application in general. Westcott 1903:271 seems to see a reference to both slaughter and blood manipulation.
[50] Hence I will call αἱματεκχυσία an "ἐκχέω compound."

between αἱματεκχυσία and ritual manipulation of blood in at least two ways. First, it may be that blood pouring, as a component of the sacrificial use of blood, may be of such atoning significance that, for Hebrews at least, it can invoke the atoning effects of the whole complex of Levitical blood manipulations. The following comments of T. G. C. Thornton seem to support such an inference: "On eight occasions the Septuagint uses the words ἐκχεῖν and αἷμα to describe the pouring out of the blood of a sin offering upon the base of the altar. This meaning of 'pouring out blood' is the only meaning of ἐκχεῖν αἷμα in Jewish sacrificial contexts in the Septuagint."[51] In support, Thornton cites Exod 29:12; Lev 4:7, 18, 25, 30, 34; 8:15; and 9:9. A similar logic seems evident in the way Moffitt groups together the effectiveness of blood "sprinkled, poured out, and applied,"[52] as well as in William Lane's suggestion that, in the LXX passages cited by Thornton, the collocation of ἐκχεῖν and αἷμα denotes "the pouring out of blood as a sin offering upon the base of the altar."[53] Elsewhere Lane writes that αἱματεκχυσία refers not to ritual slaughter "but to the final disposal of the blood upon the altar in order to effect atonement."[54] Lane thereby implies that pouring out blood at the base of the altar somehow constitutes the act as a "sin offering" and so effects atonement.

Second, it may be that ἐκχέω and its cognate ἔκχυσις are flexible enough to denote not only pouring but also a variety of blood manipulations such as sprinkling, tossing, and daubing. For instance, Thornton writes,

> There is no difficulty in regarding the root ἐκχεῖν as including the idea of sprinkling. For Rabbi Ishmael and others the general concept of 'pouring out blood' (*shefikah*) included the more particular idea of sprinkling (*zerikah*), and in the Septuagint, Philo, and Josephus the act of sprinkling sacrificial blood on the altar can be described by such general terms as προσχεῖν, χρίειν, σπένδειν, and δεύειν.[55]

---

[51] Thornton 1964:64.   [52] Moffitt 2011:292 n. 157.   [53] Lane 1991:2.232.
[54] Ibid., 2.246.
[55] Thornton 1964:65. He cites b. Zebaḥ. 36b–37a and b. Pesaḥ. 121a for the former point, and for the latter the LXX rendering of זרק as προσχέω, as well as, "Philo, *De Spec. Leg.* i. 205, iv. 125. For χρίειν cf. Philo, *De Spec. Leg.* i. 233; for σπένδειν cf. Philo, *De Vita Mosis*, ii. 150; for δεύειν cf. Josephus, *A. J.* iii. 227, 231" (ibid., 65 n. 3). We will consider all of these passages in this section.

I will answer Thornton's arguments point-by-point since, fifty years on, his remains the most substantial lexical case for αἱματεκχυσία as blood manipulation.

Regarding blood pouring in Levitical rites, I would suggest that Thornton and those who share his view have the lexical data right, but the significance of blood pouring wrong. Thornton is correct that, in sacrificial contexts in the LXX, the combination of ἐκχεῖν and αἷμα always denotes pouring out blood at the base of the altar. The problem, however, is that this is not an atoning act, but the disposal of leftover blood that was not used for any atoning purpose.[56] It is the blood that is not sprinkled, daubed, or tossed on the altar that is poured out at its base. It is the blood that does not effect atonement that is disposed of by pouring.

This understanding of blood pouring as postrequisite disposal is evident in the rabbinic discussions cited by Thornton, where, *pace* Thornton, atoning acts of blood application are clearly distinguished from the subsequent disposal of the remaining blood.[57] For instance, according to b. Pesaḥ. 89a, "whereas [the blood of] the Passover-offering must be poured out [gently], [that of] the peace-offerings requires dashing [against the altar]."[58] Here the Passover offering seems to be distinguished from the peace-offering, and in principle from other offerings, by its lack of blood manipulation: The blood is only poured out, not dashed against the altar. This is important background for b. Pesaḥ. 121a: "When you examine the matter, [you must conclude] that in R. Ishmael's opinion sprinkling [*zerikah*] is included in pouring [*shefikah*], but pouring is not included in sprinkling. Whereas in R. Akiba's opinion pouring is not included in sprinkling, nor is sprinkling included in in pouring." The question at issue is the relationship between the Passover offering and other festival offerings. The discussion presupposes that pouring and sprinkling are different acts that characterize the two offerings. Hence R. Ishmael's opinion that "sprinkling is included in pouring" does not identify the two acts, or indicate lexical equivalence, but argues that in this case the obligation to do the former can be discharged by the latter.[59]

---

[56] Wright 1987:147–48; Milgrom 1991:238–39; Janowski 2000:224 n. 200; Gane 2005:64.
[57] Rightly noted by Young 1979:180. [58] Translation from Epstein 1967.
[59] See note (4) in ibid. *ad loc.*

Further, b. Zebaḥ. 36b–37a invokes Deut 12:27, which prescribes that the blood of sacrifices be poured out on the altar, in order to discuss whether a sacrifice can be valid in which sprinkling was mandated but whose blood was in fact only poured out. Appropriating the opinion of R. Akiba in b. Pesaḥ. 121a, the passage argues: "Pouring is not included in sprinkling, nor is sprinkling included in pouring."[60] That is, such a sacrifice is invalid; pouring may not substitute for sprinkling. Again, this use of these two terms does not conflate them but instead sharply distinguishes them. Further, b. Zebaḥ. 47a–b twice mentions the residue (שירי) of blood that must be poured out, yet concludes, "but if he did not pour it out, he did not invalidate [the sacrifice]."[61] Finally, b. Zebaḥ. 51a is even more explicit: "Said R. Ishmael [This would follow] *a fortiori*: if the residue, which does not make atonement and does not come for atonement, requires the base; then surely the sprinkling itself of the [blood of the] burnt-offering, which makes atonement and comes for atonement, requires the base?" Not only does this passage distinguish sprinkled blood from the residue that is poured out, but the sprinkled blood is explicitly assigned an atoning function that the poured-out blood is just as explicitly denied. Hence, although in b. Pesaḥ. 121a one Rabbi seems to accord blood pouring more than its typical role of disposal, it is an exception rather than the norm, and does not indicate that the Hebrew words for "pouring" and "sprinkling" interchangeably designate blood manipulation. In sum, there is very little reason to think that the author of Hebrews would have fastened on the pouring out of blood at the base of the altar, at the conclusion of the sin-offering, as a theologically freighted event, such that without it there is no forgiveness. No persuasive case for equating αἱματεκχυσία with blood manipulation can be built from associating the term with pouring blood out around the altar.[62]

---

[60] Translation from Epstein 1988.   [61] Cf. b. Zebaḥ. 38a–b.

[62] Lev 8:15 (cf. 9:9) and Deut 12:27 might present *prima facie* exceptions to the relative insignificance of blood pouring, but they do not actually qualify, much less overturn, the point. In Lev 8:15, during the ordination of priests and consecration of the altar, we read, "And Moses killed [the purification offering], and took the blood, and with his finger put it on the horns of the altar round about, and purified the altar, but the blood he poured out at the base of the altar; thus he consecrated it by effecting purification for it (or: 'by effecting purgation upon it')" (translation from Sklar 2005:122 n. 45). However, rather than seeing consecration as a consequence of blood pouring, it is far more likely that "thus he consecrated it" summarizes the effect of the

But what about the argument that ἐκχέω is flexible enough to encompass acts of sprinkling, tossing, and daubing as well as pouring? We have seen that neither b. Pesaḥim nor b. Zebaḥim conflates pouring and sprinkling. However, on first reading it might appear that this is what Greek Leviticus has done, by rendering זרק, which means "throw" or "toss," with προσχέω, which typically means "pour to" or "pour on."[63] Thus Thornton takes the use of προσχέω in Greek Leviticus as evidence for lexical interchange between terms for sprinkling and pouring.[64] Further, Gäbel regards this translation as a deliberate transformation of sprinkling into pouring.[65] However, given the highly formal equivalent translation technique of Greek Leviticus, such a transformation is unlikely.[66] Instead it is far more likely, as Wevers argues, that προσχέω is a calque, a formulaic equivalent meant to preserve the sense of the Hebrew, though it departs somewhat from the Greek verb's typical semantic range.[67] In cultic contexts in the LXX, the combination of ἐκχέω and αἷμα always describes the pouring out of leftover blood as a concluding disposal, with ἐκχέω typically translating שפך.[68] By

---

whole rite, whose focal point, as in Exod 29:36–37 and Lev 16:18–19, is placing blood on the altar. Regarding Deut 12:27, the context is the prohibition against consuming blood (Deut 12:23–27). The point of the verse is that while the flesh of sacrifices is permissible to eat, the blood is poured out (יִשָּׁפֵךְ) on the altar and thereby kept from consumption. While this verb is not the one that normally denotes cultic tossing of blood on the altar (זרק; see Note 63), it is unlikely that the verse depicts an act different from tossing (see, e.g., Milgrom 1991:217, 238; for a contrasting opinion, Meshel 2014:165). Instead, שפך here likely highlights the common result of blood tossed on the altar and blood poured on the ground: consumption is foreclosed.

[63] This occurs in Lev 1:5, 11; 3:2, 8, 13; 7:2; 8:19, 24; 9:12, 18; 17:6 (cf. Exod 24:6; 29:16, 21). In twenty-two of its twenty-three uses in the LXX, προσχέω translates זרק (Wevers 1995:221). On the semantics of זרק see Gilders 2004:25–27. Scholarly consensus holds that in Levitical sacrifices blood is thrown on the sides of the altar. However, Naphtali Meshel has recently argued, in my view convincingly, that blood is instead thrown on top of the altar. See Meshel 2013; Meshel 2014:150.

[64] Thornton 1964:65.   [65] Gäbel 2006:260–61.

[66] See Büchner 2010a:111 on first the syntax, then the word choice, of Greek Leviticus: "From these few cases it can be seen that it was important for the Leuitikon translator that his produced text reflect Hebrew syntax as far as standard usage allowed for it, rather than stylish Greek ... It can be shown, at least for Leuitikon, that the provision of lexical items as corresponding matches for Hebrew items was often more crucial than the production of perfect sense."

[67] See Wevers 1997:4–5, 80 ("Clearly the verb is used with the semantic coloration of the Hebrew"). The translation in Harlé and Pralon 1988:87, "et ils apporteront le sang en cercle sur l'autel," seems to reflect the judgment that προσχέω is a calque, not a transformation of the action.

[68] Lev 4:7, 18, 25, 30, 34; 8:15; 9:9. In these last two ἐκχέω renders יצק, which also means "pour out."

contrast, while in Greek Leviticus blood is typically poured out "near the base of the altar" (παρὰ τὴν βάσιν τοῦ θυσιαστηρίου; sometimes πρός or ἐπί),[69] in passages where προσχέω renders זרק, blood is characteristically directed "to the altar round about" (ἐπὶ τὸ θυσιαστήριον κύκλῳ).[70] The adverbial dative κύκλῳ corresponds to Hebrew סָבִיב, indicating that blood is dashed in a circuit. Given how closely the Greek syntax of these phrases matches the Hebrew, and given that the action προσχέω denotes is not done near the altar but to the altar, it seems clear that, somewhat against the grain of the word's typical usage, in Greek Leviticus προσχέω denotes the tossing of blood against the altar, not its pouring out at the foot of the altar. While Greek Leviticus does use a word typically meaning "pour onto" to indicate the tossing of blood, this does not support Thornton's inference. Further, we must keep in mind that αἱματεκχυσία is cognate with ἐκχέω, not προσχέω. The latter was evidently chosen as a calque for זרק precisely because of the preposition's sense of "onto" as opposed to "out." While προσχέω is not a perfect fit for a Hebrew verb meaning "throw" or "toss," it at least conveys the sense of directing liquid to an intended destination. Further, since προσχέω in Greek Leviticus exclusively renders זרק, it is consistently distinguished from ἐκχέω, which, as we have seen, typically renders שׁפך. While Greek Leviticus uses a word for "pouring on" to denote tossing, nowhere does it use ἐκχέω, its stock verb for "pouring out," to mean tossing or sprinkling.

How then might we account for Thornton's other examples, from Philo and Josephus?[71] In *Spec. Laws* 1.205, in an allegorical interpretation of the whole burnt offering, Philo says, "The blood is poured (προσχεῖται) in a circle round the altar because the circle is the most perfect of figures, and in order that no part should be left destitute of the vital oblation (ψυχικῆς σπονδῆς). For the blood may

---

[69] Lev 4:18 has πρός, and 8:15 and 9:9 have ἐπί (cf. Exod 29:12).

[70] Every passage in Greek Leviticus with ἐκχέω and αἷμα (as well as Exod 29:12) specifies the target of pouring as "the base of the altar." The only variation is in the preposition used; see Note 69. Regarding προσχέω, every passage listed in n. 63 has κύκλῳ, and each but one has "to/on the altar" (the preposition is πρός in Exod 24:6; 29:16, 21). Lev 7:2 is the only exception, with ἐπὶ τὴν βάσιν τοῦ θυσιαστηρίου κύκλῳ. In keeping with the usual LXX sense of προσχέω, this phrase likely reflects the development of a practice in which blood was tossed at the base of the altar to avoid the possibility of spilling blood on the altar's ramp. For this suggestion, which also applies to Deut 12:27 LXX, see Dion 1987; Meshel 2014:166–67.

[71] I will also discuss several passages in Philo in addition to those noted by Thornton.

truly be called a libation of the life-principle (ψυχῆς γὰρ κυρίως εἰπεῖν ἐστι σπονδὴ τὸ αἷμα)." Philo follows the use of προσχέω in Greek Leviticus in describing the blood application on the altar during the whole burnt offering (e.g. Lev 1:5), but with a subtle difference. While Greek Leviticus uses the verb as a calque, Philo clearly has an act of pouring in view, as indicated by his use of σπονδή, "libation." Philo, unlike Greek Leviticus, actually does transform "tossing at" into "pouring out." In doing so he follows the typical sense of the verb, not its specialized LXX usage. While this results in Philo depicting a different action from that of the Hebrew text, this is unsurprising for one who would have almost exclusively read the scriptures in Greek.[72] Philo has read Greek Leviticus more as composition than as translation. Contra Thornton, Philo uses προσχέω to describe not sprinkling or tossing blood on the altar but pouring it out as a libation.

In *Spec. Laws* 4.125, Philo offers a general description of sacrificial practice in a discussion of the prohibition of consuming blood. He writes, "The blood is poured upon the altar as a libation (ὡς σπονδὴ τῷ βωμῷ προσχεόμενον)." Further, in *QG* 1.62, Philo comments that the one who offers a sacrifice "pours the blood on the altar (τὸ μὲν αἷμα τῷ βωμῷ προσχέων)." Given that in *Spec. Laws* 1.205 Philo uses similar language to describe sacrificial blood manipulations, the use of προσχέω likely denotes the same here. The action in *Spec. Laws* 4.125 is explicitly denoted a pouring-out, and *QG* 1.62 likely implies the same. Thus, as in *Spec. Laws* 1.205, in these two passages Philo uses προσχέω in its normal sense and takes sacrificial blood manipulation to be pouring, not tossing or sprinkling. Though this pouring is directed to the altar, the use of σπονδή distinguishes the motion from tossing or sprinkling. In *Heir* 1.182, Philo follows Exod 24:6 in using προσχέω to describe Moses' act of dashing blood against the altar (τὸ δὲ ἥμισυ προσέχεε πρὸς τὸ θυσιαστήριον). Given all we have seen so far, Philo likely envisions pouring rather than tossing, much less sprinkling.

Philo's final remaining use of προσχέω occurs in *Spec. Laws* 1.231. Philo says that in performing the sin offering the priest is to sprinkle blood before the veil of the inner shrine, then anoint the four horns of the altar with blood, and then, finally, "pour the rest of the blood at the foot of the altar (τὸ δ' ἄλλο αἷμα προσχεῖν παρὰ τῇ βάσει) in the

---

[72] On Philo's meager knowledge of Hebrew see, e.g., Hanson 1967.

open air." Given Philo's customary use of προσχέω to mean "pour," his use of the verb here to describe postrequisite disposal of blood is unsurprising. While the LXX consistently uses ἐκχέω for this action, distinguishing it from προσχέω as a calque for זרק ("toss"), Philo maintains no such distinction. Hence, Philo's use of προσχέω does not support Thornton's contention that this term describes "the act of sprinkling sacrificial blood on the altar."

Thornton also mentions Philo's use of χρίω in *Spec. Laws* 1.233 (cf. also 1.231). Here Philo discusses the sin offering, commenting that "the horns of the open-air altar should be anointed (χρίσαι) with the blood." Philo's scriptural sources (e.g. Lev 4:7, 18, 25) have נתן and ἐπιτίθημι: The priest dips his finger in the blood and "places" it on the horns of the altar. So Philo's use of χρίω, meaning "anoint," is an intelligible rendering that preserves the sense of manually applying blood to the altar. In Thornton's final example from Philo, *Moses* 2.150, Philo describes the consecration of the priesthood and altar, specifically the offering of the "ram of ordination" (Exod 29:19–28 // Lev 8:22–29): "He then took its blood and poured part of it round the altar (τοῦ δ' αἵματος αὐτοῦ τὸ μὲν ἐν κύκλῳ τοῦ βωμοῦ σπένδει λαβών)." The wording most closely matches Lev 8:24 LXX. There, as we would expect, the phrase προσέχεεν Μωυσῆς τὸ αἷμα ἐπὶ τὸ θυσιαστήριον κύκλῳ describes Moses' act of tossing blood around the altar, with προσχέω translating זרק. However, in *Moses* 2.150, as in *Spec. Laws* 1.205 and likely 4.125, Philo construes this not as tossing blood against the altar, but as pouring blood out as a libation (σπένδει) around the altar.

Thornton's final example is the use of δεύω ("wet") in Josephus, *Ant.* 3.226–27 and 231. In the former, "the priests drench with the blood the circuit of the altar (τὸν κύκλον τῷ αἵματι δεύουσι τοῦ βωμοῦ οἱ ἱερεῖς)." Josephus's scriptural source describes the tossing of the blood of the whole burnt offering against the altar (e.g. Lev 1:5), and he retains blood application to the altar. His use of δεύω simply describes the action of tossing blood from the standpoint of the receiving object: When blood is tossed on the altar, the altar becomes wet with it. In *Ant.* 3.231, Josephus again uses δεύω to denote blood application: "[A]nd with the blood the priest sprinkles the altar (τῷ μὲν αἵματι δεύει τὸν βωμὸν ὁ ἱερεύς)." Glossing passages such as Lev 4:7, Josephus again uses δεύω to denote blood application from the standpoint of the object. No change of action from either the Hebrew or Greek texts is discernible. Therefore, to conclude this overview of both LXX and subsequent Hellenistic Jewish usage, none of the examples Thornton adduces actually supplies evidence that verbs for pouring are used to denote blood sprinkling. None of the evidence surveyed so far should incline us to see Hebrews' use of an ἐκχέω compound to denote either sprinkling or the whole complex of atoning blood manipulations.

Another potentially relevant passage, noted by some who hold Thornton's view, is Heb 11:28, which uses πρόσχυσιν τοῦ αἵματος to describe the Passover blood application performed under Moses' leadership.[73] Greek Exodus describes this act as putting (θήσουσιν) blood on the doorposts (Exod 12:7), and as touching (καθίξετε) the lintel and doorposts with blood (Exod 12:22).[74] Why then does Hebrews use πρόσχυσις, which is cognate with προσχέω? It is noteworthy that πρόσχυσις is first attested here, and is afterward attested only in Christian writers.[75] This strongly suggests that our author coined the term. But what induced him to form a noun cognate with προσχέω in order to describe a sacrificial blood application? It is likely that he was influenced by the LXX use of προσχέω to denote tossing blood onto a cultic object.

If so, Hebrews represents a trajectory of the reception of this LXX lexeme different from either Josephus or Philo. Josephus uses a different word (δεύω) to render the same action as the Greek and Hebrew texts. Philo uses the same word, προσχέω, but in its normal sense, not as a calque. Philo thereby transforms tossing into pouring. Hebrews, in contrast to both, apparently coins a cognate noun, and deliberately retains the Septuagintal flavor of the verb from which it derives. Because in the author's Greek Bible προσχέω denotes cultic tossing of blood, Hebrews coins a noun from the same compound to indicate a similar act.

If Hebrews is indeed influenced by the LXX use of προσχέω in 11:28, this indicates neither that terms for pouring can denote sprinkling and other atoning blood applications nor that Hebrews' αἱματεκχυσία in 9:22b is influenced by LXX use of προσχέω. As we have

---

[73] Weiss 1991:482 n. 32; Koester 2001:420.

[74] The narration of the Passover in 2 Chr (2 Suppl) 35:11 speaks of the priests tossing the sacrificial blood (וַיִּזְרֹקוּ / προσέχεαν). This, of course, is because unlike the first Passover, Josiah's was performed in the temple. If Hebrews' use of πρόσχυσις in 11:28 is influenced by its verbal cognate in 2 Chr 35:11, this would simply confirm the lexical analysis above: biblical προσχέω denotes not "pouring out" but "tossing at."

[75] E.g. Justin, 2 Apol. 12.5; Gregory of Nyssa, Vit. Moys. 1.28; 2.100–101; Athanasius, Exp. Ps. (PG 27:468). (Based on a search of Thesaurus Linguae Graecae, http://stephanus.tlg.uci.edu/.)

seen, in cultic contexts in the LXX, ἐκχέω denotes only postrequisite disposal of leftover blood, not atoning blood manipulations. In fact, the likelihood that Hebrews is influenced by LXX use of προσχέω strengthens the case against identifying its ἐκχέω compound with sprinkling and other atoning blood manipulations. If the LXX consistently distinguishes ἐκχέω from προσχέω, the former denoting pouring and the latter tossing, and if Hebrews broadly follows its use of the latter in coining a noun for blood application, then it is very likely that Hebrews' use of an ἐκχέω compound is influenced by LXX usage as well. And in the LXX, when describing a cultic act involving blood, ἐκχέω consistently means "pour out."

To recap: We have examined two essentially lexical arguments in support of reading αἱματεκχυσία as denoting blood manipulation. We have seen, first, that in cultic settings in the LXX, ἐκχέω does describe pouring out blood at the foot of the altar. However, the scriptural texts present this blood pouring not as an atoning act, but as disposal. Corroborating this, rabbinic sources maintain both lexical and conceptual distinctions between atoning blood manipulations and non-atoning blood disposal via pouring out. Second, there is no relevant evidence of terms for pouring out being used to describe sprinkling or other atoning blood manipulations. The LXX does use προσχέω, whose usual sense is "pour on," to denote blood tossing, but this is a calque that preserves the sense of the Hebrew, a sense supported by this compound's preposition. Therefore there is no lexical warrant for the conclusion that Hebrews uses αἱματεκχυσία to indicate acts of blood application such as sprinkling, daubing, or tossing. Instead, our whole lexical survey creates a strong presumption against such a sense.

Positively, what sense should we assign αἱματεκχυσία in Heb 9:22b? If the verbal component provided by ἐκχέω denotes "pouring out," to what act does "the pouring out of blood" refer? I would argue, as do many, that the term describes sacrificial slaughter. First, the LXX use of both ἔκχυσις with αἷμα and especially ἐκχέω with αἷμα abundantly attests the idiom "shedding blood" for death at the hands of another. For instance, in Sir 27:15, "The strife of the proud leads to bloodshed (ἔκχυσις αἵματος)" (NRSV).[76] And dozens of passages

---

[76] 3 Kgdms (1 Kgs) 18:28 says the prophets of Baal cut themselves until blood gushed out (ἕως ἐκχύσεως αἵματος), but this bloodletting was not fatal.

combine ἐκχέω with αἷμα to describe the violent taking of life.[77] For instance, Reuben charged his brothers to "shed no blood," that is, not to kill their brother (μὴ ἐκχέητε αἷμα, Gen 37:22), and Moses instructed the Israelites to found cities of refuge so that innocent blood would not be shed in response to involuntary manslaughter (οὐκ ἐκχυθήσεται αἷμα ἀναίτιον, Deut 19:10).

Particularly noteworthy are two passages where shedding blood precipitates a life-for-life exchange, whether of retribution or redemption. In Gen 9:6, "As for the one who sheds a man's blood, in return for his blood, blood shall be shed (ὁ ἐκχέων αἷμα ἀνθρώπου ἀντὶ τοῦ αἵματος αὐτοῦ ἐκχυθήσεται)."[78] The life of one who took life must be taken. In Num 35:33, "[A]nd the land shall not be atoned for from the blood that was shed upon it, except by the blood of the one who shed it (καὶ οὐκ ἐξιλασθήσεται ἡ γῆ ἀπὸ τοῦ αἵματος τοῦ ἐκχυθέντος ἐπ' αὐτῆς ἀλλ' ἐπὶ τοῦ αἵματος τοῦ ἐκχέοντος)" (NETS). Here another talionic, life-for-life exchange is enacted. Following the retributive logic of Gen 9:6, the blood of one who sheds blood must be shed. Only in Num 35:33, the goal of this judgment is atonement. When the life of one who took life is taken, the land, which was defiled by murder, is atoned for.[79] So, in the LXX, not only does the combination of ἐκχέω and αἷμα denote violent bloodshed, but it is also used in these contexts of life-for-life exchange – including one that not only enacts justice but effects atonement. Numbers 35:33 does not prescribe a cultic practice per se, but it applies cultic logic to public justice, and indeed collapses any neat boundary between the two.[80] While I would not argue that the "blood canon" in Heb 9:22b is directly influenced by Num 35:33, the verse provides precedent for treating "bloodshed," in the sense of taking life, as a constituent element in life-for-life exchange. And life-for-life exchange lies at the heart of Lev 17:11, the passage undergirding Heb 9:22b.[81]

---

[77] Unless noted, the following describe the taking of human life: Gen 9:6; 37:22; Lev 17:4 (non-ritual animal slaughter); Num 35:33; Deut 19:10; 21:7; 1 Kgdms (1 Sam) 25:31; 3 Kgdms (1 Kgs) 2:31; 4 Kgdms (2 Kgs) 21:16; 24:4; 1 Chr 22:8; 2 Chr 36:5d; 1 Macc 1:37; 7:17; 2 Macc 1:8; Ps 78:3, 10; 105:38; Prov 1:16; 6:7; Sir 28:11; 34:22; Joel 3:19; Zeph 1:17; Isa 59:7; Jer 7:6; 22:3, 17; Lam 4:13; Ezek 16:38; 18:10; 22:3, 4, 6, 9, 12, 27; 24:7.
[78] Translation from Wevers 1993:115.
[79] Cf. Philo's comment on this passage in *Spec. Laws* 3.150, "[F]or blood is purged with blood, the blood of the willfully murdered with the blood of the slayer" (αἵματι γὰρ αἷμα καθαίρεται, τῷ τοῦ κτείναντος τὸ τοῦ ἐπιβουλευθέντος).
[80] On the ransom dynamic at work in Num 35:30–34 see especially Sklar 2005:154–56.
[81] Feder 2011:186, 266 comments on the "substitutionary" and "compensatory" functions of blood that are common to Gen 9:6, Lev 17:11, and Num 35:33.

Second, also relevant to αἱματεκχυσία is the use of ἐκχέω with αἷμα in the New Testament. In addition to denoting violent taking of life in general,[82] the combination is used in the Last Supper narratives.[83] In Matthew and Mark, Jesus mentions his "blood of the covenant, which is poured out (ἐκχυννόμενον) for many" (Matt 26:28; Mark 14:24). In Luke, "This cup that is poured out for you (ἐκχυννόμενον) is the new covenant in my blood" (Luke 22:20). It is particularly suggestive that in Matthew Jesus' blood is shed "for the forgiveness of sins" (εἰς ἄφεσιν ἁμαρτιῶν). While I do not think it can be established that Hebrews self-consciously draws on Last Supper traditions, the extent of the parallels between them and the near context of Heb 9:22 is striking. Both mention a new covenant (Luke 22:20; cf. 1 Cor 11:25 // Heb 9:15), "the blood of the covenant" (Matt 26:28; Mark 14:24 // Heb 9:20), forgiveness (Matt 26:28 // Heb 9:22), and Jesus as Isaiah's servant giving himself for "many" (Matt 26:28; Mark 14:24; cf. Luke 22:19; 1 Cor 11:24 // Heb 9:28).[84] While blood "poured out" in the Last Supper traditions may not be decisive for Hebrews' meaning, it is plausible that such traditions informed Hebrews' reasoning about the Christ-event, and therefore the cult in light of Christ. Hebrews frames its "blood canon" to highlight something the Levitical cult and Christ's saving act have in common: a life-for-life exchange enacted in death.

Third, regarding the immediate context of 9:22b, it is important to recall both the conceptual equation between death and blood in 9:18 and the argumentative function of 9:22. In 9:18, as we have seen, Hebrews draws an inference from the necessity of death for a διαθήκη to the inauguration of the Sinai covenant via bloody sacrifices. In 9:19–21 the author narrates various cult-inaugural blood sprinklings, which he conflates with the Sinai inauguration, and then draws two generalizations about the cult in 9:22: "Indeed, under the law almost everything is purified with blood, and without the shedding of blood there is no forgiveness of sins." So the immediate context of 9:22b lends twofold support to the conclusion that αἱματεκχυσία denotes ritual slaughter. First, 9:18 interprets the sacrificial use of blood as ritually enacted death. From this it is a small step to treating sacrificial death as necessary for cultically mediated forgiveness. Second, as argued earlier, the subsequently narrated blood rites illustrate this

---

[82] Matt 23:35; Luke 11:50; Acts 22:20; Rom 3:15; Rev 16:6.
[83] See also Delitzsch 1887:122.
[84] Cf. the similar analysis of Hughes 1979:55–57.

ritual enaction of death, specifically the threat of death for covenant disloyalty. Death is pervasive in the cultic exposition from which 9:22 generalizes. Thus 9:22b completes a brief conceptual arc, reiterating a cultic equation between death and blood that confirms and complements the inference of 9:18. Given the combination of these positive factors and the overwhelming improbability of αἱματεκχυσία denoting anything other than the pouring out of blood in ritual slaughter, I conclude that Heb 9:22b does indeed assert that without the bloodshed of death, there is no forgiveness of sins.

Hebrews 9:22b, Life-for-Life Exchange, and the Timing of Atonement

In this section I respond to a second argument against taking αἱματεκχυσία to denote ritual slaughter and draw out the significance of Heb 9:22b for this chapter's case. The objection is that in the biblical cultic texts, as well as roughly contemporary Jewish texts, rabbinic discussions, and Hebrews itself, it is not the slaughter of the animal that is the focal point of atonement, but rather the sprinkling, tossing, and daubing of blood.[85] Regarding Old Testament passages, in support of the objection we need only note Lev 17:11 itself, in which YHWH asserts that he has given blood "on the altar" to make atonement. Thereby Lev 17:11 underscores that blood atones by its application to the altar. For Jewish sources roughly contemporaneous with Hebrews, we might adduce Jub 6:2, where Noah "took a kid, and atoned with its blood for the sins of the earth."[86] Also relevant is the Temple Scroll, which implies that in regular and Yom Kippur sin offerings the ritual manipulation of blood effects atonement (11QT^a XVI, 14–15; XXVI, 6–7, 9–10).[87] As for rabbinic sources, b. Zebaḥ. 6a asserts that it is not the laying on of hands that makes atonement, but the blood, implying manipulation; b. Zebaḥ. 8a ties atonement in the sin offering to sprinkling;[88] and b. Zebaḥ. 26b, commenting on Lev 17:11, says, "[O]nce the blood has reached

---

[85] So Spicq 1953:265; Thornton 1964; Braun 1984:279–80; Attridge 1989:259; Lane 1991:2.232; Ellingworth 1993:474; Koester 2001:420; Gäbel 2006:418; Moffitt 2011:291–92 n. 157; Ribbens 2016:155–56.
[86] Translation from VanderKam 1989. See also Jub 6:14.
[87] For discussion of these passages from Jubilees and the Temple Scroll see Gilders 2006:85–89.
[88] Similarly b. Zebaḥ. 36a–b; 81b; 82b. See also Sifra 4:9–10; in Ginsberg 1999:69–74.

the altar, the owners are atoned for (נתכפרו בעלים)."⁸⁹ Finally, Hebrews itself says in 9:19–21 that blood sprinkling effects inaugural purification, and 9:22a asserts that under the law almost everything is purified with blood (ἐν αἵματι). In the law's cleansing rites, blood purifies on contact, and the instrumental ἐν of 9:22a indicates ritual application (cf. also 9:7, 13–14; 12:24; 13:11–12). Some argue that αἱματεκχυσία in 9:22b therefore refers to the same. So then, the objection goes, if with other early Jewish sources Hebrews regards blood application as that which effects atonement, why would it formulate a cultic maxim that seems to assign focal significance to the act of slaughter?

Here we may describe more precisely how Hebrews 9:22b appropriates Lev 17:11. Our passage does not cite this text but alludes to it. The element of the text that Hebrews particularly activates is blood as medium of life-for-life exchange. This is evident in Hebrews' one significant divergence from the rabbinic version of this maxim, with which Heb 9:22b is otherwise essentially identical. When the rabbinic version asserts, "There is no atonement except by blood," the purpose is to underscore the need for blood to reach the altar: Hand-laying, waving of sacrificial material, and so on do not suffice for atonement. However, as we have seen, Hebrews' version asserts that the shedding of blood in death is necessary for forgiveness. Given that Heb 9:22b alludes to Lev 17:11 yet focuses on the act of slaughter, I argue that the best explanation is that Hebrews appropriates from Lev 17:11 the sacrificial logic of life-for-life exchange.

Leviticus 17:11 asserts that blood atones for life by means of life, as life given for life owed. Therefore, while Lev 17:11 implies that blood achieves atonement when it is ritually applied, blood is able to effect atonement because it enacts a life-for-life exchange. In this exchange, death is not just implied but essential: Atoning blood is life-given-in-death. The following comments by Baruch Schwartz highlight this aspect of blood in Lev 17:11 in a way that, I suggest, also sheds light on Hebrews' construal of blood's atoning potential. First, commenting on the first clause of Lev 17:11, "What is useful to note is that נפש is used to mean 'life' particularly in cases when it is the *loss* of life, or the rescue of someone from *loss* of life, that is spoken of, especially when the word appears in connection with דם, whereas in other contexts the word for life is רוח."⁹⁰ Further, "The

---

⁸⁹ Altered from "the owners are forgiven" in Epstein 1988 to reflect the root כפר.
⁹⁰ Schwartz 1991:48–49, emphasis original.

statement 'The life-force of all living things is contained in the blood' is a graphic way of expressing the dependence of life upon blood. The point is not that blood *is* life, or that there is life-force, as a force distinct from the body itself, *in* blood *per se*. The point is simply that when blood is gone, there is no life. Depriving a creature of its blood ends its life."[91] Blood is life because without it a creature dies.

Therefore I take Heb 9:22b to assert that, in order for sins to be forgiven, something – eventually, someone – had to die. Hebrews 9:22b, then, does not say when blood effects atonement, whether the moment of slaughter or subsequent application. Further, Heb 9:22b does not assert that slaughter is sufficient for atonement, merely that it is necessary, and it explains why. On this reading 9:22a and 9:22b offer complementary assertions about the role of blood in the Levitical cult. The first describes blood's cleansing function, which, as we have seen, occurs through contact with defiled persons or objects. Cleansing is a goal of Levitical sacrifice, but not the only goal. As we saw earlier, the sin offering aims not only at cleansing but at forgiveness. So, the second half of 9:22 asserts that sacrificial slaughter is necessary for forgiveness. No death, no life given; no life given, no atonement for life owed. As Delitzsch observed over a century ago, "He does not say of the αἱματεκχυσία that it actually procures remission of sin, but only that without it no remission is procurable, inasmuch as nothing else but the slaughter of the victim could supply the offerer with that soul-containing blood wherewith alone atonement can be made."[92] Hebrews does not treat purification as a master category within which the interpersonal concept of forgiveness is subsumed or redefined. Instead, Hebrews figures blood as achieving the distinct, complementary goals of purification and forgiveness. According to Hebrews, blood not only cleanses on contact, it also enacts a transfer of life-given-in-death for life-liable-to-death, and thereby renders forgiveness possible.

What then is the value of Heb 9:22b for this chapter's thesis? Much in every way. Hebrews 9:22b opens a crucial window onto how Hebrews construes the Levitical cult and connects the cult to Christ. While the primary referent of Hebrews' "blood canon" is the Levitical cult, the author formulates this maxim with Christ's saving act in view. Here at the heart of Hebrews' construal of the cult, a key aspect of blood's atoning power hinges on death. Blood can enact

---

[91] Ibid., 49, emphasis original.   [92] Delitzsch 1887:122.

life-for-life exchange only when an animal gives its life in death, and thereby gives its blood for use on the altar. And it is precisely this shedding of blood in death that Hebrews highlights as a divinely ordained prerequisite to forgiveness. While Hebrews elsewhere indicates that blood's atoning efficacy is bound up with ritual manipulation, in 9:22b the author asserts that a sacrifice can only eventuate in forgiveness because it enacts death as a constituent element in life-for-life exchange.

Hebrews does in one sense equate blood with life. But it is not that Hebrews sees in blood an embodied life-force or vitality, such that life-in-blood is able to overcome or eradicate death-in-impurity.[93] Instead, insofar as 9:22b places blood in a cultic equation, both life and death can be the opposite term. Indeed, each implies the other: the death of the animal renders its blood a medium of life-for-life exchange, and the life that the blood exchanges is one that has been given in death. Hence the atoning significance Hebrews ascribes to blood is inseparable from death. It is as life-given-in-death that blood obtains forgiveness.[94]

Death, Blood, and New Covenant Inauguration in Hebrews 13:20

More briefly, we turn now to the convergence of death, blood, and new covenant inauguration in Heb 13:20. As several scholars have

---

[93] Contra the comments of Moffitt 2011:267 about how "blood's life force can overcome the impurifying force of death."

[94] Responding to Moret's critique, Moffitt 2016c:309 n. 2 writes, "Moret makes a lot of the role of ransom in Lev 17:11. This is a fair point. This text does not, however, identify the slaughter of the animal in place of the human offerer as the principal atoning or ransoming moment (the life is not given in offering when the animal dies/is slaughtered). This conclusion is clear from the fact that atonement is made 'on the altar'. But, no animals are slaughtered on any of the Jewish altars." As I will discuss in Section 6.2, Moffitt's view of Lev 17:11 and its relevance to Heb 9:22b is not entirely opposed to my own. For instance, Moffitt sees ransom at work in Lev 17:11 (2011:263–64). Nevertheless, I have attempted to open up space for precisely what Moffitt precludes. That is, one need not assert that the life of the animal is "given" only in slaughter or in blood manipulation. And one need not take the decisive role of blood manipulation in atonement to imply that the slaughter of the animal "has no particular atoning significance in and of itself" (Moffitt 2012:219). Instead, because the entire sacrificial process enacts a life-for-life exchange with blood as its medium, slaughter is not just procedurally necessary but – for lack of a better phrase – theologically integral to the rite as a whole. It is precisely as a sign of life taken in death that blood ransoms. While the effect of ransom is a function of the rite as a whole, slaughter is integral to its ransoming effect.

noted, the concluding benediction of 13:20–21 recapitulates the letter's main themes.[95] Hebrews 13:20 invokes "the God of peace who brought again from the dead our Lord Jesus, the great shepherd of the sheep, by the blood of the eternal covenant (ἐν αἵματι διαθήκης αἰωνίου)." The phrase "by the blood of the eternal covenant" could modify what follows, the request that God will equip the addressees to do his will. This is unlikely, however, because in the Greek text the prepositional phrase comes between "the great shepherd of the sheep" and its appositional modifier "our Lord Jesus."[96] Hence the phrase functions adverbially, modifying the participial phrase "who brought back (ὁ ἀναγαγών) from the dead." The prepositional phrase most likely has a causal sense: It is because of the blood of the eternal covenant – that is, because of the covenant-inaugurating force of Christ's death – that God raised Jesus from the dead.[97]

Two significant conclusions follow. First, 13:20 presents Jesus' covenant-inaugurating death as the ground of his resurrection.[98] Since Jesus was resurrected because of the blood of the eternal covenant, what "blood" denotes must precede his resurrection. And, given the links between blood and death we have discerned so far, particularly in the covenant-inaugurating context of 9:18–21, the referent of "blood" in 13:20 is clearly Jesus' death, figured as a saving, new covenant-inaugurating event. So 13:20 restates, in a covenantal and cultic idiom, a key feature of 2:9 that we discussed in Section 4.2: Jesus' resurrection and exaltation are God's response to his saving death.[99] In 13:20, the covenant inauguration Jesus'

---

[95] E.g. Grässer 1997:400, 407; Gäbel 2006:311.

[96] Cf. Ellingworth 1993:728; Gäbel 2006:314.

[97] So, e.g., Lane 1991:2.559. Many who either label this an instrumental use of ἐν or translate it "by" nevertheless offer a causal explanation (e.g., Bruce 1990:388; Ellingworth 1993:727–28; deSilva 2000:512; Gäbel 2006:314–16).

[98] So long as the "gehorsame Lebenshingabe" to which the following refers is taken to denote Christ's death, I concur with Gäbel 2006:310, "Diese ist die Erfüllung des Gotteswillens und als solche Inhalt des neuen bzw. ewigen Bundes und Grund der Erhöhung Christi."

[99] In ibid., 310–11 Gäbel argues concerning 13:20, "Die Auferstehungsvorstellung in Hebr 13,20 führt im Blick auf die Schilderung des Weges Christi nicht über die Erhöhungsaussagen des Hebr hinaus. Sie wird aufgegriffen, um im Blick auf die Auferstehung der Toten die Bedeutsamkeit des Christusgeschehens darzulegen." That is, Gäbel does not see 13:20 specifying Jesus' postmortem ontology beyond what Hebrews' other statements about Jesus' "exaltation" have said. However, I suggest this puts the burden of proof in the wrong place. Since 13:20 explicitly declares that God raised Jesus from the dead, and Hebrews elsewhere describes Jesus' deliverance from death (5:7), indestructible life (7:16), and so on, Hebrews' less ontologically specific statements about Jesus' exaltation should be read in light of the explicit

death accomplished warrants his resurrection as the "great shepherd" of his new covenant people.[100] Thus 13:20 also reaches back to 9:15, which says it is Jesus' death that inaugurates the new covenant. That the "eternal covenant" (διαθήκης αἰωνίου) of 13:20 is identical with the "new covenant" of 9:15 (also 8:6–13; 12:24; cf. 7:22) is evident in the fact that the prophets use the phrase "eternal covenant" in contexts of eschatological promise (Isa 55:3; 61:8; Ezek 16:60; cf. 2 Bar 2:35), including Jeremiah itself (50:5; LXX 27:5). In 13:20, as in 9:15, it is Jesus' death per se that inaugurates the new covenant: the verse names Jesus' death as distinct from his resurrection because it is the ground of his resurrection. It is striking that this closing thematic recapitulation of the letter underscores the saving significance of Jesus' death within a covenantal and cultic framework.[101]

The second conclusion that follows from the causal role of Jesus' "blood of the eternal covenant" in his resurrection is that, as 9:18 asserts and 9:22b explains, 13:20 uses "blood" as a metonym for Jesus' death as a saving event. And again, it does this within a covenantal and cultic conceptuality. That is, 13:20 hearkens back not only to 9:15 but also to 9:18–22. Just as the first covenant was inaugurated with blood, so also the new, everlasting covenant. What is unique about 13:20 is that, by metonymy, Jesus' death is designated the blood that inaugurates the new covenant. In this compressed closing statement, Jesus' "blood" and the inauguration of the new covenant converge on the point of his death. In light of both 9:15 and 9:22, it is not difficult to see how the author would make this connection. In 9:15 Jesus' death liberates people from liability to the old covenant's curse of death; in 9:22b blood atones because it enacts a life-for-life exchange. What 9:15 asserts by saying that Jesus' death achieved "redemption," 9:22b implies by figuring blood as a medium of life-for-life exchange. Hebrews ascribes the same logic of substitutionary soteriological exchange to Jesus' death and to his

---

affirmation of resurrection in 13:20, rather than vice versa (cf. Sections 2.2 and 2.3, "When Did Christ Offer Himself? Upon His Bodily Ascent to Heaven").

[100] Cf. Compton 2015b:134 on 13:20, "There the author says that Jesus was raised because of the efficacy of his covenant-inaugurating – and, thus, atonement-securing – death ... In other words, Jesus's death – his blood – had atoning virtue prior to his resurrection and, thus, prior to the moment at the center of Moffitt's thesis."

[101] I say "cultic framework" because Hebrews' exposition of the inauguration of both old and new covenants treats the inauguration of their respective cults (earthly and heavenly) as integral to the operation of each covenant.

sacrificial blood. That is why, here in 13:20, Hebrews uses "blood" to denote the saving, covenant-inaugurating efficacy of Jesus' death. At the epistle's conclusion death and blood converge, because at key steps in its exposition the same efficacy is ascribed to each.

Conclusions and Clarifications

This section has probed three passages at the heart of Hebrews' cultic construal of the Christ-event that ground the sacrificial significance of blood in the saving significance of Jesus' death. First, in 9:18, the author draws an inference from the necessity of death to establish a covenant to the use of blood in inaugurating the first covenant. Through this conceptual equation between death and blood, in the following verses Hebrews figures the blood rite of the Sinai inauguration as ritual self-malediction: What was done to the animals would be done to the people if they disobeyed. This meshes with presuppositions evident in 9:15, namely that the Sinai covenant stipulated death for disobedience, and that Christ died this death for his people.

Second, by alluding to Lev 17:11, Hebrews 9:22b figures sacrificial blood as a medium of life-for-life exchange. Because life depends on blood, life is given when blood is shed. Because life can be given in blood, blood can offer a life in place of a life owed. This function of blood, I have argued, is evident in the Hebrew and Greek texts of Lev 17:11, and explains the author's use of the hapax αἱματεκχυσία, which refers to ritual slaughter – primarily of an animal, but secondarily the death of Christ. Against a frequent criticism of this reading of αἱματεκχυσία, it is not that Hebrews figures slaughter as the sole, sufficient locus of atonement. Instead, Hebrews presents ritual slaughter as prerequisite to forgiveness because, in order for forgiveness to obtain, a life must be given for the life that is forfeit. In a maxim that underscores the indispensability of blood for atonement, Hebrews puts death center frame. Blood enacts a life-for-life exchange via a life given in death for a life liable to death. It is only death that renders blood a currency of life.

Third, 13:20 uses "blood of the eternal covenant" to encapsulate the saving, new-covenant inaugurating efficacy of Jesus' death. This metonymy indicates not only the effectiveness of Jesus' death that inaugurates the new covenant, but also that Hebrews deems "blood," with its cultic and covenantal connotations, to be appropriate shorthand for the efficacy of Jesus' death. In 13:20, death and blood converge, and blood emerges, even more explicitly than in the two prior passages, as a metonym for the saving efficacy of Jesus' death.

Before the next step in the argument, two clarifications are in order. First, as a metonym for Christ's death, it is specifically the saving efficacy of Christ's death that "blood" evokes. While the fact of Christ's death is not excluded, the metonymy accents what Christ's death achieves: redemption, forgiveness, and the inauguration of the new covenant. Second, I do not suggest that, in Hebrews, blood is only a metonym for the efficacy of Christ's death. We will see in Section 5.3 that, in the context of Christ's offering, blood is both his means of access into the Holy of Holies and the material he offers (9:12, 25; cf. 9:7, 14; 13:12). Further, Hebrews ascribes a cleansing function to blood, both animal blood in the old covenant (9:13, 19–21, 23) and Christ's blood in the new (9:14, 23). My point is not that this metonymy for death exhausts the significance of Christ's blood in Hebrews, but that it is one facet.

5.3 Blood and Offering

The next piece of the puzzle to put in place is the role of blood in Jesus' offering and in the Levitical offerings that prefigured it. In this section we will trace two complementary roles Hebrews assigns to blood in Levitical offerings and that of Christ: It is a means of access to the Holy of Holies and material that is offered. Regarding Levitical offerings, Hebrews explicitly attests both roles. Regarding Christ's offering, passages that figure Christ's blood as means of access also imply that it is material offered, and the latter is confirmed by passages such as 9:13–14 and 12:24.

Blood as Means of Access to the Holy of Holies

In both the Levitical Yom Kippur and its heavenly, eschatological counterpart, Hebrews treats blood as a means of access to the Holy of Holies. According to 9:7, only the high priest may enter the Holy of Holies, and he but once a year, "not without blood, which he offers for himself and for the sins-in-ignorance of the people." The high priest may only enter the Holy of Holies by bringing blood with him. Blood is a condition of his entry – his ticket of admission.[102] In

---

[102] Cf. Brooks 1970:210, "The blood is Christ's ticket of admission into the holy of holies as it was for the priests of the law." When Heb 9:7 figures blood as the Levitical

9:12, describing Jesus' entry into the heavenly Holy of Holies, Hebrews denies that Jesus entered by means of animal blood; instead, he entered by means of his own blood (διὰ δὲ τοῦ ἰδίου αἵματος).[103] In 9:25, Christ is contrasted with the Levitical high priests who yearly enter the Holy of Holies "with another's blood" (ἐν αἵματι ἀλλοτρίῳ). The presupposed commonality is that both entered by means of blood; the contrast, as in 9:12, concerns whose blood it is. Finally, 10:19 says believers have confidence to enter the Holy of Holies "by the blood of Jesus" (ἐν τῷ αἵματι Ἰησοῦ). The instrumental ἐν figures Jesus' blood as a means of access to the Holy of Holies – now access not for himself but for others. Because Christ entered the Holy of Holies by means of his own blood, believers may also, by that same blood.

Blood as Material Offered

Second, in both Levitical offerings and that of Christ, blood is material that is offered. To treat Levitical offerings first, we again observe that in 9:7, the blood that the high priest brings into the Holy of Holies he offers there. In 9:13, alluding to Num 19, blood, along with the ashes of a heifer, is sprinkled on defiled persons to cleanse them. In Hebrews' compressed narration of the inauguration of the Sinai covenant and its cult, blood of sacrifices (cf. 9:23) is sprinkled on "the book itself and all the people" (9:19), and on "the tent and all the vessels used in worship" (9:21). From this Hebrews generalizes in 9:22a, "Indeed, under the law almost everything is purified with blood (ἐν αἵματι)." Finally, in 13:11 Hebrews designates the "blood brought into the Holy of Holies" on Yom Kippur as a "sin offering."

---

high priest's means of access to the Holy of Holies, it presupposes the instructions of Lev 16:1–3, which in turn refer to the deaths of Nadab and Abihu in Lev 10. We read in Lev 16:1–3, "The LORD spoke to Moses after the death of the two sons of Aaron, when they drew near before the LORD and died, and the LORD said to Moses, 'Tell Aaron your brother not to come at any time into the Holy Place inside the veil, before the mercy seat that is on the ark, so that he may not die. For I will appear in the cloud over the mercy seat. But in this way Aaron shall come into the Holy Place: with a bull from the herd for a sin offering and a ram for a burnt offering." God permits access to the Holy of Holies only under these strictly stipulated conditions, just as Heb 9:7 says.

[103] On the instrumental sense of this second διά in 9:12, in addition to Brooks see, e.g., Delitzsch 1887:79; Spicq 1953:257, 281; Lane 1991:2.238; Weiss 1991:467; Ellingworth 1993:452; Grässer 1993:151; Backhaus 2009a:319; Moffitt 2011:212 n. 12; Kibbe 2014:32 n. 26; Ribbens 2016:117.

While the author does not report what is done with blood there, its sprinkling on the altar, per Lev 16:14–15, is assumed.

Though not stated in so many words, Hebrews also implies that Christ's blood is the sacrificial material he offers in heaven. Perhaps the most explicit evidence for this is 12:24, which says believers have come to "the sprinkled blood" (αἵματι ῥαντισμοῦ) in heaven "that speaks a better word than the blood of Abel." Given Hebrews' entire construal of Christ's self-offering in heaven and the fact that this statement follows "Jesus, the mediator of a new covenant," the phrase "the sprinkled blood" should be taken to denote the sacrificial material Jesus offered in heaven.[104] That Christ's "blood" is one way Hebrews names the sacrificial material of Christ's self-offering in heaven is also clear from the parallel assertion of 9:13–14: "For if the blood of goats and bulls, and the sprinkling of defiled persons with the ashes of a heifer, sanctify for the purification of the flesh, how much more will the blood of Christ, who through the eternal Spirit offered himself without blemish to God, purify our conscience from dead works to serve the living God." While Christ himself is the object of "offered" in 9:14, his blood is also presented as sacrificial material. Just as the sprinkled blood outwardly purged its recipients, so will the blood Christ offered cleanse the conscience.[105]

Further, each passage that compares Christ's self-offering in heaven with Levitical offerings implies that Christ's blood is what he offers in heaven. In 13:12, like the "blood brought in" on Yom Kippur, Christ's blood is said to "sanctify the people." Just as the blood the High Priest brought into the inner sanctum cleansed God's people and place, so did the blood Christ brought into the inner sanctum impart holiness. After 9:22a says that under the law almost everything was cleansed with blood, 9:23 affirms, "Thus it was

---

[104] Hence, while I am not entirely persuaded by his account of the Christ and Abel comparison in 12:24, I agree with Gäbel 2006:384 that Christ's blood plays the same role in the heavenly cult that the sprinkled blood, ash, and water of the red heifer ritual play in the earthly cult. Further, that "sprinkled blood" in heaven is something to which believers on earth "have come" (cf. 12:22) points toward the conclusion drawn at the end of this section: The role of blood as sacrificial material in Christ's offering is conceptual, not physical. For Hebrews, there is an important sense in which Christ offers his blood in heaven, but that sense is not a physical one.
[105] Cf. Ribbens 2016:131, "Further, Heb 9:14 closely associates Christ's blood and heavenly offering and complements this association by ascribing a salvific good to Christ's blood. The blood of Christ, then, must be seen as part of the heavenly sacrifice." Ribbens' arguments on this page also inform the paragraph that follows above.

necessary for the copies of the heavenly things to be purified with these rites, but the heavenly things themselves with better sacrifices than these." The comparison implies that Christ's blood, offered in heaven, is what cleanses the heavenly tabernacle. Finally, as we have often observed, the assertion of 9:7 that the high priest "offers" blood in the Holy of Holies is both singular and significant. Gäbel plausibly suggests that this description is designed to precisely anticipate Christ's offering his own blood upon entrance to the heavenly Holy of Holies.[106] In other words, Hebrews draws attention away from the specific form of the inner-sanctum blood manipulation in order to underscore that blood is the material that both earthly and heavenly high priest offered. Hence when 9:12 asserts that Jesus entered the Holy of Holies by means of his own blood, the most natural implication is that, like the earthly high priest (cf. 9:25), Christ brought his blood with him to offer it there. To argue otherwise is to fail to follow the hermeneutical direction 9:7 offers, as well as to create a discontinuity between Christ's offering and that of the earthly high priest where Hebrews repeatedly, if often implicitly, indicates continuity.

We can draw three conclusions from this survey of blood as material offered in both Levitical sacrifices and that of Christ. First, in Christ's sacrifice, as much as in Levitical sacrifices, "blood" is one way Hebrews names what Christ offers. It is true, as we will discuss later, that Hebrews does not explicitly state that "blood" is what Christ offers. However, we should not conclude from this, as many supporters of View 1 do, that Hebrews deliberately avoids saying that Christ offered his blood in heaven, since he already offered his blood in the cross.[107] Instead, Hebrews repeatedly implies that this is a point of continuity between Christ's offering and those of Levitical high priests. In Christ's offering, as in theirs, blood is both means of access to the inner sanctum and material offered there.

Second, with proper qualification we can endorse Moffitt's observation that Hebrews "employs three different terms to denote the object that Jesus offered to God as a sacrifice," namely "'himself' (7:27; 9:14, 25), his 'blood' (9:12, 14; 13:12), and his 'body' (10:10)."[108] To briefly corroborate: In 7:27, 9:14, and 9:25, the pronoun "himself" is the object of "offer." In 10:10, an objective

---

[106] Gäbel 2006:289.
[107] Again, the comments of Bruce 1990:213–14 are influential in this regard.
[108] Moffitt 2011:229.

genitive describes Christ's body as what he offers. Finally – and here is the qualification – as we have seen, several passages imply, though they do not state explicitly, that Christ brings his blood into heaven to offer it there (9:12, 14, 25; 12:24; 13:11–12).

Third, however, again with Moffitt, I do not think that Hebrews envisions Christ physically sprinkling blood in the heavenly Holy of Holies.[109] While Hebrews does name Christ's "blood" as matter he offers in heaven, I do not take Hebrews to imply that, as an act distinct from his entrance to the heavenly Holy of Holies and self-presentation before God, Jesus physically sprinkled his blood in the heavenly sanctuary. There are two reasons for this. First, Hebrews also names Jesus' body and self as what he offers. Second, Hebrews assigns the effecting of redemption to Jesus' entry to heaven itself, and accords to Jesus' entry the decisive qualifier "once for all" (9:12). Hence it seems to me that the act that constitutes Jesus' self-offering in heaven simply is his entrance there and appearance before God.

Thus I agree with Moffitt that the parallel Hebrews draws between Christ and the earthly high priest is not a matter of metaphor on the one hand, or literal identity on the other, but analogy:

> To apply these terms and categories to the resurrected and ascended Jesus is not metaphor, because the associative field of Jewish blood sacrifice is fitting for the context of Jesus's high-priestly ministry in the heavenly tabernacle, the source and subject of the earthly model. Yet this language is also not literal. That is to say, Jesus does not literally sprinkle, smear, or pour out his blood at God's throne in heaven. The fact that Hebrews describes Jesus's offering in terms of himself (Heb 7:27; 9:25–26), his body (10:10), and his blood (9:12, 14; 12:24) shows that the author is not at these points thinking literally of Jesus manipulating his blood in heaven. Rather, he is thinking in terms of analogy to the blood rituals. Just as blood, as the substance that contained life,

---

[109] On this point I differ very slightly from Ribbens 2016:130–32 and Gäbel 2006:288–90. Gäbel very cautiously affirms that Hebrews does indeed portray Christ sprinkling blood in the heavenly Holy of Holies. But he also emphasizes that Hebrews explicitly correlates Christ's act of entering the heavenly Holy of Holies, not a subsequent blood sprinkling, with the earthly high priest's inner sanctum offering. For instance: "Dem Hebr genügt es daher, zu sagen, dass Christus mit seinem eigenen Blut in das himmlische Allerheligste eingetreten ist. Typologisch entspricht das der Darbringung des Blutes durch den Hohenpriester im irdischen Allerheiligsten" (ibid., 290).

was brought by the earthly high priest into God's presence in the holy of holies on [the] Day of Atonement and was sprinkled there to effect a limited atonement, so Jesus, the heavenly high priest, took himself into God's heavenly presence and offered himself to God to effect ultimate atonement.[110]

Though my account of the overall sacrificial significance of blood in Hebrews differs from that of Moffitt, I endorse his exegetical and hermeneutical point here. The fact that Hebrews speaks virtually interchangeably of Jesus offering his blood, body, and self to God in the heavenly tabernacle indicates that the action in view is his entrance into the heavenly inner sanctum and presentation of himself to God there. So, while in Christ's offering blood is both means of access and material offered, neither role implies a physical referent distinct from Christ's self-presentation to God. In depicting Christ's heavenly offering Hebrews invokes the cultic category of blood as material offered but does not posit a distinct, corresponding act. Blood's role as sacrificial material is conceptual, not physical. "Blood" names something about the significance and effect of Christ's sacrifice without entailing a distinct act in heaven. However, whether one takes the role of blood as material Christ offers in heaven in a physical sense or, as I have argued, a merely conceptual one, the crucial point for our argument is that "blood" does indeed name what Christ offers in heaven. The significance of this blood Christ offers is the subject of the next section.

5.4 Death and Offering

The following argument presents the final substantive contribution not only of the chapter, but of the thesis. The argument of this thesis began by formally distinguishing Christ's death from his offering: The cross is not when and where Jesus offers himself. The argument will now conclude by materially reuniting Christ's death and his offering: The achievement of the cross is what he offers in heaven. In this section I will draw and corroborate an inference: The material role of Christ's blood in his offering indicates that what Christ

---

[110] Moffitt 2016b:276. Moffitt's entire chapter repays careful reading. His discussion of analogy makes a crucial methodological contribution to the study of Hebrews' sacrificial theology.

presents to God in heaven is the saving efficacy of his death. In other words, when Christ offers his blood in heaven, what he gives to God is the life he gave in death. The first subsection to follow draws primary, decisive support for this inference from the chapter's first two sections, especially the treatment of Heb 9:22b earlier. The next three subsections offer corroborating evidence that the substance of Jesus' heavenly offering is his life-given-in-death.

The Inference: Jesus' Life-Given-in-Death Is What He Offers to God in Heaven

First, then, the central contention of this chapter and of Part II as a whole: When Hebrews implies that Jesus offered his blood in heaven, this entails that Jesus' life-given-in-death is what he presents to God in heaven in the "currency" of blood. In other words, by presenting his blood to God in heaven Jesus offers what his sacrificial death achieved. We saw in Section 5.2 that, in discussing Christ's offering and its effects, Hebrews uses "blood" as a metonym for Jesus' death. The "blood" by which Jesus inaugurated the new covenant is his death (13:20), which redeemed people from liability for sins against the old covenant (9:15). Further, in Jesus' offering his "blood" is both his means of access to the Holy of Holies and the material he offers there. Regarding means of access, here again a blood-as-death metonymy is evident. Whereas the Levitical high priest first slaughtered the animal then brought its blood in, Jesus first had to die himself before bringing his own blood into the Holy of Holies (9:7, 11–14, 24–25). So, "blood" is shorthand for Jesus' sacrificial slaughter; it grants him access to the Holy of Holies; it is what he offers there.

But the key question is: In its role as sacrificial material Jesus offers in heaven, what is the primary significance or conceptual connotation of "blood"? David Moffitt, for instance, has argued that in this context "blood" signifies not death but life. On his view Levitical sacrifice, including Yom Kippur, emphasizes "the power that blood/life has to obtain redemption and make purification." Hence, "It seems highly unlikely that the author of Hebrews thinks that Jesus effected purification by bringing his death into God's presence."[111] Again: "Rather than Jesus' blood symbolizing his

---

[111] Moffitt 2011:275.

death in Hebrews, it seems more probable that, insofar as Jesus' blood functions as a symbol in the homily, Jesus' blood represents Jesus' life/living presence appearing in the presence of God."[112] In contrast, I argue that in Jesus' heavenly presentation of "blood," this blood atones not as the bearer of a force or power of life, but as currency of a life given in death. What Jesus' blood conveys to God is the value of the life he gave when he died for the redemption and forgiveness of his people.

The decisive evidence for this conclusion is the way Heb 9:22b incorporates Jesus' death into its rationale for how blood atones. As argued in Section 5.2, the verse asserts that "without the shedding of blood there is no forgiveness." This entails that Christ's sacrificial bloodshed – his death on the cross – was necessary to obtain for his people the forgiveness promised in the new covenant (cf. 10:18). With this terse maxim Hebrews, like the rabbinic tradents discussed previously, offers an allusive exegetical summary of the rationale for why blood atones offered in Lev 17:11. We saw in Section 5.2 that in Lev 17:11, blood atones by means of a life-for-life exchange. Blood renders to God a life on behalf of one who owes life. Hence, in both Lev 17:11 and in Hebrews' gloss on it, the "life" that blood gives is a life given in death. The way blood relates to "life" is not mere symbolism but currency, a medium of exchange.

Further, in formulating this maxim in 9:22b, the author goes out of his way to underline death as integral to how blood atones. In the rabbinic version of the maxim – "There is no atonement except by blood" – the implicit referent of blood's instrumental role is its application to the altar. By contrast, in what is otherwise a nearly identical saying, Hebrews asserts that the shedding of blood is necessary for forgiveness. Why this accent on death? I would suggest this deliberate focus on death explicitly activates the logic of life-for-life exchange in the text to which it alludes. When Lev 17:11 says that blood atones by means of the life, it presupposes that the blood was given in death. When Hebrews says that bloodshed is necessary for forgiveness, it makes the giving of life in death explicit.

What Heb 9:22b explicitly asserts is that the giving of life in death is necessary for forgiveness. This forgiveness is cultically mediated, a facet of "atonement" through sacrifice. What the maxim thereby implies is that death is integral to what makes blood a medium of

---

[112] Ibid., 273.

atonement. No life given in death, no blood to render as currency. No blood to render as currency, no life-for-life exchange. Like Lev 17:11 to which it alludes, Heb 9:22b offers a rationale for how it is that the blood that is manipulated does indeed accomplish its assigned atoning purpose. Given its deliberately generalizing role, Heb 9:22b is intended to apply as much to Christ's death, blood, and subsequent sacrificial presentation as it does to the Levitical precursors. Hence Christ's death is integral to his blood's ability to atone for sin. It is Christ's death that not only renders his blood available, so to speak, for subsequent use; more than that, Christ's death constitutes his "blood" a medium of exchange, whereby he can give to God in heaven that which he gave on the cross: his life, given in death in place of his people. When Hebrews implies that Jesus offered his blood to God in heaven, the key association of blood, that which renders it a medium of atonement, is that it represents the life he gave in death. In other words, to deliberately compress Hebrews' cultic idiom into a compact precis, what Jesus offered to God in heaven was his death. As the material Jesus offers in heaven, his blood presents to God what his death achieved. Jesus' death-for-others is what makes his blood atoning; his blood atones by bearing his live-given-for-others to God.

Even with this support taken into account, the idea that what Jesus offered in heaven is the life he gave in death is somewhat paradoxical or counterintuitive. One way of explicating this idea that, I would argue, reads with the grain of Hebrews' account is to consider how blood as "currency" relates both to Jesus' death and his heavenly offering. I have argued that Jesus' blood is currency of his life-given-in-death. When Jesus died he obtained this currency; when he offered himself in heaven he tendered this currency to God. On the cross Jesus gave his life for that of his people. Yet this exchange of life was completed and thereby rendered effectual by Jesus giving to God, in person, what he gave on the cross. As with most sacrifices in the Levitical cult, the sacrifice culminates with the priest giving sacrificial material to God. The offering is completed by being transferred to God's possession. Hence, by using "blood" as a metonym for Christ's death as a soteriologically effective sacrificial slaughter, Hebrews indicates that, in his heavenly self-offering, Jesus presented his life-given-in-death to God. The goal of this giving was that, through God's acceptance, Jesus' entire sacrificial self-offering would become his people's effectual, sufficient means of salvation.

The Analogy of Hebrews 2:9: Two-way Traffic between Death and Exaltation

Now for some additional evidence corroborating this conclusion, the first piece of which is an analogy. As argued in Section 4.2, in Heb 2:9 Jesus' exaltation imparts universal saving significance to his death. Christ's exaltation to heaven sets his death in force as God's effective means of deliverance from death. Therefore Hebrews 2:9 posits two-way traffic between Christ's death and exaltation. On the one hand, Christ is crowned with glory and honor because he suffered death. This parallels 13:20, where Christ is resurrected on the basis of his death's inauguration of the new covenant. On the other hand, in 2:9 Jesus is not just exalted because of his death, but his exaltation gives new scope and significance to his death. The exaltation, though temporally subsequent to Jesus' death, nevertheless does something to Jesus' death. One might say Jesus' exaltation plugs his death into a soteriological power grid from which flow its saving effects.

I here posit analogy, not identity, between the logic of Heb 2:9 and the role of Christ's death in his heavenly offering. While in Heb 2:9 Jesus' exaltation does something *to* his death, in his heavenly offering the exalted Jesus does something *with* his death, namely offer it to God. That Hebrews elsewhere posits an effective soteriological connection between Christ's death and subsequent exaltation heightens the plausibility of seeing an analogous relationship between Christ's death and heavenly self-offering.

Jesus' Death as Sacrificial Victim and Sin-Bearing Servant (Heb 9:28)

Another passage that corroborates the conclusion that Jesus' life-given-in-death is the substance of his offering in heaven is 9:28, which says Christ was "offered once to bear the sins of many" (ἅπαξ προσενεχθεὶς εἰς τὸ πολλῶν ἀνενεγκεῖν ἁμαρτίας). In this section I will argue, first, that this verse not only ascribes soteriological significance to Christ's death per se, but that it does so via the markedly cultic conceptuality of "sin-bearing." Second, by saying that Christ "was offered" in death as the slaughtered sacrificial victim, 9:28 indicates that the category of Christ's "offering" contains, rather than excludes, a distinct soteriological achievement enacted in his death. In other words, Hebrews' use of the passive "was offered" for

Christ's death, along with the active "offered himself" in heaven, further confirms that what Christ achieved when he was offered as victim is what he offers when, as high priest and victim, he offers himself in heaven.

First, as with the passages examined in Chapter 4, this verse ascribes soteriological significance to Jesus' death per se. One of the reasons I consider the passage here rather than there is that 9:28 alludes to Christ's death without mentioning it explicitly. It is important to recall, as noted in Section 2.3, that 9:28 alludes to Greek Isaiah 53:12, whose penultimate clause reads καὶ αὐτὸς ἁμαρτίας πολλῶν ἀνήνεγκεν ("and he bore the sins of many"). Hebrews' allusion to this passage affirms that, in his death, Christ bore the judicial burden of others' sins. For Christ to "bear the sins of many" is, I will argue, for him to take their place in an exclusive sense. As the substitute for "many," Christ bears the retributive consequences of their sins so that those consequences do not accrue to them. Hence 9:28 makes substantially the same point about Jesus' death as do 9:15 and 9:22.

However, not all agree with this reading of 9:28. Hence, in order to both defend this reading of 9:28 and offer support for this section's further material claims, it will be worth engaging the perspective of Otfried Hofius as a foil. First, Hofius rightly observes that, in Heb 9:28 as in Isa 53:11–12 LXX, the verb ἀναφέρω means "bear" as in "take upon oneself."[113] However, I find Hofius less persuasive when he adds,

> This formulation makes it sound as though Hebrews 9:28 is saying, fully in keeping with the sense of Isaiah 53, that Christ bore the penal consequences of sin substitutionarily for many. However, such an understanding of the clause taken from Isaiah 53 is excluded by the preceding and more important statement that Christ "was offered (as a sacrifice)." The sacrificial terminology (προσενεχθείς, from προσφέρεσθαι) shows clearly enough that the expression from Isaiah 53:12cα LXX has been incorporated into the big picture of Hebrews – that is, into the overall teaching about the self-sacrifice of Christ the high priest. The author understands this self-sacrifice as an event of atonement that sets aside the reality of sin and grants access to God.[114]

[113] Hofius 2004:184.   [114] Ibid., 184–85.

Hofius is right to discern an exclusive, substitutionary sense of "bearing sin" in Isa 53, and right to grant that this is the most natural sense of the phrase "to bear the sins of many" in Heb 9:28.[115] However, I would argue that he is wrong to pit this sense of substitutionary exchange against the sacrificial logic of the "big picture of Hebrews."

Three lines of evidence undermine Hofius's opposition between Christ "substitutionarily" bearing the retributive consequences of sin and Hebrews' cultic construal of the Christ-event. First, in the texts prescribing and describing the Levitical cult, the phrase "bear sin" denotes both objective legal culpability resulting from sin and, occasionally, a cultic process by which that culpability is removed. Out of the entire Old Testament, the phrase "bear sin" denotes the status of legal guilt and susceptibility to punishment only in the portions of Exodus, Leviticus, and Deuteronomy that describe or prescribe the Levitical cult, along with Isaiah 52:13–53:12 and Ezekiel, both of which are widely held to draw on these Levitical concepts and terms.[116] In the rest of the Old Testament, when the verb נשׂא is used with sin as its object, it denotes forgiveness, without any necessary connotation of lifting up, bearing, or carrying away.[117] The use of the phrase "bear sin" to denote legal culpability is a peculiarly Levitical idiom.[118] For instance, in Lev 5:1, one who witnesses a crime, hears an adjuration to testify, and fails to do so will bear his or

---

[115] On substitutionary place-taking in Isa 53 see, e.g., Janowski 2004.

[116] Again, as noted in Section 1.4 (n. 47), by "Levitical" I mean "pertaining to the Levitical cult as reported in the scriptural texts."

[117] For the most thorough, linguistically informed, exegetically convincing discussion of the metaphorical schema "sin is a burden" in the Hebrew Bible, see Lam 2016:16–86. Regarding the entire Hebrew Bible except for the Levitical legislation and the passages noted earlier that conceptually depend on it, Lam persuasively argues for what he calls a "lexicalization hypothesis" for the use of נשׂא with sin as object (28–40). That is, outside the Levitical material, "what we have is the *lexicalization* of *nāśā'* with the routinized meaning of 'forgive' ... giving it the status of an independent, polysemous sense of the verb" (28, emphasis original). See, e.g., Gen 18:24; 50:17; Exod 10:17; 34:7; Num 14:18; 1 Sam 15:25; Ps 32:1, 5; Isa 2:9 (full list in ibid., 233–34 n. 34). Although Lam improves upon it in key respects, Schwartz 1995 remains well worth consulting.

[118] Cf. Lam 2016:43–44, "So, then, the use of the expression *nāśā'* + *'āwōn/ḥēṭ'* to denote an objective state of legal culpability is distinctive of Priestly terminology in the Pentateuch. Not only is the phrase absent from portions of biblical law outside of the Priestly material, but even the idea of entering into a state of guilt is hardly found in any non-Priestly legal formulation."

her sin (וְנָשְׂא עֲוֹנָהּ); that is, he or she will be liable to sin's consequences.[119] One may be delivered from this state of liability by offering the אָשָׁם prescribed in the following verses (Lev 5:1–6:7). As Roy Gane observes, a person who has sinned "is in a dangerous state of bearing his own culpability ... until/unless he is relieved of it through sacrificial expiation officiated by a priest."[120] The prescribed sacrifice offers a ritual remedy for the objective judicial state of culpability denoted by "bearing sin."

Further, not only are certain sacrifices prescribed as the means by which one who "bears sin" comes to bear it no longer, but in three places the phrase "bear sin" itself arguably refers to processes by which priests and cultic items assume the burden of sin on behalf of others. The clearest of these is the goat for Azazel in Lev 16:20–22. In these verses the high priest is instructed to lay both hands on the goat and confesses over it the sins of the people, by which "he shall put them on the head of the goat" (Lev 16:21). He then sends the goat into the wilderness; the goat so laden "shall bear all their iniquities on itself (וְנָשָׂא הַשָּׂעִיר עָלָיו אֶת־כָּל־עֲוֺנֹתָם) to a barren region" (Lev 16:22). Less clear, though still significant, are Exod 28:38, in which the rosette on the high priest's forehead enables him to "bear any guilt from the holy things that the people of Israel consecrate," with the result that the people "may be accepted before the LORD"; and Lev 10:17, in which Moses reminds Aaron's sons that the sin offering is given them to consume, "that you may bear the iniquity of the congregation, to make atonement for them before the LORD."[121] In both passages a cultic process enacts "sin-bearing" in the sense that someone or something assumes the consequences of someone else's sin. Therefore, since in Levitical legislation "bear sin" refers both to a state of culpability for sin and to cultic processes by which this culpability is removed, there is no warrant for Hofius's dichotomy between cultic sacrifice and the substitutionary transfer of sin's judicial liability. Instead, by the cultic means discussed previously it is precisely the judicial liability of sin that is transferred from one person to someone (or something) else.

---

[119] See also Lev 5:17; 7:18; 17:16; 19:8, 17; 20:17, 19, 20; 22:9, 16; 24:15; Num 5:31; 9:13; Num 18:1, 22–23, 32; 30:15 (Hebrew 30:16). For discussion of many of these passages see ibid., 40–44; also Schwartz 1995:10–15.

[120] Gane 2005:102.

[121] For a variety of perspectives on these two passages see, e.g., Kiuchi 1987:46–52; Milgrom 1991:622–25; Schwartz 1995:15–17; Gane 2005:91–105; Sklar 2005:92–99; Lam 2016:22–23, 58–61.

Second, in Isa 53 itself sin-bearing arguably roots in Levitical sacrifice.¹²² For instance, in 53:10 the servant makes his life an אָשָׁם, which the Greek renders περὶ ἁμαρτίας. As we have seen, the אָשָׁם provided a cultic remedy for penal sin-bearing. And, while the LXX does not preserve a distinction between the so-called "guilt offering" and the "sin offering," it nonetheless identifies the servant's giving his life with one of the Levitical sacrifices. It is significant, therefore, that two expressions for sin-bearing follow immediately upon this designation.¹²³ Further, as Joseph Lam argues, it is precisely from the Levitical legislation that the author of Isa 53 derived the language of "bearing sin": "In sum, these verses in Isaiah 53 look to be a poetic development of the idea of 'bearing' sin for the sake of another, along the lines of the expression *nāśā' ḥēṭ'* in the Priestly material."¹²⁴ Again,

> Thus, one could say that the metaphorical schema of *sin is a burden* establishes the lines along which the writer develops the idea of the so-called suffering servant. Though this idea is not articulated with quite the same force elsewhere in the Hebrew Bible, the framework for this notion was already present (in nascent form) in the language of the Priestly literature and Ezekiel, as we have seen from other passages in which one person bears the consequences of sin for another.¹²⁵

That the servant offers himself as a "guilt offering" (or "sin offering" in the LXX) and that he bears the sins of others fit together perfectly. Isaiah 53 arguably draws from the Levitical literature not only the language of "sin bearing" but also the idea that someone or something can "bear sin" for another.¹²⁶ And if Isaiah 53 itself develops

---

¹²² For a concise summary of conceptual links between Isa 53 and Levitical legislation see, e.g., Lam 2016:241–42 n. 98. See also Blenkinsopp 2016, who argues that אָשָׁם in Isa 53:10 should be taken in its sacrificial sense, and that the analogy between the servant's death and sacrificial slaughter is crucial for the whole passage.

¹²³ In the Greek of 53:11, τὰς ἁμαρτίας αὐτῶν αὐτὸς ἀνοίσει; in 53:12, καὶ αὐτὸς ἁμαρτίας πολλῶν ἀνήνεγκεν.

¹²⁴ Lam 2016:54.

¹²⁵ Ibid., 55, emphasis original. Lam's basic point stands even if one demurs from the premise that the author of Isa 53 accessed Ezekiel.

¹²⁶ This analysis weighs against the comment of Gäbel 2006:305 that ἀναφέρω in Isa 53:12 LXX "ist ... nicht im opferkultischen Sinne zu verstehen, sondern im Sinne des Aufhebens, Auf-sich-Nehmens, was sowohl als Fortschaffen, Beseitigen auch als Erleiden, Büsen der Sünden(folge) gedeutet werden kann." Gäbel's sequence of terms does describe the effects of the servant's sin-bearing. However, the phrase's lexical

cultic conceptions, it is not surprising that Hebrews would appropriate Isa 53:12 to figure Christ's "being offered" in death as the means by which he "bore the sins of many."

Third, as I have argued throughout this chapter, Hebrews itself figures cultic offering as enacting a life-for-life exchange via the medium of blood. So there is no tension at all in Jesus having been "offered" to, in a substitutionary sense, "bear the sins of many." In this brief, allusive phrase, Hebrews names the effect of Christ's offering with respect to sin's retributive consequences. Precisely by being offered as a sacrificial victim on his people's behalf, Christ bears the penal consequences of their sins.[127] In sum, contra Hofius, when Heb 9:28 says that Christ "bore the sins of many" in his death as sacrificial victim, the idea of "substitutionarily" bearing the penal consequences of others' sin is not foreign to the overarching cultic framework but instead derives from it and depends on it. This is true not only for Heb 9:28 but also for Isa 53:12 on which it draws.

In all of Hebrews this is the only passage that ties "offering" language specifically, though still implicitly, to Christ's death. When Hebrews figures Jesus as high priest, it locates his self-offering in the heavenly sanctuary subsequent to his resurrection (7:27; 9:11–14, 23–28; 10:10, 12, 14). Yet, as we saw in Section 2.3 and have confirmed here, in 9:28 the participle προσενεχθείς ("having been offered") not only includes a reference to Jesus' death but actually focuses on it. In his death as the suffering servant, Christ "was offered" as the sacrificial victim. Therefore, while Hebrews consistently locates Christ's high-priestly self-offering in heaven, when it figures Christ as victim it can say that he *was offered* in his death on the cross. On the cross, Christ is victim; in the heavenly sanctuary he is both high priest and victim, since he offers himself to God. So 9:28 is the only place in Hebrews where Christ's "offering," specifically his being offered as sacrificial victim, is attached to his death. And in

---

contours are derived from the Levitical cult, and the phrase itself denotes the servant's receiving the burden of the (consequences of the) people's sins, in a manner broadly analogous to the goat for Azazel in Lev 16:20–22. The effects of the servant's "sin-bearing" must be distinguished from the unique lexical and metaphorical shape of the phrase itself.

[127] Cf. Ribbens 2016:201, on the parallels between 9:26 and 9:28, "Thus, the connection between the removal of sin and the suffering of Christ suggests a connection to redemption and its connoted payment through suffering and death." Further, on 9:28, "Jesus is the suffering servant who takes sin and iniquity on himself and who suffers the punishment for those sins in a vicarious and representative fashion" (ibid., 223).

9:28 Christ's "being offered" in death entails his bearing sin so that the "many" bear it no longer. So 9:28 explicitly ascribes the life-for-life exchange enacted in Christ's death to his role as both sacrificial victim and suffering servant – indeed sacrificial victim because suffering servant.

Hebrews 9:28 ascribes soteriological significance to Jesus' death per se. In his death Jesus "bears" – that is, assumes the judicial liability for and consequences of – the sins of many. Contra Hofius, substitutionary sin-bearing is not in tension with cultic sacrifice but is instead a peculiarly Levitical concept. Given 9:28, Hebrews' construal of Jesus' "offering" contains, rather than excludes, a soteriological achievement enacted in his death. The notion of substitutionary sin-bearing is not opposed to cultic offering but, in a few key instances, exemplified in it. These instances provided crucial source material for the suffering servant of Isa 53. Thus when Hebrews asserts that Jesus, in his death, "was offered" in order to bear the sins of many, he is arguably activating the cultic dimensions inscribed in the suffering servant's substitutionary death.

Hence my second conclusion: Heb 9:28 contributes to our understanding of what Christ offers when, as high priest in heaven, he offers himself to God. Hebrews 9:28 says that in his death Christ was offered as victim; after rising again and ascending to heaven, Christ then acts as both priest and victim by offering himself in the heavenly Holy of Holies. It is important to note that the participle προσενεχθείς ("was offered") does not come from Isa 53:12, but is Hebrews' own term for how Christ fulfills the servant's role. Hebrews deliberately uses the same verb, albeit in a different voice, for Christ's sin-bearing death and his subsequent self-offering in heaven. Like 9:22, 9:28 offers an account of what Christ's death as victim achieved. This verse therefore confirms that Jesus fulfills the role of sacrificial victim in two stages: First he is offered by God on the cross, and then he offers himself to God in heaven. In both stages, Christ is sacrificial victim; in the second only he is also high priest, the one offering himself as victim. Therefore I conclude that, by specifying what Christ achieved in his death as victim, Heb 9:28 sheds light on what Christ offered in heaven. What he achieved when he *was offered* as victim is what he offered when, as both high priest and victim, he presented himself to God in heaven.

Finally, to further confirm this point we can profitably link 9:28 with 10:12, "But when Christ had offered for all time a single sacrifice for sins, he sat down at the right hand of God." In the Holy of Holies in heaven, Christ offered a sacrifice (προσενέγκας θυσίαν). Since Christ's self-offering is patterned on an animal sacrifice, what he offers as a sacrifice is something that *has been slaughtered*. What is it that has been slaughtered? Himself, in his death on the cross. Not only that, but Jesus offered this sacrifice in heaven "for sins" (ὑπὲρ ἁμαρτιῶν). In 9:28 Jesus was offered for sins, to bear sins. In 10:12 he offers "for sins" a single sacrifice: himself, as the sacrificial victim who died for sins. Jesus offers for sins that which had been slaughtered for sins. This double ascription of atoning intent confirms that the sin-bearing effect of Jesus' death belongs to both his death as victim and his subsequent self-offering, and that the material he offers is what he gave in death.

Identical Saving Effects Ascribed to Jesus' Death and Offering

Another factor corroborating the conclusion that Jesus' death constitutes sacrificial material he offers to God in heaven is that in 10:26–27 saving effects are ascribed to Christ's sacrifice that are elsewhere assigned to his death. We read, "For if we go on sinning deliberately after receiving the knowledge of the truth, there no longer remains a sacrifice for sins (περὶ ἁμαρτιῶν ... θυσία), but a fearful expectation of judgment, and a fury of fire that will consume his adversaries."[128] If the hearers apostatize, abandoning Jesus' singular sacrifice on their behalf, they will no longer possess a sacrifice for sins. As a result, they will be exposed to God's wrath. This implies that it is only Jesus' sacrifice that interposes between them and God's wrath.[129] This passage portrays from yet another

---

[128] That Jesus' sacrifice (θυσία) in 10:26 has the same heavenly referent as his offering (προσφορά) does elsewhere is evident, for instance, in 10:12, where Jesus "offered (προσενέγκας) for all time a single sacrifice (θυσίαν) for sins" before sitting down at God's right hand. Cf. Section 3.2 on how 10:10–14 locates Christ's offering in heaven.

[129] See, e.g., Mora 1974:119, "No existe una posible tercera actitud de indiferencia ante el don de Dios exenta de culpa y de castigo ... El sacrificio del Señor es un juicio discriminatorio del mundo y le coloca ante una opción inevitable." Also Koester 2005:374, "Hebrews has a vivid sense of the threat of divine wrath against sin and unbelief (Heb 3:7–4:13; 10:26–31; 12:29), and the author recognizes that Christ's sacrifice delivers people from judgment precisely by removing the sin that brings divine wrath." Similarly Trompf 1971:126; Ribbens 2012:565. On the broader role of God's retributive judgment in Hebrews see, e.g., Übelacker 2007:246–51.

angle the judicial consequences of sin. God's wrath is not that of a petty tyrant, but the judge of all (12:23; cf. 6:2; 9:27; 10:30; 13:4). The consuming fire that apostates should expect expresses exactingly equitable retributive judgment (10:27–29; cf. 2:2–3). Since it is only Christ's sacrifice that averts this judgment, in 10:26–27 Christ's sacrifice is held to address the judicial consequences of sin, just as his death does in 9:15 and 9:28.

In other words, Hebrews ascribes the same soteriological ends to Jesus' death and his subsequent heavenly self-offering. This is significant because it implies more than merely that Jesus' death and heavenly self-offering are distinct elements in the unified fabric of Jesus' saving mission. Hebrews has a variety of ways of relating different moments in that mission. For instance, Jesus' incarnation itself, as a kind of foundational prerequisite, is ordered to Jesus' self-offering in heaven (10:5–14; Section 3.2). Further, Hebrews erects a series of prerequisites to Jesus' appointment to high priesthood and subsequent self-offering. Jesus not only had to become incarnate but had to suffer, triumph over temptation, die, and rise perfected by indestructible life (Section 2.2). Each of these was necessary for his appointment to high priesthood; none by itself secured or instantaneously attained it. Further, some of the soteriological payoff of these prerequisites lands elsewhere than Jesus' offering. Because Jesus was faithful in temptation, he is now a merciful and faithful high priest who is able to help those who are tempted (2:17–18; cf. 4:15). Jesus' past endurance underwrites his present intercession. Hence it is all the more striking that, in at least one key passage (10:26–27), Hebrews ascribes to Jesus' sacrifice what it elsewhere ascribes to his death. Here we are dealing not merely with a purpose that later came to fruition, or prerequisites for a status later obtained, but rather the ascription of efficient causality. What did Jesus' death do? Deliver people from sin's judicial consequences. What did Jesus' sacrificial offering of himself in heaven do? Deliver people from sin's judicial consequences.

The identity of result ascribed directly to distinct acts is conspicuous. It attests something more than coordination toward a common goal. Hence I take 10:26–27 also to confirm that Jesus' death is not merely presupposed in his heavenly self-offering but is included in it. Hebrews 10:26–27 attests that, while Jesus' death and the offering of his sacrifice are formally distinct events, the former is materially integral to the latter. How is Jesus' death included in his sacrifice? It is what he offers.

5.5 Conclusion

This chapter has connected thematic dots, as it were, between Christ's death and the substance of his heavenly self-offering. I have argued the threefold thesis that (1) in a variety of cultic contexts, Hebrews conceptually equates blood with death, including using "blood" as a metonym for Jesus' death (Section 5.2); (2) "blood" is one term for what Jesus offers in heaven, though this does not imply a physical act of sprinkling (Section 5.3); (3) therefore Jesus' death, considered as a soteriological achievement, is what he offers in heaven (Section 5.4). Jesus' death on the cross is not when and where he offers himself, but it is what he offers. When Jesus offers his blood in heaven, he gives to God the life he gave in death for his people's forgiveness.

As Section 6.2 will explore further, this chapter performs something of a reversal compared with my position on the "formal question" addressed in Part I and the range of scholarly responses to it. Regarding that question, I agree with Moffitt and other proponents of View 5 that Jesus offers himself in heaven, after his resurrection. Hence my answer to that question is diametrically opposed to that of View 1, which holds that Jesus' self-offering coincides exclusively with his death. However, on the material question of how Christ's death factors into his heavenly offering, my position differs sharply from that of Moffitt and aligns with many proponents of View 1, who take "blood" as a metonym for Christ's death.

Compared with the poles of opinion represented by Moffitt on the one hand and View 1 on the other, this chapter has offered a fuller account of the Levitical language and concepts Hebrews draws on to ascribe decisive soteriological significance to Christ's death as sacrificial victim. For instance, the author treats covenant-inaugural blood sprinkling as ritually enacting the threatened death of the covenant partner (9:18). Hebrews 9:22b highlights the necessity of sacrificial slaughter for forgiveness, deploying the logic of life-for-life exchange evident in Lev 17:11. And, drawing on language from Isa 53:12 that is itself drawn from the Levitical cult, Heb 9:28 asserts that, in being offered in death as the sacrificial victim, Christ endured the judicial consequences of others' sins. All of these conceptualities not only characterize Christ's death as a saving event; more specifically they provide theological rationales for his slaughter as victim. Much recent scholarship on Hebrews has rightly drawn on Levitical sacrifice to highlight the presence in Hebrews of an unfolding sacrificial script. In Part I, I offered just such an argument. But in this chapter I have also argued that Hebrews draws on Levitical sacrifice precisely in order to ascribe decisive atoning significance to Christ's death. Furthermore, by using "blood" as a metonym for Christ's death and assigning blood the role of sacrificial material offered in heaven, the author presents the saving significance of Jesus' death as that which he offers to God in heaven. Not only is Jesus' death a locus of atonement in its own right; it is the content of his heavenly offering.

6

CONCLUSION

6.1 Summing Up

In this final chapter I summarize the argument of the thesis, conclude both the narrow and the broad conversations, engage the question of coherence that we raised in Section 1.3, and offer suggestions regarding the place of Hebrews' sacrificial theology in the New Testament and its roots in earlier Christian tradition. First, to summarize. This thesis has addressed two related questions about Jesus' self-offering in Hebrews. First, when and where did it take place? Second, what relation does Jesus' death play in his self-offering? Before beginning the argument, in Chapter 1 we surveyed five answers to the first question that are evident in recent literature, and isolated the interpretive decisions that distinguish each from the others. To frame these decisions by the questions they answer: Does Jesus enter the heavenly sanctuary having already offered himself on the cross, or in order to offer himself there? Does Jesus' "entry" into heaven metaphorically describe the cross? Was Jesus spiritually translated to heaven or did he ascend there bodily after his resurrection?

In Part I, I answered each of these questions via exegesis of key statements in Heb 8–10, as well as other, briefer statements that figure the Christ-event in cultic terms. Hebrews presents Jesus as a high priest who carries out his ministry in the heavenly sanctuary (8:1–5), having been appointed high priest following his resurrection (7:16; cf. 5:9; 8:4). Like the Levitical high priest, Jesus entered the Holy of Holies in order to offer something there (9:7; 9:24–25). Unlike the Levitical high priest, the sanctuary Jesus entered was in heaven, and he offered himself (9:11–14, 23–26). When Hebrews reports Jesus' speech at the incarnation, "A body you have prepared for me" (10:5), it figures Christ's self-offering in heaven as a goal of his incarnation (10:5–14). Christ assumed a body prepared by God in order to offer that body to God in heaven, as living proof of the incarnate obedience that culminated in his death.

In Part II, I engaged the material question that inevitably follows my answer to the formal one: If Christ offered himself in heaven, what did his death accomplish, and how does it relate to his heavenly offering? Chapter 4 argued that in 2:9, 2:14–15, and 9:15–17 Hebrews ascribes to Jesus' death itself decisive, objective soteriological significance. In 2:9 Jesus tastes death for everyone, and his death is imbued with universal saving power precisely by his exaltation to "glory and honor," cosmic lordship (cf. 1:2, 3, 13; 8:1; 10:12–13; 12:2). In 2:14–15 Jesus' death destroys the devil's power of death and delivers people from his bondage. In 9:15–17 Jesus' death inaugurates the new covenant by bearing the curse of the old. By dying for his people Jesus bore the law's retributive sanctions that still hung over them. In Chapter 5, I argued that, via the role it ascribes to blood in Jesus' heavenly self-offering, Hebrews figures Jesus' death as sacrificial material he offers in heaven. While Jesus' death is not where and when he offers himself, it is what he offers.

In Chapter 4, we saw that Hebrews ascribes soteriological significance to Jesus' death from within a variety of conceptual networks, each of which has close parallels elsewhere in the New Testament. In Chapter 5, we saw that some of these conceptual resources contribute to how Hebrews figures Jesus' death within its predominant Levitical framework. That is to say, Hebrews not only reads the Christ-event in light of the Levitical cult, it also reads the cult in light of Christ. Hebrews sees in Jesus' death the eschatological fulfillment of the Levitical maxim that without bloodshed there is no forgiveness (9:22b). Hebrews, as it were, already knows that Jesus died for others (2:9), that his death enacted penal sanctions due to others (9:15). What fewer scholars – to my knowledge, none who affirm a heavenly offering – have noted is that this life-for-life exchange is also integral, even crucial, to Hebrews' exposition of Christ's high-priestly self-offering in heaven. As victim, Christ gives his life in death; as resurrected high priest, Christ gives that life-given-in-death to God.

Hence I materially unite what I formally distinguish. How can Jesus' death in any sense achieve "atonement" if he was not appointed high priest until after his resurrection, and he only offered himself in heaven? First, in a variety of senses shared with other New Testament texts, Hebrews affirms that Jesus' death enacted his people's deliverance from death. Second, more specifically, for

Hebrews Jesus is not just high priest but also sacrificial victim. And Hebrews' interest in Jesus' slaughter as victim is not merely procedural but theological. Drawing on the logic of life-for-life exchange in Lev 17:11, Hebrews figures Jesus' sacrificial death as a life given for life owed. And, via the "currency" of blood, this life given on the cross is what Jesus gives to God in heaven.

6.2 Concluding Both Conversations

The argument of Chapter 5 supports and completes the central claim of the thesis: Jesus' death is not where and when he offers himself, but it is what he offers. Hence, in this section I conclude both the broader and narrower conversations that structure the thesis by engaging representatives of both in light of Chapter 5. First, taking View 1 as the purest version of the view that Christ's sacrifice begins and ends on the cross, I will explore my position's material convergence with theirs, despite the formal divergence. Then, to conclude the narrow conversation, I will compare my view of the relationship of Christ's death to his self-offering with those of Moffitt and Gäbel.

We begin with View 1. Consider, for instance, William Lane's comments on "through his own blood" in 9:12: "The statement that Christ approached God by means of his own blood has specific reference to his death on the cross, which is the sacrifice of the new covenant corresponding to the animal sacrifices prescribed under the old covenant."[1] Similarly, Gareth Cockerill comments, "His shed 'blood' is his willing offering of his life through death on the cross. It was by means of this self-offering alone that he entered the heavenly presence of God."[2] Both scholars argue that Christ's self-offering begins and ends on the cross, and that "blood" is shorthand for this death-as-sacrifice. We took issue with this claim in Part I. Christ does not enter the heavenly sanctuary after having already offered himself on the cross, but in order to offer himself there. However, as argued in Chapter 5, I affirm the judgment that "blood" in Hebrews is often a metonym for death, specifically Jesus' death as sacrificial victim. So, while my stance on where and when Christ offers himself diverges from that of View 1 proponents, my take on the significance of blood has strong affinities with theirs. "Blood" does signify Christ's life-given-in-death. In the deliberately compressed

---

[1] Lane 1991:2.238.   [2] Cockerill 2012:393–94.

perspective of 9:12, it is by means of this death that Jesus enters the heavenly sanctuary.[3] Since Jesus was both high priest and victim, he needed to undergo sin's judicial consequences on his people's behalf before opening God's presence to them. He had to exchange his life for theirs, in death, in order to make for them a new and living way to God through his blood (10:19). Proponents of View 1 deny that Jesus in any sense "offered" his blood in heaven. Against this I contend that Hebrews' use of "blood" indicates that Jesus offered to God in heaven what his death on earth achieved. So I share with View 1 the judgments that "blood" is a metonym for Jesus' death and that, within Hebrews' sacrificial framework, Jesus' death itself has decisive – though not, on my view, exclusive – atoning significance. Hence emerges a material agreement within a formal disagreement.

By contrast, the relation of my position to the perspective of Moffitt is the opposite: Despite the considerable formal agreement, here we find a material disagreement. While I agree with Moffitt that Jesus offers himself in heaven, I interpret Jesus' "blood" differently than he does, and so accord a weightier role to Jesus' death itself *within Hebrews' cultic framework*. To clarify the causes of this disagreement, I here suggest five methodological and material differences in our approaches that contribute to our differing conclusions. Naturally, these either articulate or imply criticisms of Moffitt's stances.

First, Moffitt sometimes reasons directly from (modern readings of) Levitical sacrifice to what is the case in Hebrews.[4] It is possible, of course, that Hebrews' account of cleansing, blood, and so on aligns with the Levitical cult in precisely the ways Moffitt argues. But Moffitt's argument from "fit" sometimes hovers above the details of Hebrews, proceeding strictly by inference and big-picture correlation. By contrast, I have attempted to discern some of the

---

[3] That is, the instrumental significance of "blood" as death does not imply that Christ entered heaven at the moment of his death. Instead, the sacrificial framework focuses on the necessity of Christ's death as victim before his entrance into the inner sanctum to offer himself there.

[4] For instance, Moffitt frequently observes something about the logic of Levitical sacrifice and then suggests that what we see in Hebrews "accords with" or "makes good sense in view of" Leviticus. See, e.g., Moffitt 2011:257 ("accords with"; "aligns well with"), 269 ("in keeping with"), 270 ("makes good sense in view of"), and 275 ("correlates well with"). I mention "modern readings of" Levitical sacrifice because Moffitt draws directly on recent scholarly accounts of Levitical sacrifice, and engages somewhat briefly with Levitical texts themselves.

significance Hebrews ascribes to blood by tracing key seams in its central argument. More broadly, instead of reasoning directly from Levitical sacrifice to Hebrews, I have sought first to gauge Hebrews' specific interests in Levitical sacrifice; then to read the Levitical texts themselves, especially in Greek; then, finally, to consider how Hebrews appropriates Levitical paradigms.

Second, Moffitt's construal of the role of blood in Hebrews depends on a conception of purity and impurity as systematically opposing life and death; I suggest that this conception fits neither Leviticus nor Hebrews as well as Moffitt asserts. For instance, Moffitt approvingly cites Milgrom's comments that various sources of impurity have death as their "common denominator," and that "holiness stands for life."[5] Moffitt elaborates, "Within such a complex, the presentation and manipulation of blood/life before God, which is the primary means of rendering the sancta pure, participate in the battle between life and death."[6] This understanding of impurity is decisive for what Moffitt sees blood as symbolizing, and not symbolizing, in Hebrews. For instance, supporting his overall thesis that heaven is where Jesus offers himself, Moffitt writes:

> [T]his hypothesis also aligns with the emphasis in Leviticus on the place of the presentation and manipulation of blood/life on Yom Kippur (and all the other blood offerings, for that matter) and the power that blood/life has to obtain redemption and make purification. It seems highly unlikely that the author of Hebrews thinks that Jesus effected purification by bringing his death into God's presence.[7]

For Moffitt, as we have seen, insofar as Jesus' blood is a symbol in Hebrews, it does not symbolize death, but rather "Jesus' life/living presence appearing in the presence of God."[8] However, this analysis of purity and impurity as a systematic opposition of life and death has been convincingly criticized in recent literature.[9] While this view

---

[5] Ibid., 266, citing Milgrom 1991:46.   [6] Moffitt 2011:267.   [7] Ibid., 275.
[8] Ibid., 273.
[9] For influential recent arguments for understanding purity and impurity in terms of a life/death opposition, see Milgrom 1989; cf. Milgrom 1991:704–42. For critiques see, e.g., Houston 2003:147–50; Lemos 2013:268–72; Nihan 2013:326–29. For a series of studies that offer a more coherent, comprehensive account of the main types of impurity in Levitical legislation, using "disgust" as the common thread, see Kazen 2008; Kazen 2011:81–84, 93; Kazen 2014. While I would not endorse Kazen's views *tout court*, his overall case has much to commend it.

appeals primarily to Lev 12–15, it does not adequately account for all the purity laws therein. For instance, attempts to describe the defiling effects of birth and sexual intercourse in terms of "death" or "loss of life" are strained and unpersuasive.[10] And if the loss of blood is defiling because by it "life" is lost, it is not clear why only some kinds of blood loss are contaminating, and why some less severe losses of blood contaminate while more severe ones do not.[11] Levitical purity is more complex than a life/death binary allows, and the life/death binary does not adequately explain what it claims to. Thus Moffitt's a priori equation between death and impurity – such that it is "highly unlikely" that Hebrews conceives of Jesus bringing his death into God's presence – does not hold.[12]

Third, on a related note, Moffitt's construal of blood in Hebrews as the power or force of life is, at best, not as prominent in Hebrews as he takes it to be. For instance,

> The preceding discussion on the role and power of blood, particularly insofar as blood's life force can overcome the impurifying force of death, suggests that blood offering, especially that of the חטאת, has to do with enabling the divine presence and the human being to come together in close proximity because it deals with the interrelated problems of sin, impurity, and mortality.[13]

While I affirm much of this account, I question whether Hebrews ever treats blood as a "life force." I have argued that Hebrews explicitly treats sacrificial blood as enacting a life-for-life exchange, and also as a cleansing agent. However, I find no evidence in Hebrews that blood's ability to purify renders it the victorious force in a power struggle between life and death.[14]

---

[10] Nihan 2013:328.

[11] So Lemos 2013:271–72, who cites Whitekettle 1996:377, "Note that the Levitical interest in bleeding was limited to vaginal discharges. Numerous situations in which there is potentially fatal bleeding, such as wounds or accidents in the workplace, are not the subject of legislative strictures. If there is no concern with an 'aura of death' in many situations in which it would seem appropriate (e.g., a woodchopper whose hand has been cut off), it could not have been a concern in more inappropriate situations (N.B., no woman has ever menstruated to death)."

[12] Compare the criticism of Moret 2016:303, "La proposition de Moffitt trouve en fait bien peu de support dans L'Épître même, et a besoin de l'identification entre impureté et mortalité proposée par Milgrom pour tenir."

[13] Moffitt 2011:267.

[14] Compare Feder 2011:205, who argues against the understanding of blood as "life-force" in Lev 17:11, "There is no assertion whatsoever that the blood possesses

Fourth, as Jean-René Moret argues, Moffitt's view that Christ's blood represents his "living presence" – that is, his resurrection life – stretches "la métaphore" beyond what it can bear. Moret says that on Moffit's view, "Jesus would offer a blood made available by his death, the quality of which would have changed after the resurrection to become the expression of his resurrected life."[15] If Jesus' death makes his "blood" available for subsequent presentation, then that "blood" has to do with his earthly existence that terminated in death, not his subsequent glorified life.

Fifth and finally, Moffitt sets Christ's death at a certain distance from the enacting of the new covenant and its concomitant soteriological effects. Again, commenting on 9:15, Moffitt writes, "I suggest, though, that it is not necessary to assume that death itself – presumably of Jesus – is identified here as the agent that effects the redemption."[16] Because Moffitt sees "this larger understanding of how sacrifice works" at play even in the discussion of new covenant inauguration in 9:15, "[the author] is not conflating Jesus' death and the atonement."[17] Even when discussing the role of Jesus' death in inaugurating the new covenant, Moffitt maintains that "a sacrificial death is not the point at which atonement is obtained."[18] This, it

some kind of rejuvenating and vitalizing power or that it represents symbolically the concept of 'life.'"

[15] Moret 2016:303, "Jésus offrirait un sang rendu disponible par sa mort, dont la qualité aurait changé suite à la résurrection pour devenir l'expression de sa vie ressuscitée." In addition to statements already cited, compare Moffitt 2016b:276, "[I]t is his resurrection life, his now indestructible human life, that has the power to do what the life of animals could not – provide ultimate atonement."

[16] Moffitt 2011:290.   [17] Ibid.

[18] Ibid., 292. In his response to Moret's criticisms, Moffitt 2016c:308–9 n. 2 maintains, "I am not aware of any place where I claim that Jesus' death is 'only' or 'merely' anything, let alone 'only' preparation for offering his sacrifice. In fact, I speak at length about Jesus' death as, among other things, the event that inaugurates the new covenant. An inaugurating sacrifice, however, functions differently from the regular sacrifices and from those on Yom Kippur. The latter serve to maintain, not inaugurate, the covenant relationship. Remarkably, the Levitical logic that requires one to first inaugurate the Mosaic covenant and tabernacle before offering the sacrifices that maintain the covenant coheres with the notion that Jesus first died to inaugurate the new covenant and then ascended to offer the Yom Kippur sacrifice and intercession that maintains it." It is difficult for me to see how this statement represents continuity with, rather than a substantive change from, the statements in Moffitt's 2011 monograph that I have cited here. It is not clear to me that in his 2011 monograph Moffitt argues that Jesus' death is "the event that inaugurates the new covenant," since he explicitly denies that Jesus' death itself effects redemption, distinguishes "the initiating event" from the final result (290), and assimilates covenant inauguration to Yom Kippur. In his 2016 statements Moffitt seems to presuppose that covenant inauguration and Yom Kippur bring distinct, complementary conceptual frameworks to bear

seems to me, wrongly excludes the distinct conceptual contribution that new covenant inauguration makes to Hebrews' cultic construal of the Christ-event. It is certainly true that Christ's saving acts correspond in some sense to the inaugural blood sprinklings at Sinai (9:18–22; cf. 9:23). Yet in 9:15–17 the author goes out of his way to underscore emphatically the significance of Christ's death per se for the inauguration of the new covenant. In 9:15, it is precisely Christ's death that effects redemption, as efficient cause and not merely instrumental precursor; our "larger understanding of sacrifice" must accommodate rather than efface this key assertion. In other words, we should not assimilate – and thereby reduce – new covenant inauguration to the model of Yom Kippur. Instead, given how tightly interwoven are Hebrews' appropriations of covenant inauguration and Yom Kippur, we should allow Hebrews' exposition of Christ's death in the former to open up possibilities for how it functions in the latter.

Finally, we turn to the views of Gäbel. As noted briefly in Section 5.2, Gäbel argues, as do I, that by figuring Christ's "blood" as the material he offers in heaven, Hebrews portrays Christ's heavenly offering as transferring the outcome of his earthly career into the heavenly realm. Sometimes Gäbel speaks of blood as signifying Christ's life given in death, with which I concur.[19] However, sometimes Gäbel attaches blood's symbolic significance to Christ's earthly existence as a whole – which, of course, culminates in his self-giving death.[20] While I agree that the character of Christ's death as willing self-giving is crucial to the quality of his heavenly offering, I have argued that the conceptual significance of Christ's blood in Hebrews focuses on his life as given up in death – that is, as a medium of life-for-life exchange. So far as I can discern, this note of exchange is absent from Gäbel's account. Therefore, in contrast to Gäbel, I argue that the significance of Jesus' blood in Hebrews is not so much "his whole life lived" as "his life given in death."

This is related to another difference between my account and that of Gäbel, namely that Gäbel sees Hebrews as characterizing Christ's death, along with his whole earthly life, as a profane, non-cultic event.[21] For instance, Gäbel explicitly denies that Christ's death

---

in Hebrews' construal of the Christ-event, whereas in his 2011 work Moffitt emphatically subsumes the former under the latter.
[19] Gäbel 2006:279, 290, 315.   [20] Ibid., 213, 464.
[21] Ibid., 131, 172, 185–202, 253, 426, 461, 463.

corresponds to the ritual slaughter of the animal in Levitical sacrifice: "The death of Christ on earth, however, is not mentioned in the typology of 9:11ff., nor is the slaughter of the sacrificial animals as part of the Yom Kippur ritual (which would typologically correspond to Christ's death) ever mentioned by Hebrews."[22] This denial over-systematizes Hebrews' evidence and fails to reckon with the many deliberate parallels Hebrews frames between Christ's death and that of the sacrificial victim (9:11–12, 13–14, 25–26). Christ's death is a cultic act that corresponds to the slaughter of the sacrificial victim. Hebrews' cultic framework interprets not only Christ's exaltation, but the death that exaltation transfigures.

Finally, in keeping with the way Gäbel removes Christ's death from the sacrificial process, Gäbel's reading of 9:15–17 also renders Christ's death more conceptually remote from his offering than does my account. Gäbel calls 9:15–17 a "legal metaphorical insertion" indicating a considerable conceptual gap between the juridical and, as he sees it, testamentary framework of these verses and the cultic world of the rest of Heb 9.[23] In contrast to Gäbel, I have argued that Hebrews employs the logic of life-for-life exchange as a common conceptual thread that unites Jesus' covenant-inaugurating death, the covenant-inaugurating sacrifices at Sinai, and the sacrificial significance of Jesus' blood.

So, with reference to Gäbel's overall construal of the role of Christ's death in his heavenly offering, I have sought to specify and extend aspects of his position while revising others. I have sought to elaborate Gäbel's contention that "blood" is the means by which Christ offers in heaven, and so brings to effective fruition, the outcome of his saving acts on earth. However, I have specified the conceptual referent of "blood" as Jesus' life given in death as a life-for-life exchange. And I have argued that rather than being a profane event that is later transferred into the sacred realm, Jesus' death is aligned with the slaughter of the animal and therefore imbued from the outset with cultic significance. Finally, in view of the conceptual threads with which Hebrews unites covenant inauguration and the cultic significance of blood, I have argued that Jesus'

---

[22] Ibid., 286, "Das Sterben Christi auf Erden wird in der Typologie 9,11f jedoch gar nicht erwähnt, ebensowenig wie die Schlachtung der Opfertiere als Teil des Jom Kippur-Rituals (der Christi Sterben typologisch entsprechen würde) von Hebr je erwähnt wird."

[23] Ibid., 406 ("rechtsmetaphorischen Einschub").

death as a life-for-life exchange is fundamental to Hebrews' construal of how Christ's death both inaugurates the new covenant and constitutes the substance of his heavenly offering.

6.3 The Question of Coherence

This synopsis leads naturally to the question of coherence that we raised in Chapter 1. The first kind of inconsistency some scholars find in Hebrews' sacrificial theology is a narrative or sequential one. Such scholars assert that Hebrews offers no consistent answer to the question of when and where Jesus offers himself, because some passages locate that offering on earth and others in heaven.[24] However, we have argued that all but one of the passages taken to locate Christ's self-offering on the cross do not support this conclusion. Regarding the one, 9:28, we argued that this verse does indeed assert that Christ "was offered" on the cross, but this role as victim should not be conflated with Christ's subsequent appointment to high priesthood and presentation of his offering. Instead, Jesus' death as victim gives him something to offer (cf. 8:3).

A second kind of inconsistency some find in Hebrews' sacrificial theology is conceptual. For instance, in Section 5.2 we considered Christian Eberhart's comment about the transition between 9:17 and 9:18: "Here conceptual horizons are interconnected that are actually incongruent."[25] By contrast, I have argued that Hebrews discerns a logic of life-for-life exchange common to both the covenant-inaugurating sacrifices at Sinai and Christ's covenant-inaugurating death. What Sinai pictured, the cross performed. What the animals threatened would fall on the Israelites fell on Christ. For Hebrews, life-for-life exchange is integral to both covenant inauguration and the redemptive execution of covenant sanctions on the cross.

Further, we saw in Section 1.3 that for Eberhart, Hebrews' ascription to Jesus of the roles of both high priest and victim "remains ... partly contradictory"[26] However, if we allow that Hebrews invokes the category of sacrificial victim in a way that temporally precedes Christ's appointment to high priesthood, then I do not see how its

---

[24] Schenck 2003:81; Schenck 2007:8, 188; Schenck 2016; Löhr 2005:471–72; Eberhart 2013:152.
[25] Eberhart 2013:150, "Hier werden Vorstellungshorizonte miteinander verbunden, die eigentlich inkongruent sind."
[26] Ibid., 143, "... bleibt ... teilweise in sich widersprüchlich."

deployment of these two sacrificial figures, victim and priest, is necessarily contradictory. Certainly Hebrews' combining these two roles into one goes beyond anything the Levitical cult envisioned. But Hebrews constructs this combination both in light of Christ and to illumine Christ. Hebrews says something the cult never said because the cult never needed to say it. Only Christ is both high priest and victim; only Christ offered not another but himself.

6.4   Place and Roots

This much I have attempted to demonstrate conclusively. I now close with, first, a reflection on the place of Hebrews' sacrificial theology in the New Testament, and, second, a more tentative suggestion regarding its roots in the Old Testament and earlier Christian teaching. First, to locate Hebrews in relation to perhaps its nearest conceptual neighbor, my argument regarding Hebrews' sacrificial theology has discovered both difference from Paul and convergence with Paul. As is frequently noted, compared with Paul's sparse use of sacrificial terminology to interpret the saving work of Christ, Hebrews' detailed elaboration of Christ's priestly self-offering represents a substantive and original theological contribution. Further, on the reading offered in Part I, Hebrews has more to say about the soteriological impact of Jesus' ascension than does Paul. Certainly, Paul places Christ's present heavenly intercession at the climax of his crescendo of consolation in Rom 8:33–34. But in its treatment of Christ's singular, sufficient saving act, Hebrews zooms in and pauses on the moment just before Christ's session in a way that neither Paul nor any other New Testament author does. While it is dangerous to speculate, I suspect this is one reason, though by no means a sufficient one, for the popularity of View 1. For Paul, the death Christ died, he died to sin "once for all" (Rom 6:10). If we read from Paul to Hebrews, it is easy to assume that, where Hebrews does not explicitly specify the location of Christ's once-for-all offering, it must be the cross. Yet, while Hebrews in no way undercuts the singularity of Christ's death (cf. 9:26), or downplays its saving efficacy, the event it labels "once for all," and to which it devotes the most sustained attention, is the moment when Christ entered the Holy of Holies in heaven. Hence, in Part I, I have carved out a theological profile of Hebrews that differs from, though is by no means incompatible with, Paul's intense focus on the cross.

However, my argument that Christ's death is what he offers represents not only a material unity within this formal distinction, but also a material convergence with Paul. If Hebrews does indeed treat Jesus' death as a life-for-life exchange, and if Jesus offers that death to God in heaven, then even when Hebrews does not focus on Jesus' death it still focuses on Jesus' death. If Jesus' death is the substance of his heavenly offering, then Hebrews' unique account of Christ's offering does not shift attention away from Christ's death so much as elaborate its significance in a new way. Further, many of the conceptual resources Hebrews uses to figure Christ's death as integral to his heavenly offering – such as covenant sanction and life-for-life exchange – overlap extensively with Paul's theology of the cross. I say this not at all to diminish the uniqueness of Hebrews' cultic construal of the Christ-event, especially its heavenly telos. Instead, I suggest that in order to evaluate the contribution of Hebrews' sacrificial theology to the New Testament as a whole, we need to consider not just the story it tells but the significance it ascribes to each stage, and how it relates those stages to each other.

Second, I offer a tentative suggestion regarding the tradition-historical roots of Hebrews' unique cultic construal of the Christ-event. Psalm 110:1 and 4 are, of course, crucial for Hebrews' theology.[27] The former is the Old Testament passage cited most frequently in the New, a cornerstone of earliest Christian preaching. And, to put it simplistically, the author of Hebrews simply kept reading.[28] But "simply" says too much. The entire theology of Hebrews is not simply "there" in Ps 110:4, waiting to spring to life. Instead, the author of Hebrews drew on an extensive web of Old Testament passages – among which Lev 16, though only alluded to, is particularly prominent – refracted through early Christian convictions about the person and work of Christ. Yet when it comes to the *novum* of a priest who offers himself, can we say anything more about the sources of Hebrews' sacrificial theology?

Here, in closing, I want to suggest very tentatively that Isa 53 might play a more significant role in Hebrews than is often

---

[27] For instance, Compton 2015a:12 argues that Hebrews' theological argument "turns, in large part, on successive inferences drawn from Ps. 110.1 and 4."

[28] With more nuance than my deliberate caricature allows, Meier, for instance, writes, "In a sense, the whole theological achievement of the author rests on the fact that he alone among NT writers read 'theologically' beyond the first verse of Psalm 109 ... noticed the claim of v. 4, connected it with v. 1, and drew out the implications for Christology and soteriology" (1985a:184 n. 55).

recognized.[29] First, in Section 5.4 we saw that "sin-bearing" in Isa 53:11–12 is a distinctly Levitical idiom. The servant's sin-bearing not only coheres with Levitical sin-bearing but derives from it. Like the high priest with the goat for Azazel on Yom Kippur, the Lord placed all the iniquities of his people onto the servant (Isa 53:6; cf. Lev 16:21–22). Like the high priest in holy attire, and the priests who consumed the sin offering, the servant bore the people's sins (Isa 53:11–12; cf. Exod 28:38; Lev 10:17).[30] Thus it is not merely that the servant bears others' sins, a notion only attested in Levitical (and Levitically influenced) material. In addition, the passage implies that the suffering servant's sin-bearing is an act of priestly self-sacrifice. This is the only place in Israel's scripture where such a notion can be found.

On this reading the parallels between the servant's work and that of Christ in Hebrews are more extensive than is commonly noted. Not only do both bear the sins of others, but both give their lives in sacrificial slaughter. Hence, the evocation of Isa 53:12 LXX in Heb 9:28 rings with deep thematic resonance. Isaiah's servant gave his life in death as an offering; so also Christ was offered as sacrificial victim in his death. The priestly role of Isaiah's suffering servant is implicit, deriving solely from his act of offering himself to bear others' sins. By contrast, Jesus' role as high priest is a matter of explicit scriptural testimony and detailed narrative elaboration. This helps account for some of the differences between, on the one hand, the servant's self-offering in death, and, on the other, the contrast I have argued for in Hebrews between Jesus' being offered in death and offering himself

---

[29] Though dated and not compelling in detail, the work of Schaefer 1968 remains to my knowledge the most thorough discussion of this question. In contrast to my position, Schafer argues that Heb 9:28 alludes not to Isa 53:12 but to the clichéd form it presumably took in the "oral catechesis of the Church" (378). Nevertheless Schaefer argues, "Servant Christology, then, provides the point of contact between the quite singular teaching of Heb on the priesthood of Christ and the Apostolic *kerygma*" (383). Further, "It is not just a matter of priestly Christology being a major chord and servant Christology a minor one. Rather the author has reinterpreted servant Christology in terms of priestly Christology. The assumption of the former into the latter is complete" (384). Though overstated, I think there is more merit in Schaefer's former observation than in the latter. Regarding the latter, I will argue above that it is not that Hebrews has reinterpreted Isaiah's servant in priestly terms, but that Isaiah's servant provided Hebrews with priestly concepts that proved crucial for its cultic construal of Christ's saving act.

[30] Further, the Hebrew of Isa 53:10 arguably asserts that the servant gives his life as a "guilt offering," though the Greek connects "life" (ψυχή) with the following phrase and renders its possessors plural (ὑμῶν).

subsequently in heaven. Nevertheless, if we are looking for a scriptural source for the idea of a priest offering himself as a sacrifice, we have one in Isa 53.

Further, the abundance of thematic links between Heb 9 and the Last Supper narratives raises the possibility that the author was familiar with these traditions.[31] And it is arguable that in these words Jesus presented himself as the priestly suffering servant who offered himself as a sacrifice to bear the sins of many.[32] If these two premises are granted, then it is possible that the author of Hebrews was exposed to the idea of Jesus as the priest who offers himself not (or not only) from the text of Isa 53, but from the way the Last Supper traditions render Jesus as the suffering servant of Isa 53. In other words, Jesus as self-offering priest was arguably already an element of a key early Christian tradition with which our author was likely familiar. Given the close lexical parallels of Isa 53:12 with Heb 9:28, our author likely drew on firsthand knowledge of the passage. So, while the Last Supper traditions may have introduced the idea of a self-sacrificing priest to our author, he may well have deepened it through scriptural study. In any case, I offer here not a comprehensive explanation but a modest suggestion. How might we account for the flame of Hebrews' sacrificial theology? My proposal: as necessary as the kindling of Ps 110:4 was the spark of Isa 53.

---

[31] For these links see Section 4.4.
[32] For a recent argument in this direction see Pitre 2015:100–4, 115–17.

BIBLIOGRAPHY

Alexander, Philip. 2006. *Mystical Texts. CQS 7*. London: T&T Clark.
Allen, David L. 2010. *Hebrews*. NAC 35. Nashville: B&H.
Allen, David M. 2008. *Deuteronomy and Exhortation in Hebrews: A Study in Narrative Re-Presentation*. WUNT II/238. Tübingen: Mohr Siebeck.
Anderson, David R. 2001. *The King-Priest of Psalm 110 in Hebrews*. Studies in Biblical Literature 21. New York: Peter Lang.
Anderson, Gary A. 2000. "The Exaltation of Adam and the Fall of Satan." In *Literature on Adam and Eve: Collected Essays*, edited by Gary A. Anderson, Michael Stone, and Johannes Tromp, 83–110. SVTP 15. Leiden: Brill.
Andriessen, Paul. 1971. "Das grössere und vollkommenere Zelt (Hebr 9,11)." *BZ* 15: 76–92.
——— 1976. "La teneur Judéo-Chrétienne de He I 6 et II 14B–III 2." *NovT* 18: 293–313.
Asumang, Annang. 2008. *Unlocking the Book of Hebrews: A Spatial Analysis of the Epistle to the Hebrews*. Eugene, OR: Wipf & Stock.
Attridge, Harold W. 1989. *Hebrews: A Commentary on the Epistle to the Hebrews*. Hermeneia, MN: Fortress Press.
Backhaus, Knut. 2009a. *Der Hebräerbrief*. RNT. Regensburg: Friedrich Pustet.
——— 2009b. "Zwei harte Knoten: Todes- und Gerichtsangst im Hebräerbrief." *NTS* 55: 198–217.
Barnard, Jody A. 2012. *The Mysticism of Hebrews: Exploring the Role of Jewish Apocalyptic Mysticism in the Epistle to the Hebrews*. WUNT II/331. Tübingen: Mohr Siebeck.
——— 2013. "Ronald Williamson and the Background of Hebrews." *ExpTim* 124: 469–79.
Barrett, C. K. 1956. "The Eschatology of the Epistle to the Hebrews." In *The Background of the New Testament and its Eschatology*, edited by W. D. Davies and D. Daube, 363–93. Cambridge: Cambridge University Press.
Barth, Gerhard. 1992. *Der Tod Jesu Christi im Verständnis des Neuen Testaments*. Neukirchen-Vluyn: Neukirchener.
Bates, Matthew W. 2015. *The Birth of the Trinity: Jesus, God, and Spirit in New Testament and Early Christian Interpretations of the Old Testament*. Oxford: Oxford University Press.
Bauckham, Richard. 2004. "Monotheism and Christology in Hebrews 1." In *Early Jewish and Christian Monotheism*, edited by Loren T.

Stuckenbruck and Wendy E. S. North, 167–85. JSNTSup 263. London: T&T Clark.
2009. "The Divinity of Jesus Christ in the Epistle to the Hebrews." In *The Epistle to the Hebrews and Christian Theology*, edited by Richard Bauckham, Daniel R. Driver, Trevor A. Hart, and Nathan MacDonald, 15–36. Grand Rapids, MI: Eerdmans.
Behm, Johannes. 1964. "αἱματεκχυσία." In *Theological Dictionary of the New Testament*, edited by Gerhard Kittel, translated by Geoffrey W. Bromiley, 1:176–77. Vol. 1. Grand Rapids, MI: Eerdmans.
Bénétreau, Samuel. 1989a. "La mort du Christ selon l'épître aux Hébreux." *Hokhma* 39: 25–47.
———. 1989b. *L'Épître aux Hébreux: tome 1*. Commentaire Évangélique de la Bible. Vaux-sur-Seine: Édifac.
———. 1990. *L'Épître aux Hébreux: tome 2*. Commentaire Évangélique de la Bible. Vaux-sur-Seine: Édifac.
Blenkinsopp, Joseph. 2016. "The Sacrificial Life and Death of the Servant (Isaiah 52:13–53:12)." *VT* 66: 1–14.
Blomberg, Craig L. 2008. "'But We See Jesus': The Relationship between the Son of Man in Hebrews 2.6 and 2.9 and the Implications for English Translations." In *A Cloud of Witnesses: The Theology of Hebrews in Its Ancient Contexts*, edited by Richard Bauckham, Daniel Driver, Trevor Hart, and Nathan MacDonald, 88–99. LNTS 387. London: T&T Clark.
Braun, Herbert. 1984. *An die Hebräer*. HNT 14. Tübingen: Mohr Siebeck.
Brooks, Walter Edward. 1970. "The Perpetuity of Christ's Sacrifice in the Epistle to the Hebrews." *JBL* 89: 205–14.
Bruce, F. F. 1990. *The Epistle to the Hebrews*. Rev. ed. NICNT. Grand Rapids, MI: Eerdmans.
Büchner, Dirk. 2009. "A Cultic Term (ἁμαρτία) in the Septuagint: Its Meaning and Use from the Third Century B.C.E. until the New Testament." *BIOSCS* 42: 1–17.
———. 2010a. "Some Reflections on Writing a Commentary on the Septuagint of Leviticus." In *"Translation Is Required": The Septuagint in Retrospect and Prospect*, edited by Robert J. V. Hiebert, 107–17. SCS 56. Atlanta, GA: Society of Biblical Literature.
———. 2010b. "'Εξιλάσασθαι: Appeasing God in the Septuagint Pentateuch." *JBL* 129: 237–60.
Caird, G. B. 1959. "The Exegetical Method of the Epistle to the Hebrews." *CJT* 5: 44–51.
———. 1984. "Son by Appointment." In *The New Testament Age: Essays in Honor of Bo Reicke*, edited by William C. Weinrich, 1:73–81. Vol. 1. Macon, GA: Mercer University Press.
Calaway, Jared C. 2013. *The Sabbath and the Sanctuary: Access to God in the Letter to the Hebrews and Its Priestly Context*. WUNT II/349. Tübingen: Mohr Siebeck.
Calvin, John. 1963. *The Epistle of Paul the Apostle to the Hebrews and the First and Second Epistles of St. Peter*, edited by David W. Torrance and Thomas F. Torrance. Translated by W. B. Johnston. Calvin's Commentaries 12. Grand Rapids, MI: Eerdmans.

Campbell, K. M. 1972. "Covenant or Testament? Heb. 9:16, 17 Reconsidered." *EvQ* 44: 107–11.
Caraski, Michael, ed. 2005. *The Commentators' Bible: Exodus.* Philadelphia: Jewish Publication Society.
Cervera i Vallis, Jordi. 2009. "Jesús, Gran Sacerdot i Víctima, en Hebreus: Una Teologia Judeocristiana de la Mediació i de l'Expiació." *RCT* 34: 477–502.
Chester, A. N. 1991. "Hebrews: The Final Sacrifice." In *Sacrifice and Redemption: Durham Essays in Theology*, edited by S. W. Sykes, 57–72. Cambridge: Cambridge University Press.
Chrysostom, John. 1994. *Homilies on the Gospel of Saint John and the Epistle to the Hebrews*, edited by Philip Schaff. Nicene and Post-Nicene Fathers 14. Peabody, MA: Hendrickson.
Church, Philip. 2017. *Hebrews and the Temple: Attitudes to the Temple in Second Temple Judaism and in Hebrews*. NovTSup 171. Leiden: Brill.
Cockerill, Gareth Lee. 2001. "Structure and Interpretation in Hebrews 8:1–10:18: A Symphony in Three Movements." *BBR* 11: 179–201.
——— 2012. *The Epistle to the Hebrews*. NICNT. Grand Rapids, MI: Eerdmans.
Cody, Aelred. 1960. *Heavenly Sanctuary and Liturgy in the Epistle to the Hebrews: The Achievement of Salvation in the Epistle's Perspectives*. St. Meinrad, IN: Grail.
Compton, Jared. 2015a. *Psalm 110 and the Logic of Hebrews*. LNTS 537. London: Bloomsbury T&T Clark.
——— 2015b. "Review of *Atonement and the Logic of Resurrection in the Epistle to the Hebrews*, by David M. Moffitt." *TJ* 36: 133–35.
Cortez, Felix H. 2006. "From the Holy to the Most Holy Place: The Period of Hebrews 9:6–10 and the Day of Atonement as a Metaphor of Transition." *JBL* 125: 527–47.
——— 2008. "The Anchor of the Soul That Enters within the Veil: The Ascension of the 'Son' in the Letter to the Hebrews." PhD diss., Andrews University.
Croy, N. Clayton. 1998. *Endurance in Suffering: Hebrews 12:1–13 in Its Rhetorical, Religious, and Philosophical Context*. SNTSMS 98. Cambridge: Cambridge University Press.
Dahl, N. A. 1951. "A New and Living Way: The Approach to God According to Hebrews 10:19–25." *Interpretation* 5: 401–12.
Daly, Robert J. 1978. *Christian Sacrifice: The Judaeo-Christian Background before Origen.* CUASCA 18. Washington, DC: Catholic University of America Press.
Davies, J. H. 1968. "The Heavenly Work of Christ in Hebrews." In *Studia Evangelica, Vol. IV: Papers Presented to the Third International Congress on New Testament Studies Held at Christ Church, Oxford, 1965. Part I: The New Testament Scriptures*, edited by F. L. Cross, 384–89. Berlin: Akademie-Verlag.
De Wet, Chris L. 2010. "The Messianic Interpretation of Psalm 8:4–6 in Hebrews 2:6–9. Part II." In *Psalms and Hebrews: Studies in Reception*, edited by Dirk J. Human and Gert J. Steyn, 113–25. LHB/OTS 527. London: T&T Clark.
Delitzsch, Franz. 1886. *Commentary on the Epistle to the Hebrews. Vol I.* Translated by Thomas L. Kingsbury. 3rd edn. Edinburgh: T&T Clark.

1887. *Commentary on the Epistle to the Hebrews. Vol II.* Translated by Thomas L. Kingsbury. 3rd edn. Edinburgh: T&T Clark.
Dennis, John. 2002. "The Function of the חטאת Sacrifice: An Evaluation of the View of Jacob Milgrom." *ETL* 78: 108–29.
deSilva, David A. 2000. *Perseverance in Gratitude: A Socio-Rhetorical Commentary on the Epistle "to the Hebrews."* Grand Rapids, MI: Eerdmans.
2006. "The Invention and Argumentative Function of Priestly Discourse in the Epistle to the Hebrews." *BBR* 16: 295–323.
2013. "How Greek Was the Author of 'Hebrews'?" In *Christian Origins and Greco-Roman Culture: Social and Literary Contexts for the New Testament*, edited by Stanley E. Porter and Andrew W. Pitts, 629–49. TENTS 9. Leiden: Brill.
Dion, Paul E. 1987. "Early Evidence for the Ritual Significance of the 'Base of the Altar': Around Deut 12:27." *JBL* 106: 487–90.
Dunn, James D. G. 1989. *Christology in the Making: A New Testament Inquiry into the Origins of the Doctrine of the Incarnation*. 2nd edn. London: SCM.
Dunnill, John. 1992. *Covenant and Sacrifice in the Letter to the Hebrews*. SNTSMS 75. Cambridge: Cambridge University Press.
Dyer, Bryan R. 2017. *Suffering in the Face of Death: The Epistle to the Hebrews and Its Context of Situation*. LNTS 568. London: Bloomsbury T&T Clark.
Easter, Matthew C. 2014. *Faith and the Faithfulness of Jesus in Hebrews*. SNTSMS 160. Cambridge: Cambridge University Press.
Eberhart, Christian A. 2005. "Characteristics of Sacrificial Metaphors in Hebrews." In *Hebrews: Contemporary Methods – New Insights*, edited by Gabriella Gelardini, 37–64. BIS 75. Leiden: Brill.
2013. *Kultmetaphorik und Christologie: Opfer- und Sühneterminologie im Neuen Testament*. WUNT 306. Tübingen: Mohr Siebeck.
Eisele, Wilfried. 2003. *Ein unerschütterliches Reich: Die mittelplatonische Umformung der Parusiegedankens im Hebräerbrief*. BZNW 116. Berlin: de Gruyter.
Elgvin, Torlief. 2011. "From the Earthly to the Heavenly Temple: Lines from the Bible and Qumran to Hebrews and Revelation." In *The World of Jesus and the Early Church: Identity and Interpretation in Early Communities of Faith*, edited by Craig A. Evans, 23–36. Peabody, MA: Hendrickson.
Elliger, Karl. 1966. *Leviticus*. HAT 4. Tübingen: J. C. B. Mohr (Paul Siebeck).
Ellingworth, Paul. 1993. *The Epistle to the Hebrews: A Commentary on the Greek Text*. NIGTC. Grand Rapids, MI: Eerdmans.
Ellis, E. Earle. 1978. *Prophecy and Hermeneutic in Early Christianity*. WUNT 18. Tübingen: J. C. B. Mohr (Paul Siebeck).
Epstein, I., ed. 1967. *Tractate Pesaḥim*. Translated by H. Freedman. London: Soncino.
ed. 1974. *Tractate Yoma*. Translated by Leo Jung. London: Soncino.
ed. 1988. *Tractate Zebaḥim*. Translated by H. Freedman. London: Soncino.
Eskola, Timo. 2001. *Messiah and the Throne: Jewish Merkabah Mysticism and Early Christian Exaltation Discourse*. WUNT II/142. Tübingen: Mohr Siebeck.

2015. *A Narrative Theology of the New Testament: Exploring the Metanarrative of Exile and Restoration*. WUNT 350. Tübingen: Mohr Siebeck.

Feder, Yitzhak. 2011. *Blood Expiation in Hittite and Biblical Ritual: Origins, Context, and Meaning*. WAWSup 2. Atlanta, GA: Society of Biblical Literature.

Filtvedt, Ole Jakob. 2015a. "Creation and Salvation in Hebrews." *ZNW* 106: 280–303.

2015b. *The Identity of God's People and the Paradox of Hebrews*. WUNT II/400. Tübingen: Mohr Siebeck.

Freedman, H., and Maurice Simon, eds. 1939. *Midrash Rabbah: Leviticus*. Translated by J. Israelstam and Judah Slotki. London: Soncino.

Frey, Jörg. 1996. "Die alte und die neue διαθήκη nach dem Hebräerbrief." In *Bund und Tora: Zur theologischen Begriffsgeschichte in alttestamentlicher, frühjüdischer und urchristlicher Tradition*, 263–310. WUNT 92. Tübingen: J. C. B. Mohr (Paul Siebeck).

Fuhrmann, Sebastian. 2007. *Vergeben und Vergessen: Christologie und Neuer Bund im Hebräerbrief*. WMANT 113. Neukirchen-Vluyn: Neukirchener.

2010. "The Son, the Angels, and the Odd: Psalm 8 in Hebrews 1 and 2." In *Psalms and Hebrews: Studies in Reception*, edited by Dirk J. Human and Gert J. Steyn, 83–98. LHB/OTS 527. London: T&T Clark.

Gäbel, Georg. 2006. *Die Kulttheologie des Hebräerbriefes: Eine exegetisch-religionsgeschichtliche Studie*. WUNT II/212. Tübingen: Mohr Siebeck.

Gane, Roy. 2005. *Cult and Character: Purification Offerings, Day of Atonement, and Theodicy*. Winona Lake, IN: Eisenbrauns.

García Martínez, Florentino, and Eibert J. C. Tigchelaar, eds. 1998. *The Dead Sea Scrolls Study Edition, Volume Two*. Leiden: Brill.

Gathercole, Simon J. 2006. *The Preexistent Son: Recovering the Christologies of Matthew, Mark, and Luke*. Grand Rapids, MI: Eerdmans.

2015. *Defending Substitution: An Essay on Atonement in Paul*. Acadia Studies in Bible and Theology. Grand Rapids, MI: Baker.

Gelardini, Gabriella. 2007. *Verhärtet eure Herzen nicht: Der Hebräer, eine Synagogenhomilie zu Tischa be Aw*. BIS 83. Leiden: Brill.

2012. "The Inauguration of Yom Kippur According to the LXX and Its Cessation or Perpetuation According to the Book of Hebrews: A Systematic Comparison." In *The Day of Atonement: Its Interpretations in Early Jewish and Christian Traditions*, edited by Thomas Hieke and Tobias Nicklas, 225–54. TBN 15. Leiden: Brill.

Geller, Stephen A. 1992. "Blood Cult: Toward a Literary Theology of the Priestly Work of the Pentateuch." *Prooftexts* 12: 97–124.

Gheorghita, Radu. 2003. *The Role of the Septuagint in Hebrews: An Investigation of its Influence with Special Consideration to the Use of Hab 2:3–4 in Heb 10:37–38*. WUNT II/160. Tübingen: Mohr Siebeck.

Gilders, William K. 2004. *Blood Ritual in the Hebrew Bible: Meaning and Power*. Baltimore, MD: Johns Hopkins University Press.

2006. "Blood and Covenant: Interpretive Elaboration on Genesis 9.4–6 in the Book of *Jubilees*." *JSP* 15: 83–118.

Ginsberg, Morris. 1999. *Sifra: With Translation and Commentary*. SFSHJ *194*. Atlanta, GA: Scholars Press.

Gordon, Robert P. 2000. *Hebrews. Readings*. Sheffield: Sheffield Academic.
Gorman, Frank H. 1990. *The Ideology of Ritual: Space, Time and Status in the Priestly Theology*. JSOTSup 91. Sheffield: JSOT Press.
Grässer, Erich. 1990. *An die Hebräer: 1. Teilband, Hebr 1–6*. EKK 17/1. Zurich: Benziger.
— 1992a. "Beobachtungen zum Menschensohn in Hebr 2,6." In *Aufbruch und Verheißung: Gesammelte Aufsätze zum Hebräerbrief*, edited by Martin Evang and Otto Merk, 155–65. BZNW 65. Berlin: de Gruyter.
— 1992b. "Die Heilsbedeutung des Todes Jesu in Hebräer 2, 14–18." In *Aufbruch und Verheißung: Gesammelte Aufsätze zum Hebräerbrief*, edited by Martin Evang and Otto Merk, 181–200. BZNW 65. Berlin: de Gruyter.
— 1993. *An die Hebräer: 2. Teilband, Hebr 7,1–10,18*. EKK 17/2. Zurich: Benziger.
— 1997. *An die Hebräer: 3. Teilband, Hebr 10,19–13,25*. EKK 17/3. Zurich: Benziger.
Gray, Patrick. 2003. *Godly Fear: The Epistle to the Hebrews and Greco-Roman Critiques of Superstition*. SBLABib 16. Atlanta, GA: Society of Biblical Literature.
Grogan, Geoffrey W. 1969. "Christ and His People: An Exegetical and Theological Study of Hebrews 2.5–18." *Vox Evangelica* 6: 54–71.
Gurtner, Daniel M. 2009. *Second Baruch: A Critical Edition of the Syriac Text*. JCTCRS. New York: T & T Clark.
Guthrie, George H. 1994. *The Structure of Hebrews: A Text-Linguistic Analysis*. NovTSup 73. Leiden: Brill.
— 1998. *Hebrews*. NIVAC. Grand Rapids, MI: Zondervan.
— 2007. "Hebrews." In *Commentary on the New Testament Use of the Old Testament*, edited by G. K. Beale and D. A. Carson, 919–95. Grand Rapids, MI: Baker Academic.
Guthrie, George H., and Russell D. Quinn. 2006. "A Discourse Analysis of the Use of Psalm 8:4–6 in Hebrews 2:5–9." *JETS* 49: 235–46.
Guzmán, Ron, and Michael W. Martin. 2015. "Is Hebrews 5:11–6:20 Really a Digression?" *NovT* 2015: 295–310.
Haber, Susan. 2005. "From Priestly Torah to Christ Cultus: The Re-Vision of Covenant and Cult in Hebrews." *JSNT* 28: 105–24.
Hahn, Scott W. 2004. "A Broken Covenant and the Curse of Death: A Study of Hebrews 9:15–22." *CBQ* 66: 416–36.
— 2009. *Kinship by Covenant: A Canonical Approach to the Fulfillment of God's Saving Promises*. AYBRL. New Haven, CT: Yale University Press.
Hanson, Anthony. 1967. "Philo's Etymologies." *JTS* 18: 128–39.
Harlé, Paul, and Didier Pralon. 1988. *Le Lévitique. La Bible d'Alexandrie 3*. Paris: Cerf.
Harris, Murray J. 2012. *Prepositions and Theology in the Greek New Testament*. Grand Rapids, MI: Zondervan.
Hartenstein, Friedhelm. 2005. "Zur symbolischen Bedeutung des Blutes im Alten Testament." In *Deutungen des Todes Jesu im Neuen Testament*, edited by Jörg Frey and Jens Schröter, 119–37. WUNT 181. Tübingen: Mohr Siebeck.

Hay, David M. 1973. *Glory at the Right Hand: Psalm 110 in Early Christianity.* SBLMS 18. Nashville, TN: Abingdon.
Hays, Richard B. 1989. *Echoes of Scripture in the Letters of Paul.* New Haven, CT: Yale University Press.
2009. "'Here We Have No Lasting City': New Covenantalism in Hebrews." In *The Epistle to the Hebrews and Christian Theology*, edited by Richard Bauckham, Daniel R. Driver, Trevor A. Hart, and Nathan MacDonald, 151–73. Grand Rapids, MI: Eerdmans.
Hegermann, Harald. 1988. *Der Brief an die Hebräer.* THNT. Berlin: Evangelische Verlagsanstalt.
Heininger, Bernhard. 1997. "Sündenreinigung (Hebr 1,3). Christologische Anmerkungen zum Exordium des Hebräerbriefs." *BZ* 41: 54–68.
Hengel, Martin. 1995. "'Sit at My Right Hand!' The Enthronement of Christ at the Right Hand of God and Psalm 110:1." In *Studies in Early Christology*, 119–225. Edinburgh: T&T Clark.
Hermann, Markus-Liborius. 2013. *Die "hermeneutische Stunde" des Hebräerbriefes: Schriftauslegung in Spannungsfeldern.* HBS 72. Freiburg: Herder.
Hofius, Otfried. 1970a. "Inkarnation und Opfertod Jesu nach Hebr 10,19f." In *Der Ruf Jesu und die Antwort der Gemeinde: Exegetische Untersuchungen Joachim Jeremias zum 70. Geburtstag gewidmet von seinen Schülern*, edited by Eduard Lohse, Christoph Burchard, and Berndt Schaller, 132–41. Göttingen: Vandenhoeck & Ruprecht.
1970b. *Katapausis: Die Vorstellung vom endzeitlichen Ruheort im Hebräerbrief.* WUNT 11. Tübingen: Mohr Siebeck.
1972. *Der Vorhang vor dem Thron Gottes: Eine exegetisch-religionsgeschichtliche Untersuchung zu Hebräer 6,19f und 10,19f.* WUNT 14. Tübingen: Mohr Siebeck.
2004. "The Fourth Servant Song in the New Testament Letters." In *The Suffering Servant: Isaiah 53 in Jewish and Christian Sources*, edited by Bernd Janowski and Peter Stuhlmacher, translated by Daniel P. Bailey, 163–88. Grand Rapids, MI: Eerdmans.
Houston, Walter J. 2003. "Towards an Integrated Reading of the Dietary Laws of Leviticus." In *The Book of Leviticus: Composition and Reception*, edited by Rolf Rendtorff and Robert A. Kugler, 142–61. VTSupp 93. Leiden: Brill.
Hughes, John J. 1979. "Hebrews IX 15ff. and Galatians III 15ff.: A Study in Covenant Practice and Procedure." *NovT* 21: 27–96.
Hughes, Philip Edgcumbe. 1973. "The Blood of Jesus and His Heavenly Priesthood in Hebrews: Part II: The High-Priestly Sacrifice of Christ." *BibSac* 130: 195–212.
Hundley, Michael B. 2011. *Keeping Heaven on Earth: Safeguarding the Divine Presence in the Priestly Tabernacle.* FAT II/50. Tübingen: Mohr Siebeck.
Hurst, L. D. 1987. "The Christology of Hebrews 1 and 2." In *The Glory of Christ in the New Testament: Studies in Christology in Memory of George Bradford Caird*, edited by L. D. Hurst and N. T. Wright, 151–64. Oxford: Oxford University Press.
1990. *The Epistle to the Hebrews: Its Background of Thought.* SNTSMS 65. Cambridge: Cambridge University Press.

Isaacs, Marie E. 1992. *Sacred Space: An Approach to the Theology of the Epistle to the Hebrews.* JSNTSup 73. Sheffield: JSOT Press.
Jamieson, R. B. 2016. "Hebrews 9.23: Cult Inauguration, Yom Kippur and the Cleansing of the Heavenly Tabernacle." *NTS* 62: 569–87.
———. 2017. "When and Where Did Jesus Offer Himself? A Taxonomy of Recent Scholarship on Hebrews." *CBR* 15: 338–68.
Janowski, Bernd. 2000. *Sühne als Heilsgeschehen: Traditions- und religionsgeschichtliche Studien zur Sühnetheologie der Priesterschrift.* 2nd ed. WMANT 55. Neukirchen-Vluyn: Neukirchener.
———. 2004. "He Bore Our Sins: Isaiah 53 and the Drama of Taking Another's Place." In *The Suffering Servant: Isaiah 53 in Jewish and Christian Sources,* edited by Bernd Janowski and Peter Stuhlmacher, 48–74. Grand Rapids, MI: Eerdmans.
Jenson, Philip Peter. 1992. *Graded Holiness: A Key to the Priestly Conception of the World.* JSOTSup 106. Sheffield: JSOT Press.
Jeremias, Joachim. 1949. "Zwischen Karfreitag und Ostern: Descensus und Ascensus in der Karfreitagstheologie des Neuen Testamentes." *ZNW* 42: 194–201.
———. 1971. "Hebräer 10:20: τοῦτ' ἔστιν τῆς σαρκὸς αὐτοῦ." *ZNW* 62: 131.
Jipp, Joshua W. 2010. "The Son's Entrance into the Heavenly World: The Soteriological Necessity of the Scriptural Catena of Hebrews 1.5–14." *NTS* 56: 557–75.
Johnson, Luke Timothy. 2006. *Hebrews: A Commentary.* NTL. Louisville, KY: Westminster John Knox.
Johnson, Richard W. 2001. *Going Outside the Camp: The Sociological Function of the Levitical Critique in the Epistle to the Hebrews.* JSNTSup 109. Sheffield: Sheffield Academic Press.
Johnsson, William G. 1973. "Defilement and Purgation in the Book of Hebrews." PhD diss., Vanderbilt University.
———. 1978. "The Cultus of Hebrews in Twentieth-Century Scholarship." *Expository Times* 89: 104–108.
Joslin, Barry C. 2007. "Christ Bore the Sins of Many: Substitution and the Atonement in Hebrews." *SBJT* 11: 74–103.
———. 2008. *Hebrews, Christ, and the Law: The Theology of the Mosaic Law in Hebrews 7:1–10:18.* PBM. Milton Keynes: Paternoster.
Jürgens, Benedikt. 2001. *Heiligkeit und Versöhnung: Levitikus 16 in seinem literarischen Kontext.* HBS 28. Freiburg: Herder.
Karrer, Martin. 2008. *Der Brief an die Hebräer: Kapitel 5,11–13,25.* ÖTK 20/2. Gütersloh: Gütersloher.
———. 2010. "LXX Psalm 39:7–10 in Hebrews 10:5–7." In *Psalms and Hebrews: Studies in Reception,* edited by Dirk J. Human and Gert J. Steyn, 126–46. LHB/OTS 527. London: T&T Clark.
Käsemann, Ernst. 1961. *Das wandernde Gottesvolk: Eine Untersuchung zum Hebräerbrief.* FRLANT 55. Göttingen: Vandenhoeck & Ruprecht.
Kazen, Thomas. 2008. "Dirt and Disgust: Body and Morality in Biblical Purity Laws." In *Perspectives on Purity and Purification in the Bible,* edited by Baruch J. Schwartz, David P. Wright, Jeffrey Stackert, and Naphtali S. Meshel, 43–64. LHB/OTS 474. London: T&T Clark.

2011. *Emotions in Biblical Law: A Cognitive Science Approach.* HBM 36. Sheffield: Sheffield Phoenix.
2014. "The Role of Disgust in Priestly Purity Law: Insights from Conceptual Metaphor and Blending Theories." *JLRS* 3: 62–92.
Kibbe, Michael. 2014. "Is It Finished? When Did It Start? Hebrews, Priesthood, and Atonement in Biblical, Systematic, and Historical Perspective." *JTS* 65: 25–61.
2016. *Godly Fear or Ungodly Failure? Hebrews 12 and the Sinai Theophanies.* BZNW 216. Berlin: de Gruyter.
Kilpatrick, G. D. 1977. "Διαθήκη in Hebrews." *ZNW* 68: 263–65.
Kinzer, Mark Stephen. 1995. "'All Things Under His Feet': Psalm 8 in the New Testament and in Other Jewish Literature of Late Antiquity." PhD diss., University of Michigan.
Kiuchi, Nobuyoshi. 1987. *The Purification Offering in the Priestly Literature: Its Meaning and Function.* JSOTSup 56. Sheffield: JSOT Press.
Klawans, Jonathan. 2006. *Purity, Sacrifice, and the Temple: Symbolism and Supersessionism in the Study of Ancient Judaism.* Oxford: Oxford University Press.
Kleinig, John W. 1999. "The Blood for Sprinkling: Atoning Blood in Leviticus and Hebrews." *Lutheran Theological Journal* 33: 124–35.
Kline, Meredith G. 1963. *Treaty of the Great King.* Grand Rapids, MI: Eerdmans.
Knibb, Michael A. 1976. "The Exile in the Literature of the Intertestamental Period." *HeyJ* 17: 253–72.
Knöppler, Thomas. 2001. *Sühne im Neuen Testament: Studien zum urchristlichen Verständnis der Heilsbedeutung des Todes Jesu.* WMANT 88. Neukirchen-Vluyn: Neukirchener.
Koester, Craig R. 1989. *The Dwelling of God: The Tabernacle in the Old Testament, Intertestamental Literature, and the New Testament.* CBQMS 22. Washington, DC: Catholic Biblical Association of America.
2001. *Hebrews: A New Translation with Introduction and Commentary.* AB 36. New York: Doubleday.
2005. "God's Purposes and Christ's Saving Work According to Hebrews." In *Salvation in the New Testament: Perspectives on Soteriology*, edited by Jan G. van der Watt, 361–87. NovTSup 121. Leiden: Brill.
Kögel, Julius. 1904. *Der Sohn und die Söhne: Eine exegetische Studie zu Hebräer 2,5–18.* Beiträge zur Förderung christlicher Theologie 8.5–6. Gütersloh: Bertelsmann.
Kraus, Wolfgang. 1991. *Der Tod Jesu als Heiligtumsweihe: Eine Untersuchung zum Umfeld der Sühnevorstellung in Römer 3,25–26a.* WMANT 66. Neukirchen-Vluyn: Neukirchener.
2014. "Die Bedeutung von διαθήκη im Hebräerbrief." In *The Reception of Septuagint Words in Jewish-Hellenistic and Christian Literature*, edited by Eberhard Bons, Ralph Brucker, and Jan Joosten, 67–83. WUNT II/367. Tübingen: Mohr Siebeck.
Kuma, Herman V. A. 2012. *The Centrality of Αἷμα (Blood) in the Theology of the Epistle to the Hebrews: An Exegetical and Philological Study.* Lewiston, NY: Edwin Mellen.

Kurianal, James. 2000. *Jesus Our High Priest*. EUS 693. Frankfurt am Main: Peter Lang.

Lam, Joseph. 2016. *Patterns of Sin in the Hebrew Bible: Metaphor, Culture, and the Making of a Religious Concept*. New York: Oxford University Press.

Lane, William L. 1991. *Hebrews*. 2 vols. WBC 47A–B. Dallas: Word.

Laub, Franz. 1980. *Bekenntnis und Auslegung: Die paränetischen Funktion der Christologie im Hebraërbrief*. Biblische Untersuchungen 15. Regensburg: Pustet.

———. 1991. "'Ein für allemal hineingegangen in das Allerheiligste' (Hebr 9,12) – Zum Verständnis des Kreuzestodes im Hebraërbrief." *BZ* 35: 65–85.

Lausberg, Heinrich. 1998. *Handbook of Literary Rhetoric: A Foundation for Literary Study*, edited by David E. Orton and R. Dean Anderson. Translated by Matthew T. Bliss, Annemiek Jansen, and David E. Orton. Leiden: Brill.

Lee, Aquila H. I. 2005. *From Messiah to Preexistent Son: Jesus' Self-Consciousness and Early Christian Exegesis of Messianic Psalms*. WUNT II/192. Tübingen: Mohr Siebeck.

Lehne, Susanne. 1990. *The New Covenant in Hebrews*. JSNTSup 44. Sheffield: JSOT Press.

Lemos, T. M. 2013. "Where There Is Dirt, Is There System? Revisiting Biblical Purity Constructions." *JSOT* 37: 265–94.

Leschert, Dale F. 1994. *Hermeneutical Foundations of Hebrews: A Study in the Validity of the Epistle's Interpretation of Some Core Citations from the Psalms*. NABPR Dissertation Series 10. Lewiston, NY: Edwin Mellen.

Levine, Baruch A. 1989. *Leviticus*. JPSTC. Philadelphia: Jewish Publication Society.

Lindars, Barnabas. 1991. *The Theology of the Letter to the Hebrews*. Cambridge: Cambridge University Press.

Linebaugh, Jonathan A. 2013. *God, Grace, and Righteousness in Wisdom of Solomon and Paul's Letter to the Romans: Texts in Conversation*. NovTSup 152. Leiden: Brill.

Loader, William R. G. 1981. *Sohn und Hoherpriester: Eine traditionsgeschichtliche Untersuchung zur Christologie des Hebräerbriefes*. WMANT 53. Neukirchen-Vluyn: Neukirchener.

Löhr, Hermut. 1991. "Thronversammlung und preisender Tempel. Beobachtungen am himmlischen Heiligtum im Hebräerbrief und in den Sabbatopferliedern aus Qumran." In *Königsherrschaft Gottes und himmlischer Kult: im Judentum, Urchristentum und in der hellenistischen Welt*, edited by Martin Hengel and Anna Maria Schwemer, 185–205. WUNT 55. Tübingen: Mohr Siebeck.

———. 1994. *Umkehr und Sünde im Hebräerbrief*. BZNW 73. Berlin: de Gruyter.

———. 1997. "Anthropologie und Eschatologie im Hebräerbrief: Bemerkungen zum theologischen Interesse einer frühchristlichen Schrift." In *Eschatologie und Schöpfung: Festschrift für Erich Gräßer zum siebzigsten Geburtstag*, edited by Martin Evang, Helmut Merklein, and Michael Wolter. BZNW 89. Berlin: de Gruyter.

———. 2005. "Wahrnehmung und Bedeutung des Todes Jesu nach dem Hebräerbrief: Ein Versuch." In *Deutungen des Todes Jesu im Neuen Testament*,

edited by Jörg Frey and Jens Schröter, 455–76. WUNT 181. Tübingen: Mohr Siebeck.
Long, Thomas G. 1998. "Bold in the Presence of God: Atonement in Hebrews." *Interpretation* 52: 53–69.
Luck, Ulrich. 1963. "Himmlisches und irdisches Geschehen im Hebräerbrief: Ein Beitrag zum Problem des 'historischen Jesus' im Urchristentum." *NovT* 6: 192–215.
Mackie, Scott D. 2007. *Eschatology and Exhortation in the Epistle to the Hebrews*. WUNT II/223. Tübingen: Mohr Siebeck.
——— 2011. "Heavenly Sanctuary Mysticism in the Epistle to the Hebrews." *JTS* 62: 77–117.
MacRae, George W. 1978. "Heavenly Temple and Eschatology in the Letter to the Hebrews." *Semeia* 12: 179–99.
Maré, Leonard P. 2010. "The Messianic Interpretation of Psalm 8:4–6 in Hebrews 2:6–9. Part I." In *Psalms and Hebrews: Studies in Reception*, edited by Dirk J. Human and Gert J. Steyn, 99–112. LHB/OTS 527. London: T&T Clark.
Marshall, I. Howard. 2009. "Soteriology in Hebrews." In *The Epistle to the Hebrews and Christian Theology*, edited by Richard Bauckham, Daniel R. Driver, Trevor A. Hart, and Nathan MacDonald, 253–77. Grand Rapids, MI: Eerdmans.
März, Claus-Peter. 1996. "'...nur für kurze Zeit unter die Engel gestellt' (Hebr 2,7): Anthropologie und Christologie in Hebr 2,5–9." In *Von Gott Reden in säkularer Gesellschaft. Festschrift für Konrad Feiereis zum 65. Geburtstag*, edited by Emerich Coreth, Wilhelm Ernst, and Eberhard Tiefensee, 29–42. Erfurter Theologische Studien 71. Leipzig: Benno.
Mason, Eric F. 2008. *"You Are a Priest Forever": Second Temple Jewish Messianism and the Priestly Christology of the Epistle to the Hebrews*. STDJ 74. Leiden: Brill.
——— 2012. "'Sit at My Right Hand': Enthronement and the Heavenly Sanctuary in Hebrews." In *A Teacher for All Generations: Essays in Honor of James C. VanderKam*, edited by Eric F. Mason, Kelley Coblentz Bautch, Angela Kim Harkins, and Daniel A. Machiela, 901–16. JSJSup 2/153. Leiden: Brill.
McCruden, Kevin B. 2008. *Solidarity Perfected: Beneficent Christology in the Epistle to the Hebrews*. BZNW 159. Berlin: de Gruyter.
McDonough, Sean M. 2009. *Christ as Creator: Origins of a New Testament Doctrine*. Oxford: Oxford University Press.
McKnight, Scot. 1992. "The Warning Passages of Hebrews: A Formal Analysis and Theological Conclusions." *TJ* 13: 21–59.
Meier, John P. 1985a. "Structure and Theology in Heb 1,1–14." *Biblica* 66: 168–89.
——— 1985b. "Symmetry and Theology the Old Testament Citations of Heb 1,5–14." *Biblica* 66: 504–33.
Meshel, Naphtali S. 2013. "The Form and Function of a Biblical Blood Ritual." *VT* 63: 276–89.
——— 2014. *The "Grammar" of Sacrifice: A Generativist Study of the Israelite Sacrificial System in the Priestly Writings with A "Grammar" of Σ*. Oxford: Oxford University Press.

Michel, Otto. 1966. *Der Brief an die Hebräer*. 12th edn. KEK 13. Göttingen: Vandenhoeck & Ruprecht.
Milgrom, Jacob. 1976. "Israel's Sanctuary: The Priestly 'Picture of Dorian Gray.'" *RB* 83: 390–99.
———. 1989. "Rationale for Cultic Law: The Case of Impurity." *Semeia* 45: 103–9.
———. 1991. *Leviticus 1–16: A New Translation with Introduction and Commentary*. AB 3. New York: Doubleday.
———. 2000. *Leviticus 17–22: A New Translation with Introduction and Commentary*. The Anchor Bible. New York: Doubleday.
Moffatt, James. 1924. *A Critical and Exegetical Commentary on the Epistle to the Hebrews*. ICC 40. Edinburgh: T&T Clark.
Moffitt, David M. 2010. "Unveiling Jesus' Flesh: A Fresh Assessment of the Relationship between the Veil and Jesus' Flesh in Hebrews 10:20." *PRSt* 37: 71–84.
———. 2011. *Atonement and the Logic of Resurrection in the Epistle to the Hebrews*. NovTSup 141. Leiden: Brill.
———. 2012. "Blood, Life, and Atonement: Reassessing Hebrews' Christological Appropriation of Yom Kippur." In *The Day of Atonement: Its Interpretations in Early Jewish and Christian Traditions*, edited by Thomas Hieke and Tobias Nicklas, 211–24. TBN 15. Leiden: Brill.
———. 2016a. "Hebrews and the General Epistles." In *T&T Clark Companion to the Doctrine of Sin*, edited by Keith L. Johnson and David Lauber, 111–25. London: Bloomsbury T&T Clark.
———. 2016b. "Serving in the Tabernacle in Heaven: Sacred Space, Jesus's High-Priestly Sacrifice, and Hebrews' Analogical Theology." In *Hebrews in Contexts*, edited by Gabriella Gelardini and Harold W. Attridge, 259–79. AGJU 91. Leiden: Brill.
———. 2016c. "The Role of Jesus' Resurrection in the Epistle to the Hebrews, Once Again: A Brief Response to Jean-René Moret." *NTS* 62: 308–14.
———. 2017. "Jesus' Heavenly Sacrifice in Early Christian Reception of Hebrews: A Survey." *JTS* 68: 46–71.
Moore, Nicholas J. 2013. "Review of *Atonement and the Logic of Resurrection in the Epistle to the Hebrews*, by David M. Moffitt." *JTS* 64: 673–75.
———. 2014. "Jesus as 'The One Who Entered His Rest': The Christological Reading of Hebrews 4.10." *JSNT* 36: 383–400.
———. 2015. *Repetition in Hebrews: Plurality and Singularity in the Letter to the Hebrews, Its Ancient Context, and the Early Church*. WUNT II/388. Tübingen: Mohr Siebeck.
Mora, Gaspar. 1974. *La Carta a los Hebreos como Escrito Pastoral*. CSP 20. Barcelona: Herder.
Morales, Rodrigo J. 2010. *The Spirit and the Restoration of Israel: New Exodus and New Creation Motifs in Galatians*. WUNT II/282. Tübingen: Mohr Siebeck.
Moret, Jean-René. 2014. "Ancienne et Nouvelle Alliance dans l'épître aux Hébreux." *Hokhma* 106: 41–58.
———. 2016. "Le rôle du concept de purification dans l'Épître aux Hébreux: une réaction à quelques propositions de David M. Moffitt." *NTS* 62: 289–307.

Mosser, Carl. 2004. "No Lasting City: Rome, Jerusalem and the Place of Hebrews in the History of Earliest 'Christianity.'" PhD thesis, University of St. Andrews.
Nairne, Alexander. 1913. *The Epistle of Priesthood: Studies in the Epistle to the Hebrews*. Edinburgh: T. & T. Clark.
Nelson, Richard D. 2003. "'He Offered Himself': Sacrifice in Hebrews." *Interpretation* 57: 251–65.
Neusner, Jacob. 1979. *The Tosefta: Fifth Division; Qodoshim*. New York: Ktav.
Nihan, Christophe. 2007. *From Priestly Torah to Pentateuch: A Study in the Composition of the Book of Leviticus*. FAT II/25. Tübingen: Mohr Siebeck.
— 2013. "Forms and Functions of Purity in Leviticus." In *Purity and the Forming of Religious Traditions in the Ancient Mediterranean World and Ancient Judaism*, edited by Christian Frevel and Christophe Nihan, 311–67. DHR 3. Leiden: Brill.
— 2015. "The Templization of Israel: Some Remarks on Blood Disposal and Kipper in Leviticus 4." In *Text, Time, and Temple: Literary, Historical, and Ritual Studies in Leviticus*, edited by Francis Landy, Leigh M. Trevaskis, and Bryan D. Bibb, 94–130. HBM 64. Sheffield: Sheffield Phoenix.
Nongbri, Brent. 2003. "A Touch of Condemnation in a Word of Exhortation: Apocalyptic Language and Graeco-Roman Rhetoric in Hebrews 6:4–12." *NovT* 45: 265–79.
Origen. 1990. *Homilies on Leviticus 1–16*. Translated by Gary Wayne Barkley. The Fathers of the Church 83. Washington, DC: Catholic University of America Press.
Ounsworth, Richard. 2012. *Joshua Typology in the New Testament*. WUNT II/328. Tübingen: Mohr Siebeck.
Owen, John. 1991. *The Works of John Owen*. Edited by William H. Goold. Vol. 22. Edinburgh: Banner of Truth.
Parsons, Mikeal C. 1988. "Son and High Priest: A Study in the Christology of Hebrews." *EvQ* 60: 195–216.
Peeler, Amy L. B. 2014. *You Are My Son: The Family of God in the Epistle to the Hebrews*. LNTS 486. London: Bloomsbury T&T Clark.
Peterson, David. 1982. *Hebrews and Perfection: An Examination of the Concept of Perfection in the "Epistle to the Hebrews."* SNTSMS 47. Cambridge: Cambridge University Press.
Philip, Mayjee. 2011. *Leviticus in Hebrews: A Transtextual Analysis of the Tabernacle Theme in the Letter to the Hebrews*. Frankfurt: Peter Lang.
Pitre, Brant. 2005. *Jesus, the Tribulation, and the End of the Exile*. WUNT II/204. Tübingen: Mohr Siebeck.
— 2015. *Jesus and the Last Supper*. Grand Rapids, MI: Eerdmans.
Propp, William H. C. 2006. *Exodus 19–40: A New Translation with Introduction and Commentary*. AB 2A. New York: Doubleday.
Pursiful, Darrell J. 1993. *The Cultic Motif in the Spirituality of the Book of Hebrews*. Lewiston, NY: Edwin Mellen.
Rascher, Angela. 2007. *Schriftauslegung und Christologie im Hebräerbrief*. BZNW 153. Berlin: de Gruyter.

Reinmuth, Ekart. 2006. *Anthropologie im Neuen Testament*. UTB 2768. Tübingen: Francke.
— 2012. "Der Hebräerbrief vor dem Horizont politischer Philosophie: Ausgrenzung und Solidarität." In *Neues Testament, Theologie und Gesellschaft: Hermeneutische und diskurstheoretische Reflexionen*. Stuttgart: Kohlhammer.
Reynolds, Benjamin E. 2008. *The Apocalyptic Son of Man in the Gospel of John*. WUNT II/249. Tübingen: Mohr Siebeck.
Ribbens, Benjamin J. 2012. "Forensic-Retributive Justification in Romans 3:21–26: Paul's Doctrine of Justification in Dialogue with Hebrews." *CBQ* 74: 548–67.
— 2016. *Levitical Sacrifice and Heavenly Cult in Hebrews*. BZNW 222. Berlin: de Gruyter.
Richardson, Christopher A. 2012. *Pioneer and Perfecter of Faith: Jesus' Faith as the Climax of Israel's History in the Epistle to the Hebrews*. WUNT II/338. Tübingen: Mohr Siebeck.
Riggenbach, Eduard. 1987. *Der Brief an die Hebräer*. 3rd edn. KNT 24. Wuppertal: Brockhaus.
Rissi, Mathias. 1987. *Die Theologie des Hebräerbriefs: Ihre Verankerung in der Situation des Verfassers und seiner Leser*. WUNT 41. Tübingen: Mohr Siebeck.
Rooke, Deborah W. 2000. "Jesus as Royal Priest: Reflections on the Interpretation of the Melchizedek Tradition in Heb 7." *Biblica* 81: 81–94.
Rose, Christian. 1994. *Die Wolke der Zeugen: Eine exegetisch-traditionsgeschichtliche Untersuchung zu Hebräer 10,32–12,3*. WUNT II/60. Tübingen: J. C. B. Mohr (Paul Siebeck).
Rosenbaum, Stephen E. 1986. "How to Be Dead and Not Care: A Defense of Epicurus." *APQ* 23: 217–25.
Rowe, Galen O. 1997. "Style." In *Handbook of Classical Rhetoric in the Hellenistic Period (330 B.C.–A.D. 400)*, edited by Stanley E. Porter, 121–57. Leiden: Brill.
Rowland, Christopher, and Christopher R. A. Morray-Jones. 2009. *The Mystery of God: Early Jewish Mysticism and the New Testament*. CRINT 12. Leiden: Brill.
Sargent, Benjamin. 2014. *David Being a Prophet: The Contingency of Scripture upon History in the New Testament*. BZNW 207. Berlin: de Gruyter.
Schaefer, J. R. 1968. "The Relationship between Priestly and Servant Messianism in the Epistle to the Hebrews." *CBQ* 30: 259–85.
Scharbert, Josef. 1970. "Blood." In *Encyclopedia of Biblical Theology*, edited by Johannes B. Bauer, 1:75–79. Vol. 1. London: Sheed and Ward.
Schenck, Kenneth L. 1997. "Keeping His Appointment: Creation and Enthronement in Hebrews." *JSNT* 66: 91–117.
— 2001. "A Celebration of the Enthroned Son: The Catena of Hebrews 1." *JBL* 120: 469–85.
— 2003. *Understanding the Book of Hebrews: The Story behind the Sermon*. Louisville, KY: Westminster John Knox.
— 2007. *Cosmology and Eschatology in Hebrews: The Settings of the Sacrifice*. SNTSMS 143. Cambridge: Cambridge University Press.

2016. "An Archaeology of Hebrews' Tabernacle Imagery." In *Hebrews in Contexts*, edited by Gabriella Gelardini and Harold W. Attridge, 240–58. AGJU 91. Leiden: Brill.
Scholer, John M. 1991. *Proleptic Priests: Priesthood in the Epistle to the Hebrews*. JSNTSup 49. Sheffield: JSOT Press.
Schreiner, Thomas R. 2015. *Commentary on Hebrews*. BTCP. Nashville, TN: B&H.
Schunack, Gerd. 1994. "Jesu 'Opfertod' im Hebräerbrief." In *Der bezwingende Vorsprung des Guten: Exegetische und theologische Werkstattberichte*, edited by Ulrich Schoenborn and Stephan Pfürtner, 209–31. Münster: Lit.
— 2002. *Der Hebräerbrief*. ZBK 14. Zürich: Theologischer Verlag.
Schwartz, Baruch J. 1991. "The Prohibitions Concerning the 'Eating' of Blood in Leviticus 17." In *Priesthood and Cult in Ancient Israel*, edited by Gary A. Anderson and Saul M. Olyan, 34–66. JSOTSup 125. Sheffield: JSOT Press.
— 1995. "The Bearing of Sin in the Priestly Literature." In *Pomegranates and Golden Bells: Studies in Biblical, Jewish, and Near Eastern Ritual, Law, and Literature in Honor of Jacob Milgrom*, edited by David P. Wright, David Noel Freedman, and Avi Hurvitz, 3–21. Winona Lake, IN: Eisenbrauns.
Scott, James M. 1993. "'For as Many as Are of Works of the Law Are under a Curse' (Galatians 3.10)." In *Paul and the Scriptures of Israel*, edited by Craig A. Evans and James A. Sanders, 187–221. JSNTSup 83. Sheffield: JSOT Press.
Silva, Moisés. 1976. "Perfection and Eschatology in Hebrews." *WTJ* 39: 60–71.
Sklar, Jay. 2005. *Sin, Impurity, Sacrifice, Atonement: The Priestly Conceptions*. HBM 2. Sheffield: Sheffield Phoenix.
Small, Brian C. 2014. *The Characterization of Jesus in the Book of Hebrews*. BIS 128. Leiden: Brill.
Söding, Thomas. 2005. "'Hoherpriester nach der Ordnung des Melchisedek' (Hebr 5,10): Zur Christologie des Hebräerbriefes." In *Ausharren in der Verheißung: Studien zum Hebräerbrief*, edited by Rainer Kampling, 63–109. Stuttgarter Bibelstudien 204. Stuttgart: Katholishces Bibelwerk.
Soskice, Janet Martin. 1985. *Metaphor and Religious Language*. Oxford: Clarendon.
Sowers, Sidney G. 1965. *The Hermeneutics of Philo and Hebrews: A Comparison of the Interpretation of the Old Testament in Philo Judaeus and the Epistle to the Hebrews*. BasST 1. Zürich: EVZ.
Spicq, Ceslas. 1953. *L'Épître aux Hébreux: II. Commentaire*. EBib. Paris: Gabalda.
Stanley, Steve. 1995. "Hebrews 9:6–10: The 'Parable' of the Tabernacle." *NovT* 37: 385–99.
Stegemann, Ekkehard W., and Wolfgang Stegemann. 2005. "Does the Cultic Language in Hebrews Represent Sacrificial Metaphors? Reflections on Some Basic Problems." In *Hebrews: Contemporary Methods – New Insights*, edited by Gabriela Gelardini, 13–23. BIS 75. Leiden: Brill.

Bibliography

Sterling, Gregory E. 2001. "Ontology versus Eschatology: Tensions between Author and Community in Hebrews." *SPhilo* 13: 190–211.
Stewart, Alexander. 2010. "Cosmology, Eschatology, and Soteriology in Hebrews: A Synthetic Analysis." *BBR* 20: 545–60.
Stökl ben Ezra, Daniel. 2003. *The Impact of Yom Kippur on Early Christianity: The Day of Atonement from Second Temple Judaism to the Fifth Century*. WUNT 163. Tübingen: Mohr Siebeck.
Stott, Wilfred. 1962. "The Conception of 'Offering' in the Epistle to the Hebrews." *NTS* 9: 62–67.
Strack, Hermann L., and Paul Billerbeck. 1926. *Kommentar zum Neuen Testament aus Talmud und Midrasch. Dritter Band: Die Briefe des Neuen Testaments und die Offenbarung Johannis*. Munich: Beck.
Svendsen, Stefan Nordgaard. 2009. *Allegory Transformed: The Appropriation of Philonic Hermeneutics in the Letter to the Hebrews*. WUNT II/269. Tübingen: Mohr Siebeck.
Swetnam, James. 1965. "A Suggested Interpretation of Hebrews 9,15–18." *CBQ* 27: 373–90.
———. 1966. "Greater and More Perfect Tent: A Contribution to the Discussion of Hebrews 9:11." *Biblica* 47: 91–106.
Telscher, Guido. 2007. *Opfer aus Barmherzigkeit: Hebr 9,11–28 im Kontext biblischer Sühnetheologie*. FB 112. Würzburg: Echter.
Theodoret of Cyrus. 2001. *Commentary on the Letters of St. Paul*. Translated by Robert Charles Hill. Brookline, MA: Holy Cross Orthodox Press.
Thompson, James W. 1982. *The Beginnings of Christian Philosophy: The Epistle to the Hebrews*. CBQMS 13. Washington, DC: Catholic Biblical Association of America.
———. 2008. *Hebrews*. Paideia. Grand Rapids, MI: Baker.
Thornton, T. G. C. 1964. "The Meaning of αἱματεκχυσία in Heb. IX.22." *JTS* 15: 63–65.
Tov, Emanuel. 1975. *The Book of Baruch. Texts and Translations/Pseudepigrapha Series 8/6*. Missoula, MT: Scholars Press.
Trompf, G. W. 1971. "The Conception of God in Hebrews 4:12–13." *ST* 25: 123–32.
Tuckett, C. M. 1992. "Atonement in the NT." In *The Anchor Bible Dictionary*, edited by David Noel Freedman, 1:518–22. Vol. 1. New York: Doubleday.
Übelacker, Walter. 2007. "Die Alternative Leben oder Tod in der Konzeption des Hebräerbriefs." In *Lebendige Hoffnung – ewiger Tod?!*, edited by Michael Labahn and Manfred Lang, 235–63. ABG 24. Leipzig: Evangelische Verlagsanstalt.
———. 2010. "Anthropologie und Vollendung – Perspektiven im Hebräerbrief." In *Anthropology in the New Testament and Its Ancient Context: Papers from the EABS-Meeting in Piliscsaba/Budapest*, 209–40. CBET 54. Leuven: Peeters.
VanderKam, James C. 1989. *The Book of Jubilees*. CSCO 511/Scriptores Aethiopici 88. Leuven: Peeters.
———. 1997. "Exile in Jewish Apocalyptic Literature." In *Exile: Old Testament, Jewish, and Christian Conceptions*, edited by James M. Scott, 89–109. JSJSup 56. Leiden: Brill.

Vanhoye, Albert. 1963. *La structure littéraire de L'Épitre aux Hébreux*. Paris: Desclée de Brower.
——— 1965. "Par la tente plus grande et plus parfaite ..." *Bib* 46: 1–28.
——— 1969. *Situation du Christ: Hébreux 1–2*. Lectio divina 58. Paris: Cerf.
——— 1996. "La 'Teleiôsis' du Christ: Point capital de la Christologie sacerdotale d'Hébreux." *NTS* 42: 321–38.
——— 2011. *A Different Priest: The Epistle to the Hebrews*. Rhetorica Semitica. Miami, FL: Convivium.
Vervenne, Marc. 1993. "'The Blood Is the Life and the Life Is the Blood': Blood as Symbol of Life and Death in Biblical Tradition (Gen. 9,4)." In *Ritual and Sacrifice in the Ancient Near East*, edited by Jan Quaegebeur, 451–70. OLA 55. Leuven: Peeters.
Vos, Geerhardus. 1915. "Hebrews, the Epistle of the Diatheke." *PTR* 13: 587–632.
Wallace, Daniel B. 1996. *Greek Grammar beyond the Basics: An Exegetical Syntax of the New Testament*. Grand Rapids, MI: Zondervan.
Wallis, Ian G. 1995. *The Faith of Jesus Christ in Early Christian Traditions*. SNTSMS 84. Cambridge: Cambridge University Press.
Walter, Nikolaus. 1997. "Christologie und irdischer Jesus im Hebräerbrief." In *Praeparatio Evangelica: Studien zur Umwelt, Exegese und Hermeneutik des Neuen Testaments*, edited by Wolfgang Kraus and Florian Wilk, 151–68. WUNT 98. Tübingen: J. C. B. Mohr (Paul Siebeck).
Walton, John H. 2001. "Equilibrium and the Sacred Compass: The Structure of Leviticus." *BBR* 11: 293–304.
Watson, Francis. 2000. "The Triune Divine Identity: Reflections on Pauline God-Language, in Disagreement with J.D.G. Dunn." *JSNT* 80: 99–124.
Webster, John. 2009. "One Who Is Son: Theological Reflections on the Exordium to the Epistle to the Hebrews." In *The Epistle to the Hebrews and Christian Theology*, edited by Richard Bauckham, Daniel R. Driver, Trevor A. Hart, and Nathan MacDonald, 69–94. Grand Rapids, MI: Eerdmans.
Weiss, Hans-Friedrich. 1991. *Der Brief an die Hebräer*. 15th ed. KEK 13. Göttingen: Vandenhoeck & Ruprecht.
Wenham, Gordon J. 1979. *The Book of Leviticus*. NICOT. Grand Rapids, MI: Eerdmans.
Westcott, Brooke Foss. 1903. *The Epistle to the Hebrews: The Greek Text with Notes and Essays*. 3rd edn. London: Macmillan.
Wevers, John William. 1993. *Notes on the Greek Text of Genesis*. SCS 35. Atlanta, GA: Scholars Press.
——— 1995. *Notes on the Greek Text of Deuteronomy*. SCS 39. Atlanta, GA: Scholars Press.
——— 1997. *Notes on the Greek Text of Leviticus*. SCS 44. Atlanta, GA: Scholars Press.
Whitekettle, Richard. 1996. "Levitical Thought and the Female Reproductive Cycle: Wombs, Wellsprings, and the Primeval World." *VT* 46: 376–91.
Whitlark, Jason A. 2014. "Cosmology and the Perfection of Humanity in Hebrews." In *Interpretation and the Claims of the Text: Resourcing New*

Testament Theology, edited by Jason A. Whitlark, Bruce W. Longenecker, Lidija Novakovic, and Mikeal C. Parsons, 117–28. Waco, TX: Baylor University Press.
Wiid, J. S. 1992. "The Testamental Significance of διαθήκη in Hebrews 9:15–22." *Neot* 26: 149–56.
Williamson, Paul R. 2007. *Sealed with an Oath: Covenant in God's Unfolding Purpose*. NSBT 23. Nottingham: Apollos.
Willi-Plein, Ina. 2005. "Some Remarks on Hebrews from the Viewpoint of Old Testament Exegesis." In *Hebrews: Contemporary Methods – New Insights*, edited by Gabriela Gelardini, 25–36. BIS 75. Leiden: Brill.
Witherington, Ben. 1991. "The Influence of Galatians on Hebrews." *NTS* 37: 146–52.
Wright, David P. 1987. *The Disposal of Impurity: Elimination Rites in the Bible and in Hittite and Mesopotamian Literature*. SBLDS 101. Atlanta, GA: Scholars Press.
——— 1992. "Day of Atonement." In *The Anchor Bible Dictionary*, edited by David Noel Freedman, 2:72–76. Vol. 2. New York: Doubleday.
Young, Norman H. 1973. "ΤΟΥΤ' ΕΣΤΙΝ ΤΗΣ ΣΑΡΚΟΣ ΑΥΤΟΥ (Heb. x. 20): Apposition, Dependent, or Explicative?" *NTS* 20: 100–104.
——— 1979. "Αἱματεκχυσία: A Comment." *ExpTim* 90: 180.
——— 1981. "The Gospel according to Hebrews 9." *NTS* 27: 198–210.
Zesati Estrada, Carlos. 1990. *Hebreos 5,7–8: estudio histórico-exegético*. AnBib 113. Rome: Editrice Pontificio Istituto Biblico.
Zuckermandel, M. S. 1937. *Tosephta: Based on the Erfurt and Vienna Codices*. Jerusalem: Bamberger & Wahrmann.
Zwiep, A. W. 1997. *The Ascension of the Messiah in Lukan Christology*. NovTSup 87. Leiden: Brill.

SUBJECT INDEX

access
  to God, 89
  to the Holy of Holies, 37–39, 54, 61, 91, 160–61, 166
Adam
  dominion granted to, 101
  fall of, 102
apocalyptic, 56
ascension, 1, 16–17, 64, 127, 190
atonement
  Day of, see *Yom Kippur*
  in the Levitical cult, 36–47, 135–41, 150, 170–74
  lexical issues surrounding, 17–19, 133–34, 137–38, 141–53
  timing of, 47–86, 91–94, 153–56

blood
  application of, 18, 39–41, 46, 130–33, 141–50, 153–56
  of Jesus, 4, 20, 38, 59, 61–62, 70, 85–86, 94, 128–29, 152, 156–68, 178–79
  as means of access to the Holy of Holies, 160–61
  as medium of life-for-life exchange, 132–56, 159
  as ritually enacted death, 129–32
  pouring out of, 141–50, 152
  shedding of in ritual slaughter, 132, 135, 152, 156, 159, 167
  sprinkling or tossing of, 39, 42, 130, 132–33, 142–50, 153, 161–62, 164

covenant
  inauguration of, 122–26, 129–33, 152, 156–59, 186–87
  new, 80, 122–23, 134, 152, 156–59, 162, 186–87
  old, 54, 63, 118–22
  sanctions of, 116–19, 122–25, 129–31

death of Jesus
  as bearing others' sins, 169–76
  as defeat of the devil, 110–14
  as life given for life owed, 153–56
  as means of deliverance from death, 99–114
  as redemptive enaction of covenant sanctions, 121–26
  as slaughter of the sacrificial victim, 153–56, 166–76
  as substance of his heavenly offering, 165–79

faith, 122, 126
forgiveness, 132–35, 137, 144, 152–56, 159–60, 167–68, 171, 178, 181

glory, 26, 68–69, 99–109, 169, 181

Heaven
  tabernacle in, 51–57, 59–60, 86–91
  veil in, 54, 68, 86–91
high priest
  Jesus as, see *Jesus as high priest*
  levitical, 36–47, 85–86, 160–63, 172
Holy of Holies
  in the earthly tabernacle, 36–47
  in heaven, 47–62, 66–68, 86–89, 160–64
humanity
  exaltation of, 107–9

inheritance, 122–23
Israel, 119–20, 122, 131

Jesus
  appointment to high priesthood, 10–11, 23–35
  as high priest, 47–94
  as suffering servant, 169–76, 191–93

Subject Index

body of, 163–65, 180–81
enthronement of, 27–28
entrance to heaven of, 1–19, 48–51, 57–63, 67–70, 85, 89, 93, 164
exaltation of, 5, 8–12, 16–17, 24, 68–69, 77, 82, 93, 99, 104–9, 115–16, 157, 169, 181, 188
faithfulness of, 27, 80–81, 108, 114, 177
heavenly session of, 8, 27, 76–78, 83, 175
incarnation of, 78–83, 112–13, 177
intercession of, 30, 57, 177, 190
perfection of, 35–58, 108–9
resurrection of, 8–12, 16–17, 23–25, 28, 30–35, 54, 64, 69–70, 77–78, 157–58
second coming of, 63, 67, 92
judgment, 63, 102–4

Last Supper, 125–26, 152, 193

Melchizedek, 30
messiah, 27

offering(s)
covenant-inaugural, 36, 129–32, 152, 161, 189
daily, 36
postrequisite disposal of, 4, 38, 85, 143–44, 148, 150
presentation of, 17–18, 75, 77, 80–82, 86, 92, 165–68, 186, 189
purification/sin, 18, 38, 40, 43–46, 59, 85–86, 134, 142, 144, 147, 153–54, 161, 172, 192

red heifer, 36
reparation/guilt, 134, 173
whole burnt, 44–45, 146–48

Paul, 90, 102, 109–10, 125–26, 190–91
purification
of the earthly tabernacle, 40–44
of the heavenly tabernacle, 51
of the people (new covenant), 63
of the people (old covenant), 41, 44–46
purity, 133–34, 184–85

ransom, 137–41, 156
redemption, 18, 38, 58–59, 63, 92–93, 118, 121–26, 151, 158, 160, 164, 166–67, 187

tabernacle
earthly, 37, 41–42, 44–46, 51, 54–56, 131–32
temple in Jerusalem, 120, 149
throne of God, 52, 67–68, 78, 115

Yom Kippur
Hebrews' appropriation of, 35–66, 76–77, 84–86, 92–93, 160–65, 187
inner-sanctum cleansing rite in, 39–40, 42–44, 46, 58–59, 85, 162–63
scapegoat rite in, 39, 43–44
twofold purpose of, 40–41, 44–47, 162
unified ritual sequence of, 43

SCRIPTURE INDEX

Genesis
  1:26–28, 102
  2:17, 102
  3, 102, 110
  3:9, 102
  9:6, 151
  18:24, 171
  32:21, 46
  37:22, 151
  50:17, 171
Exodus
  3:12, 114
  3:16–17, 114
  10:17, 171
  12:7, 149
  12:12, 114
  12:22, 149
  14:4, 114
  14:17–18, 114
  15:1, 114
  15:1–12, 114
  15:21, 114
  24:1–11, 36
  24:3–8, 130–31
  24:6, 145–47
  24:8, 126
  25:8, 43
  25:40, 55–56
  28:38, 172, 192
  29, 131
  29:12, 142, 146
  29:16, 145–46
  29:19–28, 148
  29:21, 145–46
  29:36–37, 145
  29:38–42, 36
  29:45–46, 43
  30:10, 41, 42, 76
  30:12, 137
  30:15–16, 137
  34:7, 171
  40, 131
Leviticus
  1:2–3, 17
  1:5, 17, 39–40, 145, 147–48
  1:10, 17
  1:11, 145
  2:1, 17
  3:2, 145
  3:8, 145
  3:13, 145
  4–5, 134
  4:3, 40
  4:7, 142, 145, 148
  4:14, 40
  4:18, 142, 145–46, 148
  4:20, 134
  4:25, 142, 145, 148
  4:26, 134
  4:30, 142, 145
  4:31, 134
  4:34, 142, 145
  4:35, 134
  5, 134
  5:1, 171
  5:1–6:7, 172
  5:6, 40
  5:7, 40
  5:8, 40
  5:9, 40
  5:10, 134
  5:11–13, 132
  5:13, 134
  5:16, 134
  5:17, 172
  5:18, 134
  5:26, 134
  6:18, 40
  7:2, 145–46
  7:18, 172

Scripture Index

7:33, 17, 40
8, 131
8:15, 142, 144–46
8:19, 145
8:22–29, 148
8:24, 145, 148
9:9, 17, 142, 144–46
9:12, 145
9:18, 145
10, 161
10:17, 172, 192
12–15, 185
14:7–8, 132
15:5–12, 132
15:31, 43
16, 35, 42, 45–47, 140, 191
16:1–3, 161
16:2, 43
16:3, 40, 42
16:5, 40
16:6, 40, 44–45
16:9, 40
16:11, 39–40, 44–45
16:12, 43
16:14, 39
16:14–15, 162
16:15, 39, 40, 42–43
16:15–16, 51
16:15–17, 43
16:16, 43–46, 140
16:17, 44
16:18, 43
16:18–19, 39, 145
16:20, 42–43, 45
16:20–22, 39, 172, 174
16:21, 172
16:22, 172
16:24, 44–45
16:26, 132
16:27, 39–40, 42, 85
16:28, 132
16:29, 39
16:30, 41, 44–45
16.30–34, 44
16:31, 39
16:33, 40, 43–45
16:33–34, 45–46
17:4, 151
17:6, 145
17:10, 138
17:10–12, 138
17:11, 132, 135–41, 151, 153–54, 156, 159, 167–68, 178, 182, 185
17:12, 138
17:16, 172
16:34, 42, 45, 76
18:24–25, 44
19, 134
19:8, 172
19:17, 172
19:22, 134
20:3, 44
20:17, 172
20:19, 172
20:20, 172
22:6, 132
22:9, 172
22:16, 172
24:15, 172
24:18, 139
26:14–39, 119
26:17, 119
26:22, 119
26:25, 119
26:33, 119
28:38, 119
Numbers
5:31, 172
7, 131
9:13, 172
14:18, 171
15, 134
15:25, 134
15:26, 134
15:28, 134
18:1, 172
18:22–23, 172
18:32, 172
19, 161
19:1–13, 36
19:13, 44
19:20, 44
28:1–8, 36
30:15, 172
31:19–24, 132
31:50, 137
35:30–34, 151
35:33, 135, 151
Deuteronomy
4:17, 55
4:27, 119
12:23–27, 145
12:27, 144–46
17:2 **LXX**, 119
17:6, 119
19:10, 151

Deuteronomy (cont.)
  21:7, 151
  28–30, 119
  28:15–68, 119
  28:20–22, 119
  28:24, 119
  28:26, 119
  28:45, 119
  28:48, 119
  28:51, 119
  28:61, 119
Joshua
  7:11–15, 119
  23:15–16, 119
1 Samuel
  15:25, 171
  25:31, 151
1 Kings
  2:31, 151
  18:28, 150
2 Kings
  21:16, 151
  24:4, 151
1 Chronicles
  22:8, 151
2 Chronicles
  35:11, 148
Psalms
  2:7, 27–28, 34
  8, 101–2, 106–8
  8:5–7 LXX, 99–102, 107
  8:6, 102
  8:7 LXX, 100
  32:1, 171
  32:5, 171
  39 LXX, 73, 82
  39:2 LXX, 73
  39:3 LXX, 73
  39:4–6 LXX, 73
  39:7–9 LXX, 74, 83
  39:9 LXX, 74
  39:10 LXX, 73
  40, 39
  40:7–8, 80
  40:7–9, 72, 81–82
  78:3, 151
  78:10, 151
  105:38, 151
  110:1, 8, 34, 52, 68, 191
  110:4, 27–28, 30, 32–34, 36, 191, 193
Proverbs
  1:16, 151
  6:7, 151

Isaiah
  2:9, 171
  26:20, 73
  52:13–53:12, 171
  53, 170–71, 173, 175, 191, 193
  53:6, 192
  53:8, 64
  53:9, 64
  53:10, 65, 173, 192
  53:11, 173
  53:11–12, 64–65, 170, 192
  53:12, 4, 63–64, 170, 173–75, 178, 192–93
  55:3, 158
  59:7, 151
  61:1–2, 133
  61:8, 158
Jeremiah
  7:6, 151
  22:3, 151
  22:8–12, 119
  22:17, 151
  30:3, 123
  31:31–34, 81, 118, 121
  31:32, 118
  31:33, 81
  32:37, 123
  32:37–41, 123
  32:39, 123
  32:40, 123
  34:17–22, 119
  38:33 LXX, 74
  50:5, 158
Lamentations
  4:13, 151
Ezekiel
  8–11, 44
  8:10, 55
  11:16–20, 123
  11:17, 119
  16:60, 158
  16:38, 151
  18:10, 151
  22:3, 151
  22:4, 151
  22:6, 151
  22:9, 151
  22:12, 151
  22:27, 151
  24:7, 151
  36:22–26, 123
  36:24, 119
  37:15–28, 123
  39:25–29, 123

Scripture Index

43:20, 43
44:7, 40
44:15, 40
Daniel
 9:7, 120
Joel
 3:19, 151
Habakkuk
 17:27, 48
Zephaniah
 1:17, 151
Matthew
 10:15, 103
 11:22–24, 103
 17:27, 48
 23:35, 152
 25:31–46, 103
 26:26, 126
 26:28, 126, 133, 152
Mark
 1:4, 133
 3:29, 133
 10:45, 123
 14:22, 126
 14:24, 126, 152
Luke
 1:77, 133
 4:18, 133
 11:50, 152
 22:19, 152
 22:19–20, 126
 22:20, 126, 152
 24:47, 133
John
 3:14, 69
 5:22–29, 103
 8:28, 69
 12:23, 69
 12:28, 69
 12:31, 111, 113
 12:32, 69
 13:31, 69
 13:31–32, 69
 13:32, 69
 17:5, 69
 19:28, 48
Acts
 1, 17
 2:38, 133
 5:31, 133
 10:42, 103
 10:43, 133
 13:38, 133
 17:31, 103

22:20, 152
24:25, 103
26:18, 111, 133
Romans
 2:1–11, 103
 2:16, 103
 3:6, 103
 3:15, 152
 3:24, 123, 125
 3:24–26, 125
 5:6, 109
 5:8, 109
 5:12, 102, 110
 5:14, 110
 5:17, 110
 5:20, 110
 6:9–10, 110
 6:10, 77, 190
 8:20, 102
 8:21, 102
 8:33–34, 190
 10:8, 90
 14:10–12, 103
 14:15, 109
1 Corinthians
 4:4–5, 103
 5:5, 103
 11:24, 152
 11:25, 152
 11:32, 103
 15:25–27, 102
2 Corinthians
 5:10, 103
 5:14–15, 109
Galatians
 3:10, 125
 3:10–14, 125
 3:13, 126
 3:14, 126
Ephesians
 1:7, 123, 133
 2:2, 111
 6:12, 111
Philippians
 2:8–9, 104
 2:9, 106
Colossians
 1:13, 111
 1:14, 123, 133
 2:15, 113
1 Thessalonians
 5:10, 109
2 Thessalonians
 1:5–10, 103

2 Timothy
  1:10, 79, 113
  4:1, 103
  4:14, 103
Hebrews 1–2, 116
  1:1–14, 115
  1:2, 122, 181
  1:3, 4, 8, 34, 41, 52, 54, 62, 68, 71, 77, 83–84, 92, 116, 181
  1:3–4, 27–28
  1:4, 107
  1:5, 27–28, 34
  1:5–14, 107
  1:6–7, 74
  1:13, 34, 54, 68, 181
  1:14, 74, 122
  2, 116
  2:2, 118–19
  2:2–3, 177
  2:3, 115
  2:5, 100–1, 107–8
  2:5–8, 100–2
  2:5–9, 74, 99, 102, 104, 107–10
  2:5–16, 115
  2:5–18, 107, 110, 112, 114–15
  2:6, 100
  2:6–7, 100
  2:7–8, 100
  2:8, 100–1, 106–8
  2:8–9, 107
  2:9, 4, 14, 19, 26, 68–69, 77, 98–102, 104–10, 112–14, 116, 127, 157, 169, 181
  2:9–10, 28–29
  2:9–1 **4**, 4
  2:10, 4, 26, 29, 32–34, 84, 107–9, 115
  2:10–11, 115
  2:10–18, 108, 115
  2:11, 26
  2:11–12, 27
  2:12, 73
  2:11–13, 68–69
  2:13, 27, 114
  2:14, 4, 27, 32, 62, 79, 110, 113
  2:14–15, 14, 19, 62, 98, 102, 104, 110, 112–14, 116, 127, 181
  2:14–16, 116
  2:14–3:2, 114
  2:15, 102, 110–12
  2:16, 26
  2:17, 4, 26–27, 41, 62, 71, 84, 115, 129
  2:17–18, 27, 29, 33, 79–80, 84, 177
  2:18, 27, 84, 108
  3:1, 129

3:7–4:13, 176
4:12–13, 103
4:14, 54
4:14–16, 115
4:15, 31, 33, 80, 177
4:16, 57, 68
5:1, 11, 17, 23–24, 34, 39, 52, 66, 70
5:1–3, 30
5:1–10, 29
5:1–7:28, 52
5:1–10:18, 3, 115
5:3, 17, 29–30, 39
5:5, 27–28
5:5–6, 25, 28, 34
5:5–10, 27, 34
5:6, 27, 30, 34
5:7, 17, 28, 29–30, 69, 73, 105, 157
5:7–8, 103
5:7–10, 4, 28–30, 32–34, 52, 68–69, 106, 108
5:8, 28–29
5:8–10, 26, 80
5:9, 29, 109, 180
5:9–10, 28–29, 84
5:10, 27
5:11, 52
5:11–6:20, 52
6:2, 103, 177
6:4–8, 104
6:6, 4
6:7–8, 103
6:8, 103–4
6:12, 122
6:13–15, 122
6:17, 122
6:19, 37–38, 68, 89
6:19–20, 4, 7, 37, 39, 54, 56, 60, 68, 88–89, 92
6:20, 27, 38, 88, 92, 108
7, 30–31, 33–34
7–10, 13
7:3, 30
7:8, 30–31, 69, 103
7:11, 115
7:11–12, 115
7:11–28, 52
7:13–14, 33
7:15, 33
7:16, 27, 30–32, 69, 157, 180
7:17, 32
7:18–19, 115
7:19, 121
7:22, 80, 121, 158
7:23, 30, 103

7:23–24, 30–31
7:23–25, 31–33, 69, 121
7:24–25, 31
7:25, 30, 57, 84, 129
7:26, 54
7:26–28, 31
7:27, 4, 17, 30–31, 36, 57, 60, 71, 76, 79, 84, 163–64, 174
7:28, 26, 29–34
8–9, 77, 84
8–10, 180
8:1, 52–53, 92, 181
8:1–2, 4, 52–53, 56–57
8:1–5, 19, 34, 38, 42, 47, 51, 56–57, 59, 62–63, 66, 70, 77, 92, 180
8:1–6, 55
8:2, 53–54, 56, 59
8:3, 11, 17, 23–24, 34, 39, 57, 65–66, 70, 74, 129, 189
8:3–10:18, 52–53
8:3–4, 4, 82
8:3–5, 52, 56
8:4, 17, 33–35, 39, 52, 57, 180
8:5, 16, 52–57, 87
8:6, 51, 80
8:6–13, 158
8:7, 118, 121
8:7–13, 51, 80
8:8, 115, 118, 121
8:9, 118, 121–22
8:8–12, 81, 118
8:13, 121
9, 188, 193
9:1, 80, 121
9:1–5, 37
9:1–8, 54
9:1–10, 37
9:2, 121
9:2–3, 54
9:3, 37, 39, 54, 89, 121
9:6, 37, 54, 121
9:6–7, 58
9:6–10, 16, 38, 59, 121
9:7, 6–7, 17–18, 36, 37, 39–40, 42, 48, 51, 58, 59–61, 66, 70, 76, 85–86, 91–92, 121, 154, 160–61, 163, 166, 180
9:8, 54, 80, 89, 121
9:9, 17, 37, 39
9:9–10, 37, 59, 63
9:11, 56, 59–60, 68, 188
9:11–12, 4, 53–54, 56–59, 61–62, 64, 67, 70, 85, 87, 92, 188
9:11–14, 7, 17, 19, 47, 57, 63, 72, 77, 82, 166, 174, 180

9:11–10:18, 38, 41
9:12, 7, 37–38, 57, 59–63, 76, 86, 89, 92, 124, 128, 160–61, 163–64, 182–83
9:13, 62, 160–61
9:13–14, 36, 57, 62–64, 154, 160, 162, 188
9:14, 4, 7, 17, 38–40, 62–63, 65, 79, 115, 128, 160, 162–64
9:15, 4, 14, 80, 117–19, 121–27, 129–31, 152, 158–59, 166, 170, 177, 181, 186–87
9:15–16, 131
9:15–17, 14, 19, 98, 116, 118, 126, 129–31, 181, 187–88
9:15–18, 97
9:15–22, 125
9:16, 129, 130
9:16–17, 117–18, 124–25, 129
9:17, 124, 129–30, 189
9:18, 80, 129, 131, 152, 153, 158–59, 178, 189
9:18–21, 36, 132, 136, 157
9:18–22, 129, 131, 158, 187
9:19, 161
9:19–21, 129, 152, 154, 160
9:19–22, 131
9:20, 130–32, 152
9:21, 54, 132, 161
9:22, 129, 131–37, 140–41, 148, 150–56, 158, 161–62, 166–68, 170, 175, 178, 181
9:23, 13, 16–17, 40–42, 49, 51, 55, 160–62, 187
9:23–24, 53, 62, 87
9:23–25, 63
9:23–26, 50, 51, 180
9:23–28, 19, 77, 84, 132, 174
9:24, 4, 7, 12, 38, 40, 48–51, 54, 56, 59, 67, 92
9:24–25, 17, 47–49, 51, 57, 64, 66, 70, 77, 82, 84, 86, 127, 166, 180
9:24–26, 7, 40, 49, 64
9:24–28, 72
9.25, 4, 12, 17, 38–39, 48–49, 54, 61–62, 64–65, 79, 160–61, 163–64
9:25–26, 6, 10, 38, 49–50, 164, 188
9:26, 4, 17, 47–48, 50, 57, 60, 62–64, 75–76, 79–80, 174, 190
9:27, 103, 109, 177
9:27–28, 6, 12, 64
9:28, 4, 17, 39, 47, 54, 57, 60, 62–65, 67, 70, 75–76, 92, 127, 152, 169–71, 174–78, 189, 192–93
10, 73–74, 82

Hebrews 1–2, (cont.)
  10:1, 16–17, 37, 39, 115
  10:1–4, 119
  10:2, 17, 39
  10:5, 17, 39, 72–75, 79–82, 93, 180
  10:5–10, 74, 80, 83
  10:5–14, 19, 47, 70–72, 74–75, 78–82, 127, 177, 180
  10:7, 80
  10:8, 17, 39, 80
  10:9, 80–81
  10:10, 4, 10, 17, 39, 57, 60, 62, 72–73, 75–77, 79, 81–82, 91, 93, 163–64, 174
  10:10–14, 73, 75–76, 83, 176
  10:11, 17, 39, 76
  10:11–13, 76
  10:12, 4, 8, 17, 38–39, 62, 73, 75–78, 82–84, 174–76
  10:12–13, 38, 54, 68, 76, 92, 181
  10:14, 4, 17, 38–39, 72–73, 75–77, 82, 115, 174
  10:15–17, 81
  10:15–18, 80
  10:16, 74
  10:18, 83, 133–34, 167
  10:19, 4, 62, 88, 161, 183
  10:19–20, 19, 68, 71, 89–91
  10:19–25, 82, 115
  10:19–39, 103
  10:20, 38, 39, 68, 86–92
  10:26, 17, 176
  10:26–27, 176–77
  10:26–29, 103
  10:26–31, 103, 176
  10:26–38, 73
  10:27–29, 177
  10:28, 118–19
  10:29, 104
  10:30, 103–4, 177
  10:31, 103
  10:38, 82
  10:39, 103–4
  11, 119
  11:4, 17, 103
  11:5, 103
  11:8, 122
  11:10, 122
  11:12, 103
  11:13, 103
  11:13–16, 122
  11:17, 17
  11:19, 103
  11:21, 103
  11:28, 149
  11:29, 103
  11:31, 103
  11:35, 103
  11:37, 103
  11:40, 119
  12:2, 4, 54, 68–69, 77, 92, 105–8, 181
  12:7, 17
  12:22, 162
  12:23, 103, 119, 177
  12:24, 38, 80, 154, 158, 160, 162, 164
  12:25–29, 103
  12:28, 113
  12:29, 103, 176
  13:4, 177
  13:10, 10, 54, 93
  13:11, 18, 38–40, 54, 58, 85–86, 161
  13:11–12, 38, 154, 164
  13:11–13, 4, 71, 85–86
  13:12, 4, 13, 38, 85–86, 93, 160, 162–63
  13:12–13, 107
  13:13, 85
  13:15, 17
  13:16, 17
  13:20, 11, 28, 69, 73, 129, 156–59, 166, 169
  13:20–21, 157
James
  5:9, 103
1 Peter
  1:17, 103
  1:18–20, 79
  2:21, 109
  2:23, 103
  3:18, 77
  4:5, 103
2 Peter
  2:4, 103
  3:7, 103
1 John
  3:5, 79
  3:8, 113
  3:16, 109
  4:17, 103
Jude
  6, 103
Revelation
  11:18, 103
  16:16, 152
  19:31, 48
  20:11–13, 103

INDEX OF OTHER ANCIENT SOURCES

Old Testament Apocrypha

Baruch
  1:20, 120
  2:13, 120
  2:26, 120
  3:8, 120
  4:24–25, 120
1 Maccabees
  1:37, 151
  7:17, 151
2 Maccabees
  1:8, 151
Tobit
  13:1–18, 120
  13:3–4, 120
  13:5–6, 120
  13:10, 120
  13:13, 120
Sirach
  14:11, 17
  27:15, 150
  28:11, 151
  34:22, 151
  40:1–7, 111
  41:1–4, 111
Sirach Prologue
  13, 111
Wisdom of Solomon
  2:23–24, 111
  4:20–5:23, 103

Old Testament Pseudepigrapha

Apocalypse of Moses
  24, 102
2 Baruch
  2:35, 158
  4:2–7, 56
  14:17–19, 56
  14:18–19, 101
  15:7–8, 101
  17:2–3, 102
  23:4, 102
  51:1–6, 103
  54:14, 102
1 Enoch
  9:1, 56
  12:4, 56
  14:8–25, 56
  15:3, 56
  71:5–9, 56
  90:28–29, 56
2 Enoch
  30:11–12, 101
  31:1–6, 101
  58:3, 101
4 Ezra
  3:7, 1-2
  6:53–54, 101
  6:59, 101
  7:118, 102
  7:26, 56
  7:33–44, 103
  8:38, 103
  9:10–12, 103
  8:52, 56
  13:36, 56
  14:35, 103
Jubilees
  1:15–23, 119
  1:16, 119–20
  1:16–18, 56
  1:27–29, 56

Jubilees (cont.)
  6:2, 153
  6:14, 153
  31:12–17, 56
Testament of Gad
  7:2, 30
Testament of Levi
  3:2–3, 103
  3:8, 30
  16:5, 120

Dead Sea Scrolls

1QS 3:17–18a, 101
4Q400, 56
4Q403, 56
4Q405, 56
4Q504 (4Q Words of the Luminaries[a])
  1–2 III, 8–13, 120
  1–2 V, 9–16, 120
  1 – 2 VI, 10–13, 120
11Q17 21–22, 56
11QT[a]
  XVI, 14–15, 153
  XXVI, 6–7, 153
  XXVI, 9–10, 153

Philo of Alexandria

On Dreams
  2.3, 55
On the Confusion of Tongues
  1.64, 55
On the Creation of the World
  84, 101
On the Life of Joseph
  1.40, 30
On the Life of Moses
  2.77–108, 56
  2.150, 142, 148
On the Posterity of Cain
  1.122, 55
On the Special Laws
  1.66–67, 56
  1.205, 142, 146–48
  1.231, 147–48
  1.233, 142, 148
  3.150, 151
  4.125, 147–48
Questions and Answers on Exodus
  2.68–97, 56

Questions and Answers on Genesis
  1.45, 102
  1.62, 147
That Every Good Person Is Free
  22, 111
Who Is the Heir?
  1.182, 147
  1.256, 55

Josephus

Antiquities
  2.42, 30
  2.45, 30
  2.148, 30
  3.122–24, 56
  3.179–87, 56
  3.226–27, 148
  3.227, 142
  3.231, 142, 148
  4.107, 30
Jewish War
  1.374, 55
  1.507, 55
  3.353, 30
  5.207–18, 56

Rabbinic Literature

b. Menaḥim
  93b, 136
b. Pesaḥim
  89a, 143
  121a, 142–44
b. Sanhedrin
  38b, 101
b. Yoma
  5a, 136
b. Zebaḥim
  6a, 136
  8a, 153
  26b, 153–54
  36a–b, 153
  36b–37a, 142, 144
  38a–b, 144
  47a–b, 144
  51a, 144
  81b, 153
  82b, 153
Leviticus Rabbah
  6:5, 130

Sifra
 4:9–10, 153
 4:10, 136
t. Našim Soṭah
 6.5, 101
t. Zebaḥim
 8:17, 136

Early Christian Commentaries on Hebrews

Chrysostom, 60
Ps.-Oecumenius, 49
Theodoret of Cyrus, 78
Theophylact, 49

Other Early Christian Authors

Athanasius
 Expositions on the Psalms, 149
Gregory of Nyssa
 De vita Moysis
  1.28, 149
  2.100–101, 149
Hippolytus
 Against Noetus
  4, 78
Justin Martyr
 Dialogue with Trypho
  118.3, 90
 Second Apology
  12.5, 149
Origen
 Homilies on Leviticus
  9.2.3, 78
  9.5.4, 78

Classical Authors

Achilles Tatius
 Leucippe and Clitophon
  7.1.3, 30

Cicero
 Tusculan Disputations
  1, 111
 Letters to Atticus
  9.2a, 111
Dio Chrysostom
 Orations
  6.42, 111
Dionysius of Halicarnassus
 De compositione verborum
  17, 55
Epictetus
 Discourses
  1.17.25, 111
  1.27.7–10, 111
  2.18.30, 111
  3.26.38–39, 111
  4.7.6, 111
  4.7.17–18, 111
Euripides
 Orestes
  1520–24, 111
Longus
 Daphnis and Chloe
  2.33.1, 30
Lucian
 The Passing of Peregrinus
  13, 111
  23, 111
  33, 111
Lucretius
 De rerum natura
  1.102–26, 111
Marcus Aurelius
 Meditations
  11.3, 111
Plutarch
 Moralia
  34B, 111
Polybius
 Histories
  6.54.6, 55
Seneca
 Epistulae morales
  3.1.23–25, 111
Xenophon
 Cyropaedia
  3.1.23–25, 111

AUTHOR INDEX

Alexander, Philip, 56
Allen, David L., 6
Allen, David M., 5, 117, 131
Anderson, David R., 24, 28, 31
Anderson, Gary A., 101
Andriessen, Paul, 60–61, 87–88, 114
Asumang, Annang, 7
Attridge, Harold W., 7, 25, 30, 40–41, 54, 55, 60, 64, 72, 80, 83–84, 88, 90, 101, 104–6, 111, 113–14, 117, 132–33, 137, 141, 153

Backhaus, Knut, 8, 28, 56, 58, 60, 72, 81, 101, 113, 117, 161
Barnard, Jody A., 11, 24–25, 54, 56, 60, 83
Barrett, C. K., 11
Barth, Gerhard, 8
Bates, Matthew W., 24, 69
Bauckham, Richard J., 79, 116
Behm, Johannes, 141
Bénétreau, Samuel, 6, 84, 87
Billerbeck, Paul, 136
Blenkinsopp, Joseph, 173
Blomberg, Craig L., 100–2
Braun, Herbert, 6, 49, 84, 87, 115, 117, 133, 141, 153
Brooks, Walter Edward, 11, 13, 25, 97, 160
Bruce, F. F., 6–7, 27, 31, 59, 72, 117, 137, 157, 163
Büchner, Dirk, 40, 42, 46, 140, 145

Caird, G. B., 37, 79
Calaway, Jared C., 11
Calvin, John, 7
Campbell, K. M., 117
Caraski, Michael, 130
Cervera i Vallis, Jordi, 9
Chester, A. N., 9
Church, Philip, 6, 56

Cockerill, Gareth Lee, 6–7, 24, 29, 49, 56, 59–60, 62, 72, 117, 128, 130, 133, 141, 182
Cody, Aelred, 9, 10, 24, 60
Compton, Jared, 6, 14, 25, 31, 60, 62, 101, 107–8, 115, 117, 119, 158, 191
Cortez, Felix H., 9–10, 24, 37–38
Croy, N. Clayton, 69

Dahl, N. A., 87
Daly, Robert J., 78
Davies, J. H., 4, 11, 24
De Wet, Chris L., 101
Delitzsch, Franz, 9, 49, 105–7, 111, 135, 136, 141, 152, 155
Dennis, John, 44, 45
deSilva, David, 9, 31, 34, 49, 93, 101, 137, 157
Dion, Paul E., 146
Dunn, James D. G., 79
Dunnill, John, 5
Dyer, Bryan R., 5

Easter, Matthew C., 5, 25, 69, 101–2, 104, 108
Eberhart, Christian A., 13, 17, 25, 39, 44, 72, 128–31, 189
Eisele, Wilfried, 8, 56
Elgvin, Torlief, 56
Elliger, Karl, 44
Ellingworth, Paul, 6–7, 27–28, 49, 64, 68, 72, 83–84, 88, 104–5, 112, 115, 117, 133, 136, 137, 141, 153, 157, 161
Ellis, E. Earle, 82
Epstein, I., 136, 143–44, 154
Eskola, Timo, 11, 13–14, 17, 25, 56, 78, 97

Feder, Yitzhak, 137, 139, 185
Filtvedt, Ole Jakob, 5, 85–86, 88, 101, 117, 122

Author Index

Freedman, H., 130
Frey, Jörg, 117
Fuhrmann, Sebastian, 6, 24, 58, 60, 63, 72, 84, 111, 117

Gäbel, Georg, 3, 11–12, 24–25, 27–28, 30, 34, 37, 39–40, 45, 47, 49, 55–56, 58, 60–62, 64, 68–69, 71–73, 75, 77, 79, 81, 83–85, 87, 89–91, 99–102, 104–7, 113–15, 117, 128, 130–31, 133, 136–37, 141, 145, 153, 157, 162–64, 173, 187–88
Gane, Roy, 38, 43–45, 85, 134–35, 143, 172
García Martínez, Florentino, 120
Gathercole, Simon J., 79, 109
Gelardini, Gabriela, 5, 68
Geller, Stephen A., 44
Gheorgita, Radu, 117
Gilders, William K., 44, 130, 135, 137, 139, 145, 153
Ginsberg, Morris, 136, 153
Gordon, Robert P., 133, 141
Gorman, Frank H., 44, 135
Grässer, Erich, 8, 24, 49, 54, 56, 58, 64, 68–69, 72, 79, 81, 83–84, 100, 102, 109, 113, 115, 117, 131, 133, 135, 137, 141, 157, 161
Gray, Patrick, 28, 103, 110
Grogan, Geoffrey W., 101
Gurtner, Daniel M., 101
Guthrie, George H., 9, 27–28, 38, 52–53, 82, 101, 108
Guzmán, Ron, 52

Haber, Susan, 11
Hahn, Scott W., 64, 117, 119, 122–23, 125–26, 130
Hanson, Anthony, 147
Harlé, Paul, 46, 145
Harris, Murray J., 109
Hartenstein, Friedhelm, 43–44
Hay, David M., 6, 24, 28, 31, 78
Hays, Richard B., 31, 73
Hegermann, Harald, 105–7, 122, 141
Heininger, Bernhard, 41
Hengel, Martin, 17
Hermann, Markus-Liborius, 7, 72
Hofius, Otfried, 8, 42, 54, 60, 68, 80, 88–89, 90, 112, 170
Houston, Walter J., 184
Hughes, John J., 117, 122, 126, 152
Hughes, Philip Edgcumbe, 6

Hundley, Michael B., 44
Hurst, L. D., 5, 55–56, 79, 89–90, 100

Isaacs, Marie E., 6, 72, 87

Jamieson, R. B., 4, 41, 50–51, 131
Janowski, Bernd, 143, 171
Jenson, Philip Peter, 44
Jeremias, Joachim, 8, 88, 90
Jipp, Joshua W., 5, 28
Johnson, Luke Timothy, 9, 25, 31, 68, 104, 109–11, 117, 133
Johnson, Richard W., 5
Johnsson, William G., 5, 87, 133
Joslin, Barry C., 6, 59
Jürgens, Benedikt, 44, 45, 137

Karrer, Martin, 31, 72, 79, 81, 117, 135
Käsemann, Ernst, 56
Kazen, Thomas, 184
Kibbe, Michael, 11, 14, 25, 29, 67, 161
Kilpatrick, G. D., 117
Kinzer, Mark Stephen, 100–2
Kiuchi, Nobuyoshi, 172
Klawans, Jonathan, 56
Kleinig, John W., 6
Kline, Meredith G., 117
Knibb, Michael A., 120
Knöppler, Thomas, 8, 18, 72, 86
Koester, Craig R., 9–10, 16, 25, 29, 56, 58, 60, 72, 83–84, 88, 93, 101, 104, 111, 113, 117, 133, 135, 141, 148, 153, 176
Kögel, Julius, 107
Kraus, Wolfgang, 44, 64, 117
Kuma, Herman V. A., 6, 128
Kurianal, James, 25–26, 28–29, 31

Lam, Joseph, 171–73
Lane, William L., 6–7, 24, 26–27, 29, 31, 40–41, 49, 58–60, 62, 64, 68, 72, 80–81, 83–84, 88, 102, 104–5, 107, 110–11, 117, 128, 130, 133, 135, 141–42, 153, 157, 161, 182
Laub, Franz, 2–3, 7–8, 24, 56, 58, 60, 83, 87
Lausberg, Heinrich, 88
Lee, Aquila H. I., 24
Lehne, Susanne, 5
Lemos, T. M., 184–85
Leschert, Dale F., 101
Levine, Baruch, 43–44, 137
Lindars, Barnabas, 6–7, 116
Linebaugh, Jonathan A., 125

Loader, William R. G., 6–7, 24, 27, 41, 60, 62, 64, 72, 83, 87, 104–5, 113, 131
Löhr, Hermut, 12–13, 25, 41, 56, 60, 72, 86–87, 90, 99, 101, 103, 116, 124, 189
Long, Thomas G., 114
Luck, Ulrich, 7, 56

Mackie, Scott D., 9–10, 24, 54, 56, 60, 64, 68, 83, 86, 93–94, 125
MacRae, George W., 56
Maré, Leonard P., 101
Marshall, I. Howard, 99
Martin, Michael W., 52
März, Claus-Peter, 101
Mason, Eric F., 11, 56, 68
McCruden, Kevin B., 5
McDonough, Sean M., 79
McKnight, Scot, 104
Meier, John P., 24, 27–28, 79, 191
Meshel, Naphtali S., 145–46
Michel, Otto, 9, 27, 49, 87, 105, 115, 117, 135–36, 141, 145
Milgrom, Jacob, 38–39, 43–45, 85, 135, 137, 143, 145, 172, 184
Moffatt, James, 6, 56, 60, 87, 105, 111, 114, 117, 133, 141
Moffitt, David M., 2, 9, 11, 14–15, 17, 20, 25, 28–29, 31, 33–35, 49, 56, 60–61, 64, 69, 71, 73–75, 77, 78, 81–82, 84, 86, 88, 91–93, 97, 117, 124, 128, 131, 133, 141–42, 153, 156, 161, 163–67, 178, 183–87
Moore, Nicholas J., 9–10, 14, 16, 25, 31, 49, 60, 68, 80, 84, 93
Mora, Gaspar, 176
Morales, Rodrigo J., 120, 125
Moret, Jean-René, 6, 14, 117, 185, 186
Morray-Jones, Christopher R. A., 8, 56, 69
Mosser, Carl, 15

Nairne, Alexander, 117
Nelson, Richard D., 9–10, 24, 35, 72, 93, 94
Neusner, Jacob, 136
Nihan, Christophe, 44–45, 135, 137, 184–85
Nongbri, Brent, 104

Ounsworth, Richard, 8, 37–38
Owen, John, 6, 60

Parsons, Mikeal C., 79
Peeler, Amy L. B., 5, 24–25, 27, 69, 79, 111, 114
Peterson, David, 24–25, 31, 56
Philip, Mayjee, 6
Pitre, Brant, 123, 193
Pralon, Didier, 46, 145
Propp, William H. C., 130
Pursiful, Darrell, J., 9, 25

Quinn, Russell D., 101

Rascher, Angela, 5, 16, 24, 104
Reinmuth, Ekart, 103
Reynolds, Benjamin E., 69
Ribbens, Benjamin, 2, 11, 24, 34–35, 54, 56–57, 60–61, 64, 78, 84, 123, 125, 133, 135, 141, 153, 161–62, 164, 174, 176
Richardson, Christopher A., 6, 24, 29, 62–64, 69, 72, 77, 84, 86, 128
Riggenbach, Eduard, 131
Rissi, Mathias, 6, 24
Rooke, Deborah W., 31
Rose, Christian, 8
Rosenbaum, Stephen E., 111
Rowe, Galen O., 88
Rowland, Christopher, 8, 56, 69

Sargent, Benjamin, 24
Schaefer, J. R., 192
Scharbert, Josef, 130
Schenck, Kenneth L., 12, 25, 56, 60, 65, 72, 79, 87, 101–2, 189
Scholer, John M., 9, 24, 26, 29, 54
Schreiner, Thomas R., 6, 31, 88, 117
Schunack, Gerd, 6
Schwartz, Baruch J., 137–39, 154–55, 171–72
Scott, James M., 120
Silva, Moisés, 28
Simon, Maurice, 130
Sklar, Jay, 44, 45, 135, 137–39, 144, 172
Small, Brian C., 6, 24–25, 32, 68, 72, 99, 104–5, 114, 117
Söding, Thomas, 113
Soskice, Janet Martin, 93
Sowers, Sidney G., 56
Spicq, Ceslas, 6, 27, 60, 72, 83–84, 115, 117, 133, 141, 153, 161
Stanley, Steve, 37
Stegemann, Ekkehard W., 8, 56
Stegemann, Wolfgang, 8, 56
Sterling, Gregory E., 56

Author Index

Stewart, Alexander, 5
Stökl ben Ezra, Daniel, 6, 7, 25, 30, 56
Stott, Wilfred, 6
Strack, Hermann L., 136
Svendsen, Stefan Nordgaard, 56
Swetnam, James, 60, 117

Telscher, Guido, 6, 60, 69
Thompson, James W., 7, 8, 24, 56, 87, 105, 117
Thornton, T. G. C., 141-43, 145, 153
Tigchelaar, Eibert J. C., 120
Tov, Emanuel, 120
Trompf, G. W., 176
Tuckett, C. M., 18-19

Übelacker, Walter, 102-3, 176

VanderKam, James C., 119-20, 153
Vanhoye, Albert, 6, 27, 31-32, 60, 84, 104, 115, 117
Vervenne, Marc, 130
Vos, Geerhardus, 117

Wallace, Daniel B., 91
Wallis, Ian G., 24

Walter, Nikolaus, 11, 24, 27, 128
Walton, John H. 44
Watson, Francis B. 107
Webster, John, 79
Weiss, Hans-Friedrich, 6, 26-27, 41, 49, 58, 60, 64, 68, 79, 84, 88, 104-11, 115, 117, 128, 131, 133, 137, 141, 148, 161
Wenham, Gordon J., 44
Westcott, Brooke Foss, 6, 60, 72, 87, 91, 100, 110, 117, 133, 137, 141
Wevers, John William, 45, 140, 145, 151
Whitekettle, Richard, 185
Whitlark, Jason A., 24
Wiid, J. S., 117
Williamson, Paul R., 117
Willi-Plein Ina, 11, 43
Witherington, Ben, 126
Wright, David P., 38, 43, 85, 143

Young, Norman H., 6, 7, 40, 49, 59-60, 63, 88, 90, 141, 143

Zesati Estrada, Carlos, 29
Zuckermandel, M. S., 136
Zweip, A. W., 17

For EU product safety concerns, contact us at Calle de José Abascal, 56–1°,
28003 Madrid, Spain or eugpsr@cambridge.org.

www.ingramcontent.com/pod-product-compliance
Ingram Content Group UK Ltd.
Pitfield, Milton Keynes, MK11 3LW, UK
UKHW042302220226
468302UK00010B/142